D0127660

Tools for Facilitating Team Meetings

Easy Tools That Help Plan, Organize, Conduct, and Evaluate Team Meetings

Johnna L. Howell

Integrity **Integrity Publishing**
Seattle, Washington

Tools for Facilitating Team Meetings

Easy Tools That Help Plan, Organize Conduct, and Evaluate Team Meetings

By Johnna L. Howell

© 1995, **Integrity Publishing**
Printed in the United States of America

All rights reserved. No part of this publication, except those pages specifically designated, and found in the Appendix, may be reproduced, stored in a retrieval system, or transmitted in any form or by any means, electronic, mechanical, photocopying, recording, or otherwise, without the prior written permission of the publisher.

Library of Congress Cataloging-in-Publication Data

Howell, Johnna L.
    Tools for facilitating team meetings: easy tools that help plan, organize, conduct, and evaluate team meetings / Johnna L. Howell. -- 1st ed.
    p. cm.
    Includes Index
    Preassigned **LCCN**: 94-96899
    ISBN 1-886671-00-1
        1. Meetings. 2. Work groups.   I. Title.
    HF5734.5.H69 1995   658.4'56
                          QBI95-228

Copy Editing: Betsy Wilcox
                  Weadonne Littrell

Cover design and book design: Jointly with Maria Ostrand

 Integrity Publishing and Consulting
7456 E. Greenlake Drive North
Seattle, WA 98115
(206) 524-5348 • Fax (206) 524-5527

Acknowledgments

A number of individuals have contributed greatly to the completion of this book. They have my sincere gratitude and thanks.

Peer Reviewers:

These individuals provided invaluable insights that have enhanced the end product. They did this during the November and December holidays when work pressures and personal demands were at their peak.

> Warren Carlisle, Westin Hotels and Resorts
> Rose Cohan, Rose Cohan & Associates
> Carol Kirsch, Health Plan Institute, Kaiser Permanente
> Nancy Kuhn, Charles Drew Biomedical Institute, American Red Cross
> Laura Marshall-deJong, Westin Hotels and Resorts
> Donna Treat, Northwest Natural Gas
> Dianna Upthegrove, Corning Nichols Institute

Copy Editors:

> Betsy Wilcox, Independent Consultant
> Weadonne Littrell, Independent Consultant

Cover design and book design:

> Jointly with Maria Ostrand

A special thanks also goes to Maria Ostrand for her tireless efforts in coaching and mentoring me through the design and desktop publishing aspects of this project. Her professionalism and patience with my novice efforts is greatly appreciated.

This book is dedicated to my FAMILY — Jerry, Jeff and Christine. They are my dearest friends, supporters, teachers and confidants.

Contents

Introduction i

SECTION I.   MEETING PLANNING 1

Overview 3
Planning the Meeting 4
15 Steps 5
Agenda 9
Process and Tool Selection 10
Evaluation 14
Meeting Planning Checklist 15
Summary Steps for Planning a Successful Meeting 18

SECTION II. TOOLS 19

Tools 21
Materials Selection Matrix 22

   Gather Data 23
     Brainstorming 24
     Observation 27
     Questions/Surveys 31
     Mystery Shopper 36
     Interviews 38

   Organize Data 43
     T-Charts 44
     Double T-Charts (TT-Chart) 47
     Matrix Chart 51
     Consensus Card Method 59
     Paired-Choice Matrix 62
     Multi-Voting 65
     Force Field Analysis 68
     Worksheet 72
     Check/Tally Sheets 74

   Group Data 81
     Affinity Diagram 82
     Interrelationship Diagram 85
     Venn Diagram 88
     Quadrant Diagram 92

   Sequence Data 95
     Continuums 96
     Stages 100
     Levels 103
     Gantt Chart 106

Breakdown Data **109**
   Tree Diagram 110
   Work Breakdown Structure (WBS) 114
   Link Pin Diagram 116
   Circles (Relationships) 118
   Iceberg Diagram 123

Map Data **127**
   Storyboard 128
   Process Flow Chart 131
   Deployment Process Flow Chart 134
   Work Flow Diagram 138

Display Data **141**
   Area Graph 142
   Bar Graph 144
   Line Graph/Run Graph 148

SECTION III.   CASE STUDIES **153**
Overview 155
Service - Hotel Company - Guest Check-In Process Action Plan 157
Finance - Investment Banking - Sales and Marketing Strategic Planning 183
Manufacturing - Heavy Equipment - Valve Production Process Improvement 209

APPENDIX **237**
How to Use 239
Organization 239
Tools - Reproducible 240

TOOL INDEX **351**

Introduction

Background

Total quality, continuous improvement, re-engineering, re-inventing and re-organizing efforts have spurred literally hundreds of thousands of teams to be formed in companies throughout the world. The range of these team activities is varied. Some companies have done as little as form *ad hoc work teams* to address specific work problems. Others have broadened their commitment by forming *cross-functional teams* from which information from all sources can be obtained and utilized. Still others have taken the more empowering approach of forming *self-directed work teams* in which all aspects of the work are planned and performed by the work team.

Whether the company is implementing one of the above team approaches or some other approach, this new emphasis on teams has forced many individuals into unfamiliar team roles. *Employees who once attended meetings as passive listeners are now encouraged to become active participants in all aspects of team activities. This often includes leading the team by providing the team facilitation. These individuals typically are not prepared.*

To address this emerging movement toward team activities, a number of books have been written over the last several years. These books address such topics as: how to go about forming teams, handling team conflict, managing meetings, stages of teams, types of teams, team roles, team training, and team reward and recognition strategies. The topic of team meeting facilitation is handled in a similar manner. Facilitation that is discussed in current publications include such topics as: the role of the facilitator, room set up, media techniques, meeting planning, record keeping and managing group process.

Why This Book

Because team facilitation tools are either embedded within the text of current team literature, or absent altogether, they are difficult to track down for readily available usage. Without easily accessible tools, preparation for team meetings becomes cumbersome and lengthy. Ill-prepared facilitators produce unfocused meetings which waste the time of all involved.

This book provides easy-to-use facilitation tools for anyone. Facilitation *tools* are simply a combination of words and lists that are organized around lines, circles, boxes, graphs and pictures. They are used to enable groups, to bring together ideas and make decisions. With this book, the novice facilitator will learn the tools and how to use them, while the expert facilitator will use the tool kit as a quick reference guide and an expansion of personal facilitation methods.

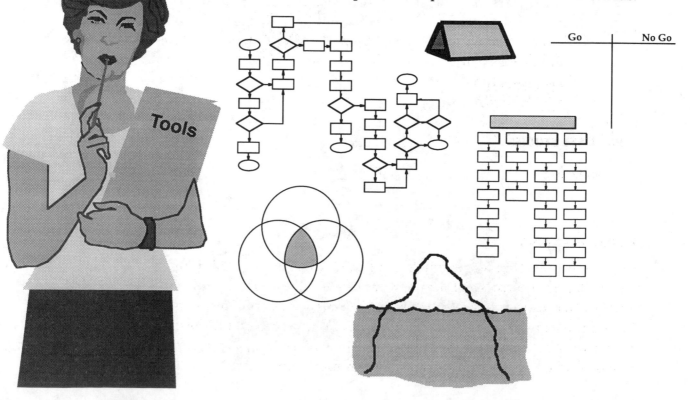

How This Book Is Organized

The book is divided into three major sections with the tool section as the primary focus.

INTRODUCTION

I. MEETING PLANNING

II. TOOLS

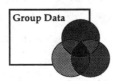

III. CASE STUDIES

APPENDIX

MEETING PLANNING

A successful meeting starts with thoughtful planning. The *15 Steps to Facilitating a Successful Meeting* provide an integrated approach to utilization of the tools. By following a series of steps directed at planning, organizing, conducting and evaluating a successful meeting, users will learn how to apply the same process to addressing their own team issues and to choosing the most appropriate tools.

TOOLS

Materials that are needed to facilitate meetings are described at the beginning of the Tool section. This includes a matrix of basic techniques including: Flip Charts, Overhead Projectors, White/Chalk Boards, Butcher Paper, and Computer-assisted tools. The matrix organizes the materials into the following categories: Description, Uses For, Advantages and Disadvantages. Special materials that are unique to the usage of a particular tool are not included in the matrix, but are mentioned with the particular tool.

Although the tools are placed into one of seven different groups, many can be used in multiple ways. They are grouped for easy access, although many of the tools could be included in different groupings.

The *Tool* section describes each of the tools in detail using the following format.

WHAT
What the tool is.

WHEN
When to use it.

HOW
How to use it.

TIMING
Timing for using the tool.

MATERIALS
Materials required.

VARIATIONS
Variations of usage.

In addition, many of these tools also have practical advantages for use at home, as well as work. Tool usage examples are given for both.

CASE STUDIES

Case Studies provide examples from a variety of organizations. Each example utilizes several of the tools so that the reader can see how they are used in an integrated fashion within a team meeting. The tools are linked visually through the use of icons. The icons provide the reader with a quick reference to the tool grouping from which the tool was taken. Referring to the tool grouping can generate alternative choices since other tools in the same grouping could also be considered as possible solutions.

How To Use This Book

This book is designed as a facilitation *planning* resource. It enables quick access and utilization of facilitation tools used for focusing teams on the desired problem, issue, process or project outcomes. The more advanced team facilitator should skip around the book for new and renewed ideas. The novice, however, should follow the steps below.

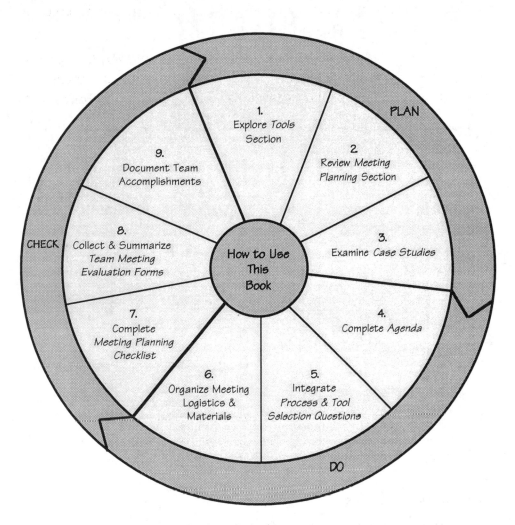

Meeting Planning

15 STEPS TO
FACILITATING A
SUCCESSFUL
MEETING

◆

AGENDA

◆

PROCESS AND
TOOL SELECTION
QUESTIONS

◆

TEAM MEETING
EVALUATION
FORM

◆

MEETING
PLANNING
CHECKLIST

Overview

Mastering team facilitation tools is one of the most troublesome elements of team meetings because teams seldom receive instructions on how to use the tools and are rarely given practical examples of how the tools can be purposefully integrated throughout the meeting. Because of this lack of instruction, teams often use the same one or two tools over and over again. They reason that, "If a *Process Flow Chart* worked last time, it should surely work again this time."

This chapter is written in response to the above predicament. It provides a step-by-step method for planning a meeting and choosing the "best" tool for the problem, process, issue, or project that the team is trying to address. Later, will be examples, through case studies, of teams who have been able to improve meeting outcomes by using the tools described in this book.

There are many ways to plan meetings. This book offers an effective comprehensive planning method. This method was developed to be used specifically with teams who are seeking to address a **problem**, **process**, **issue** or **project**. Traditional information sharing meetings, such as those that use "round robin" (information sharing around the table) techniques and those that address "old" and "new" business activities, are not covered in this discussion.

In addition, many meetings include a number of activities directed at team building, confronting issues, building trust and just plain "having fun" together. Since the primary focus of the book is on team facilitation tools, the above activities are also not included in the examples.

Planning the Meeting

The first step in planning is to identify the various elements that are needed to facilitate a successful meeting.

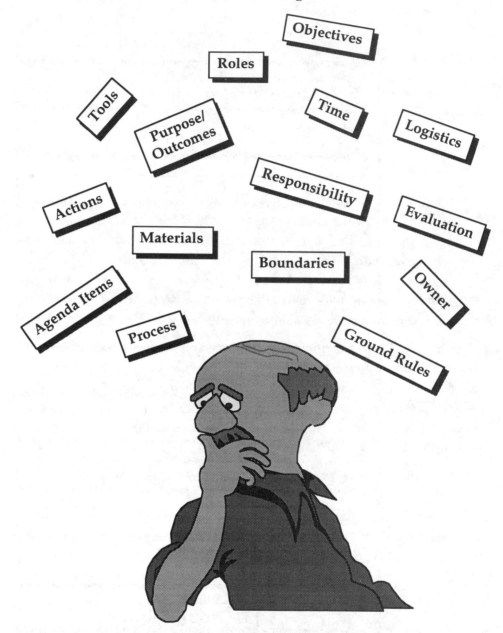

Once these elements have been identified, it is necessary to organize them into a usable process. These steps should be followed in an orderly manner because decisions that are made early on will effect the decisions that will need to be made later in the planning process.

Unfortunately, too often, the problem is defined early on and time to address the problem is scheduled. The Facilitator is then brought in and told what the problem is and how much time the team has been given to work on it. Instead of the meeting being planned around the time needed to work on the problem, the meeting ends up being squeezed or expanded to fit the pre-established time frame.

15 Steps

This book uses a 15-step process to plan, organize, conduct, and evaluate a meeting.

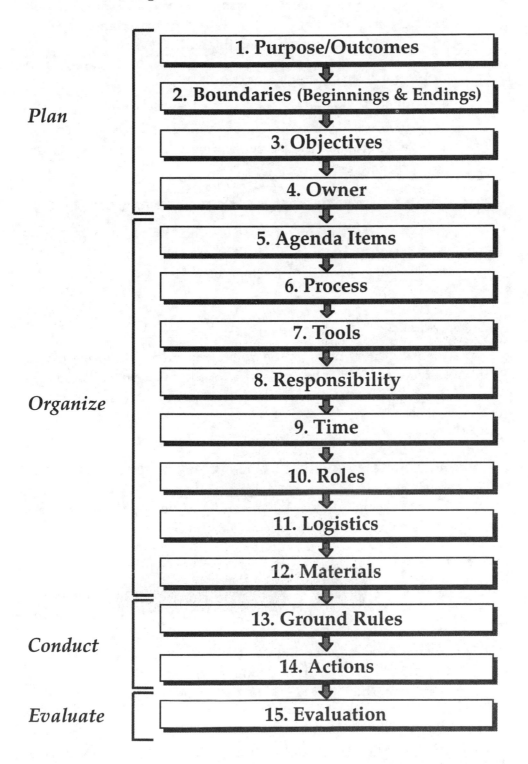

Plan

1. Purpose/Outcomes
2. Boundaries (Beginnings & Endings)
3. Objectives
4. Owner

Organize

5. Agenda Items
6. Process
7. Tools
8. Responsibility
9. Time
10. Roles
11. Logistics
12. Materials

Conduct

13. Ground Rules
14. Actions

Evaluate

15. Evaluation

Plan

1. **MEETING PURPOSE/OUTCOME(S)**

   What is the problem/process/issue/project the team is addressing? Determine what the team is trying to accomplish in the meeting. What is/are the meeting outcome(s)?

2. **BOUNDARIES (BEGINNINGS AND ENDINGS)**

   Establish the boundaries of the problem/issue/process/project to be addressed. What is the beginning and what is the ending of the problem/issue/process/project that the team is going to work on?

3. **MEETING OBJECTIVES (THESE BECOME THE AGENDA ITEM(S) BELOW.)**

   List 3 - 6 meeting objectives based on the problem/issue/process/project to be addressed. What are the primary things that need to be done in order to accomplish the purpose listed above?

4. **OWNER(S)**

   Identify the owner(s) of the problem/issue/process/project. Who is responsible for the outcome(s) of the meeting? Who has the most risk if the meeting does not accomplish its purpose?

Organize

5. **AGENDA ITEM(S) (THESE ARE TAKEN FROM THE MEETING OBJECTIVES ABOVE.)**

   Set the Agenda Items. What are the primary things that need to be done in order to accomplish the purpose?

6. **PROCESS**

   Determine the process to be used to address the Agenda Items. Use the *Process and Tool Selection Questions* to select appropriate processes. Do you have data? Is the data organized? Is the data grouped? Is there a sequence implied by the data? Is the data broken down in a manner that is usable? Should the team map the data? Is the data displayed in a manner that is usable?

7. **TOOL(S)**

   Choose a tool within the process area that will be used to address the action item. What tool(s) should be used to Gather, Organize, Group, Sequence, Breakdown, Map, and/or Display the data?

8. **RESPONSIBILITY**

Assign responsibility for each action item. This could be an individual or group outside of the team, a member of the team, or the entire team. Who is responsible for this activity? Is the activity a presentation, panel discussion, debate, or team effort?

9. **TIME**

Allocate time for each Agenda Item. Based on the above information, determine the amount of time needed to accomplish the Agenda. How much time will be needed to complete each activity?

10. **ROLES**

Identify the *Leader, Facilitator, Recorder, Presenter(s)* (if any), and the *Participants*. Who is responsible for planning and setting the direction of the meeting? Who will move the meeting along and keep it focused? Who will document the process, decisions, actions and outcomes? Are presentations needed? Who will be responsible for them? Who needs to be included in the meeting? How many people should be included?

11. **LOGISTICS**

Confirm the meeting logistics such as date, time and location. Have conflicting activities such as company activities, holidays, vacations, and schedules of critical members been considered?

12. **MATERIALS NEEDED**

Obtain the necessary meeting materials, such as flip charts, chalk boards, white boards, overhead projectors. Is the room configured in a way that will maximize the interactions? Will the facility accommodate the needs of the group for breaks and lunches?

Conduct

13. GROUND RULES

Agree on meeting expectations, behaviors, performance and evaluation. Has the team determined and agreed to the meeting guidelines? Should the team sign the Rules to show their support and accountability?

14. ACTIONS

Take action. Agree on next steps, create action plans, plan further meetings, write reports and/or change the way business is done. Does everyone know *who* is responsible for *what*, by *when*?

Evaluate

15. EVALUATION

Evaluate self, team, leader, facilitator, process and outcomes. Provide feedback where appropriate. How well did I contribute to the success of the meeting? How well did the team, the leader, and the facilitator contribute? Were the processes that were used successful? Did the outcomes meet the originally stated purpose and outcomes?

These steps and descriptions provide the directions for completion of the meeting *Agenda*. Steps 1 through 12 correspond to the *Agenda* item with the same number. The *Agenda* should be completed by following these steps.

Agenda

In order to complete steps 6 and 7, the *Process and Tool Selection Questions* worksheets should be used.

Agenda

1. Meeting Purpose/Outcome(s):

2. Boundaries (Beginning and Ending):

3. Meeting Objectives (These become the Agenda Item(s) below.):

4. Owner(s):

5. Agenda Item(s)	*6. Process*	*7. Tool(s)*	*8. Responsibility*	*9. Time*

9a. Total Time Needed:

10. Roles:

    Leader: _____   **Facilitator:** _____   **Recorder:** _____

    Presenter(s): _____

    Participants:

1. _____	5. _____	9. _____
2. _____	6. _____	10. _____
3. _____	7. _____	11. _____
4. _____	8. _____	12. _____

11. Logistics:

    Date: **Time:**   **Location:**

12. Materials Needed:

Process and Tool Selection

The following worksheets are designed to help the team or facilitator focus on the primary processes and tools to be used in order to accomplish the meeting objectives. The results of these worksheets should be placed on the Agenda next to steps 6 and 7.

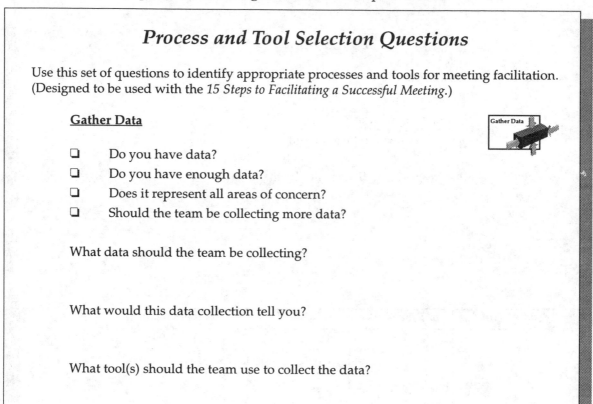

Process and Tool Selection Questions

Use this set of questions to identify appropriate processes and tools for meeting facilitation. (Designed to be used with the *15 Steps to Facilitating a Successful Meeting*.)

Gather Data

❑   Do you have data?
❑   Do you have enough data?
❑   Does it represent all areas of concern?
❑   Should the team be collecting more data?

What data should the team be collecting?

What would this data collection tell you?

What tool(s) should the team use to collect the data?

Organize Data

❑   Is the data organized?
❑   Is it organized in a manner that is usable for the team?
❑   Should the team better organize the data?

How could the team better organize the data?

What would this organized data tell you?

What tool(s) should the team use to organize the data?

Group Data

❏   Is the data grouped?

❏   Is it grouped in a manner that is usable for the team?

❏   Does the data need to be grouped?

How could the data be grouped in order to facilitate clarity around the issues?

What would this grouped data tell you?

What tool(s) should the team use to group the data?

Sequence Data

❏   Is there a sequence implied by the data?

❏   Are there steps, phases, levels, stages, timelines associated with the data?

❏   Should the team sequence the data?

How could the team better sequence the data?

What would this sequenced data tell you?

What tool(s) should the team use to sequence the data?

Breakdown Data

- ❏   Is the data in manageable chunks?
- ❏   Should it be broken down so that the various parts become evident?
- ❏   Are the components and relationships among the data in their simplest form?
- ❏   Is the data broken down in a manner that is usable?

How could the data be broken down in order to facilitate clarity around the issues?

What would this broken down data tell you?

What tool(s) should the team use to break down the data?

Map Data

- ❏   Is it important to understand the flow of the data and/or process being addressed?
- ❏   Can the data and/or processes be mapped to visually show the flow?
- ❏   Should the team map the data?

How could the data be mapped in order to facilitate clarity around the issues?

What would this mapped data tell you?

What tool(s) should the team use to map the data?

Display Data

❏   Is the data easy to understand in its current form?

❏   Should it be displayed so that the various parts become evident?

❏   Are the components and relationships among the data evident?

❏   Is the data displayed in a manner that is usable?

How could the data be displayed in order to facilitate clarity around the issues?

What would this displayed data tell you?

What tool(s) should the team use to display the data?

Evaluation

A sample *Team Meeting Evaluation Form* is provided in order to address step 15. This form should be used to evaluate participation, process and outcomes.

Team Meeting Evaluation Form

Please complete and return to the Facilitator within one week of the meeting. Place a check mark (✔)next to each observation that applies to you, theTeam, the Leader, the Facilitator, the Process and the Outcomes.

Participation	Myself	Team	Leader	Facilitator
Listened to others	❑	❑	❑	❑
Participated generously	❑	❑	❑	❑
Sought additional facts	❑	❑	❑	❑
Encouraged others	❑	❑	❑	❑
Came prepared	❑	❑	❑	❑
Explored alternatives	❑	❑	❑	❑
Problem solved effectively	❑	❑	❑	❑
Suggested solutions	❑	❑	❑	❑
Agreed to actions	❑	❑	❑	❑
Agreed to accountability	❑	❑	❑	❑

Process & Outcomes	Yes	No
Meeting notice helpful	❑	❑
Agenda followed	❑	❑
Tools used appropriately	❑	❑
Entire team participated	❑	❑
Actions clear and targeted	❑	❑
Outcomes useful and targeted	❑	❑

What were the most positive aspects of this meeting?_____

_____

_____

What needs improving?_____

_____

_____

Meeting Planning Checklist

Finally, the *Meeting Planning Checklist* has been included. This check list should be used upon completion of the 15 steps and Agenda. It will provide a quick check on the completeness of the meeting plan.

Meeting Planning Checklist

❑ **Determine if the meeting is necessary.**
Team process needed
Alternatives examined and eliminated

❑ **Establish Meeting Purpose/Outcomes.**
Problem/Issue/Process/Project identified
Problem/Issue/Process/Project Boundaries specified (Beginning & Ending)
Objectives stated
Problem/Issue/Process/Project Owner(s) established

❑ **Prepare Agenda.**
Sequenced topics/steps/information/activities listed
Process(es) to be used identified
Tools/Methods for accomplishing outcomes (e.g. debate, panel, presentation,
         open discussion, facilitation) selected
Responsible person for each item named
Time allocations specified

❑ **Identify Group Roles.**
Leader - Plan the meeting, set direction and establish accountability
Facilitator - Move the meeting along and keep it focused
Recorder - Document process, decisions, actions, and outcomes
Presenters - Prepare and present specific information
Participants - Participate through input, discussion, and feedback

❑ **Identify meeting participants.**
Those with pertinent information included
Those with authority to act considered
Those with a stake in the outcome included
Those needing development in this particular area considered
Those with pertinent expertise included
Those with functional responsibility for outcomes included
Number of people necessary to accomplish goals selected

❑ **Establish Meeting Schedule/Date/Time.**
Before, during, after work, or over weekends explored
Consecutive days considered
A few hours a week over a period of time examined
Conflicting company activities accounted for
Conflicting holidays or vacations accounted for
Conflicting schedules of critical members accommodated

❑ **Select a Meeting Location.**
Away from the work environment considered
Near the work environment examined
In an office contemplated
In a conference room analyzed
Shop facilities investigated
Restaurant accommodations scrutinized
Hotel facilities explored
Conference center facilities researched

❑ **Prepare Pre-Meeting Materials.**
Participant pre-work assignments considered
Presentation data prepared
Individual assignments requested
Information and data documentation obtained and assimilated

❑ **Determine Room Set-up.**
Audio-visual equipment needs reviewed
Flip Charts, Chalk Board, White Board needs examined
Table and chair configuration(s) explored
Comfort accounted for
Lighting/Heating scrutinized
Break and lunch facilities investigated
Walls to display team's work inspected

❑ **Establish Ground Rules.** (Teams often sign to show their commitment.)
Expectations agreed to:
   Frequency of meetings
   Time of meetings
   Attendance at meetings
   Objectives for meetings
   Biggest hopes/worries
   Prioritization of work/activities
Behaviors agreed to:
   Resolution of problems/conflicts
   Decision making process
   Communication styles/methods
Team performance evaluated:
   Measurement of productivity/quality
   Improvement continuous and ongoing
Accountability established:
   Feedback individual performance
New team-member expectations set

❑ **Conduct Meeting.**
Agenda followed
Ground Rules followed
Time managed
All team members heard from
Meeting facilitation tools used

❑ **Agree on Next Steps.**
Work completed - no next steps
Action plans developed
Further meetings planned
Report written
The way business is done is changed

❑ **Evaluate the Meeting.**
Self evaluated
Team evaluated
Leader evaluated
Facilitator evaluated
Process evaluated
Outcomes evaluated

❑ **Feedback Meeting Data.**
Minutes furnished
Presentation materials supplied
Decisions made
Actions taken
Information shared
Contributions rewarded and/or recognized

❑ **Clean-up.**
Equipment returned
Room configuration reconstructed

Summary

The following steps should be taken for planning a successful meeting.

AaBbCcDdEeFfGgHhIiJjKkLlMmNn

Steps for
Planning a Successful Meeting

1. Complete the *Agenda* by following steps 1-12 of the *15 Steps to Facilitating a Successful Meeting*. Questions 13-15 will be completed during the meeting. Include your responses to the *Process and Tool Selection Questions* when completing steps 6. Process, and 7. Tools.

2. Study the facilitation tools that you have selected for the meeting so that you will be able to properly integrate them into the meeting facilitation process.

3. Use the *Meeting Planning Checklist* to evaluate the completeness of your planning.

II

Tools

GATHER DATA

◆

ORGANIZE DATA

◆

GROUP DATA

◆

SEQUENCE DATA

◆

BREAKDOWN
DATA

◆

MAP DATA

◆

DISPLAY DATA

Tools

Significant meeting time is saved when a knowledgeable, equipped facilitator focuses the team and leads them toward quicker decision-making. Equipping the facilitator with the correct tools for addressing the team's problem, issue, process or project is the focus of this chapter.

There are over 100 examples and variations of meeting facilitation tools given in the following seven tool groupings. These tool groupings have been assigned to organize the information and make it more accessible. The seven groupings include: Gather Data, Organize Data, Group Data, Sequence Data, Breakdown Data, Map Data, and Display Data.

Each grouping is organized in the same way. It describes: **WHAT** the tool is, **WHEN** to use it, **HOW** to use it, **TIMING** for usage, **MATERIALS** required, and **VARIATIONS** of usage. Step-by-step instructions for the use of each tool are given. Details around timing, materials requirements and variability of usage provide the reader with a thorough understanding of the tool and its use.

Following each tool description are examples which demonstrate the use of the tool. All of the examples begin with Problem and Goal Statements. This is done to put the examples in a team meeting context. The team should always define why it is doing what it is doing. This is critical for facilitating the team and targeting its efforts.

Many of the examples are completed in full. They not only show the process or form that the team would use, but show a completed document so the reader can better understand the process. Other examples simply show the process or form, and are easy enough to understand without the additional detail.

Conclusions that the team would draw from the data in the examples are not given. The point of the example is to show the process and how it works. The reader should examine the Case Studies for examples of conclusions drawn.

A *Materials Selection Matrix* follows. The Matrix gives additional information on the types of materials commonly used by team facilitators.

Materials Selection Matrix

Description	Usage	Advantages	Disadvantages
Flip Chart An easel with a blank pad of paper that attaches. Information is recorded on it with felt tip markers. Post-its can be placed on this to organize data.	• Small groups (under 25) • Informal learning • Meeting facilitation • Teaching rules & concepts • Organizing & displaying information • Highlighting important points	• Easy to use • Readily available • Portable • Display work around room • Grids allow easy writing • Flexible	• Group size • Speaker's back to audience • No permanent record until transposed • Limited space for writing
Overhead Projector Acetate sheets are used with an overhead projector. Information is added with felt tip markers.	• Small to medium groups (20 - 75) • Meeting facilitation • Organizing & displaying information • Displaying graphs/charts • Projecting to a large audience	• Easy to use • Readily available • Flexible • Facilitator faces group • Can be done ahead with color, pictures, graphics, charts, etc.	• Distracting if presenter blocks view of material • Fan noise • Requires special equipment • Can be glaring • Room lighting can deter from visuals
White/Chalk Board A board that is either hung on a wall or mounted on rollers. Information is recorded using either chalk or felt tip markers. Post-its can be placed on the white board to organize data.	• Small groups (under 25) • Informal learning • Meeting facilitation • Organizing & displaying information • Adapting & changing information as needed • Organizing sticky notes	• Easy to use • Erasable • Portable • Flexible • Readily available • Surface to place Post-its	• Group size • Limits eye contact • Summary information done after-the-fact • No permanent record until transposed
Butcher Paper Paper that comes in a roll. It is either white or like a brown paper bag. The paper rolls out and can be used to cover a wall . It can be written on with felt tip markers. Post-its can be placed on this to organize data.	• Small groups (under 25) • Informal learning • Meeting facilitation • Organizing & displaying information • Organizing sticky notes • Organizing large space items such as time lines, process mapping, stages, continuums, etc.	• Easy to use • Large surface • Readily available • Surface to place Post-its • Easy to see • Can involve entire group in process	• Group size • Cumbersome • Difficult to hang • Summary information done after-the-fact • Difficult to copy information afterward
Computer Interface Computers can be used to display information when a projection interface system is used.	• Small to medium groups (20 - 75) • Organizing & displaying information • Adapting & changing information as needed • Printing out quickly • Meeting facilitation	• Fast • Easy to see • Portable • Flexible • Can be done ahead of time • Changes can be made real time • Quick feedback	• Difficult to use • Requires special equipment • Room lighting can deter from visuals • One-person involvement • Expensive

Gather Data

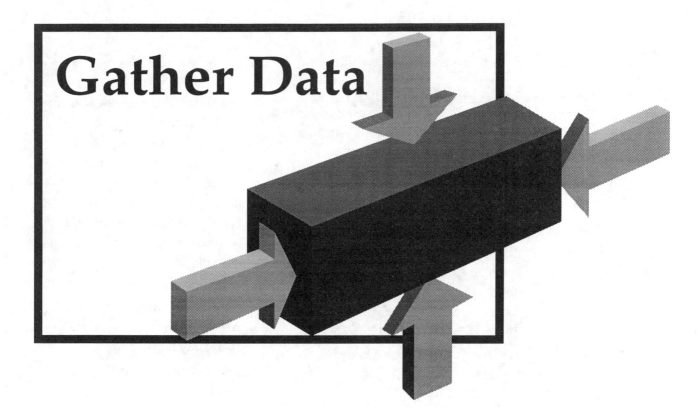

Brainstorming

Observation

Questions/Surveys

Mystery Shopper

Interviews

BRAINSTORMING

What

One of the easiest ways to gather data is to generate creative and divergent thinking about an idea, topic or decision by creating a list in a structured way. Brainstorming puts all of the data in one place. The group can then evaluate, combine, delete and converge the data as generated, or utilize it in conjunction with other team facilitation tools. Brainstorming is subjective and non-judgemental. It must be supported by real data.

When

Brainstorming can serve several purposes for the team:

- get all ideas out in the open
- allow team members to build on each other's ideas
- document everyone's input
- promote creative thinking
- surface problems, issues and opportunities
- document information, issues, ideas or data
- focus team thinking
- segregate issues

How

In generating your list(s), you should:

1. Define the problem.
2. Set goals for the session.

3. Generate the list either independently on 3 X 5 cards or sticky notes, or as a group with one person recording all ideas. There should be no judgment, discussion, or criticism of the ideas at this point. If the contribution is too long, ask the contributor to shorten. Build on each others ideas.

4. Observe, discuss and fine-tune the content of the list. All members should understand each contribution.

5. Set action plan(s) for next steps.

Timing

Lists can be generated in a relatively short period of time if the team is dealing with simple issues. If the list is being generated real time, then it should take no more than 15 - 30 minutes to develop.

Brainstorming

Problem: There are a lot of things to accomplish today.
Goal: Develop a check list so that none of the *"To Dos"* will be forgotten.

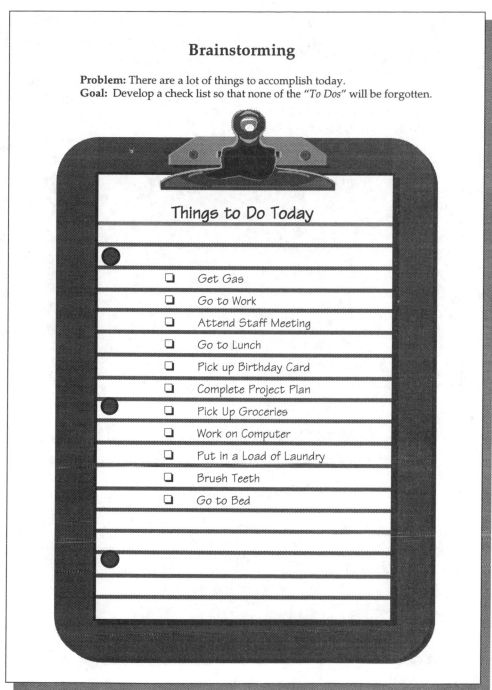

Things to Do Today

- ❑ Get Gas
- ❑ Go to Work
- ❑ Attend Staff Meeting
- ❑ Go to Lunch
- ❑ Pick up Birthday Card
- ❑ Complete Project Plan
- ❑ Pick Up Groceries
- ❑ Work on Computer
- ❑ Put in a Load of Laundry
- ❑ Brush Teeth
- ❑ Go to Bed

Materials

Something to write on that can be seen by all participants:

- Flip Chart (including masking tape or push pins for hanging)
- Overheads and Projector
- Butcher Paper
- White Board
- Chalk Board
- 3 X 5 Cards or Sticky Notes
- Worksheets
- Questionnaires
- Logs
- Computer

Something to write with:

- Felt Tip Pens (different types for Flip Charts, Overheads and White Boards)
- Chalk
- Pens/Pencils

Gather Data

Brainstorming

Problem: Not all of the organization's managers are qualified to manage.
Goal: Identify the management development needs of the management staff.

Management Development Needs

- ☑ Managing performance
- ☑ Managing problem performance
- ☑ Team development
- ☑ Decision making
- ☑ Delegation
- ☑ Interviewing
- ☑ Organizing
- ☑ Strategic planning
- ☑ Project planning
- ☑ Rewards and recognition
- ☑ Managing diversity
- ☑ Continuous improvement
- ☑ Organizational priorities
- ☑ Communication

Variations

Lists are as varied as the needs for generating them. Here are different ways of using lists:

- Generate Ideas
- Document Different Points of View
- Input Agenda Items
- Formulate Questions
- Select Data
- Name Items, People, Things
- Furnish Citations
- Pinpoint Opportunities
- Relate Information
- Record Ideas

OBSERVATION

What

Data can be gathered through observation. When something is observed, it is then recorded so as not to be omitted from the activity when performed.

When

Observation should be used when teams want to collect data with minimal disturbance to the regular work flow. Through observation, information can be collected and recorded on:

- processes
- activities
- behaviors
- service
- frequency
- order
- changes over time
- displayed materials
- groupings and clusters
- linkages
- work flow
- history
- methods

How

1. Define the problem.
2. Set the goals of the observation.
3. Identify the observations that you will be targeting.
4. Set a schedule for observation(s).
5. Record your observations in a consistent manner.
6. Analyze information, seek solutions, verify, and/or document.
7. Set action plans for next steps.

Timing

The variation of timing on this tool is extensive. In very simple, fast moving situations, observations and record keeping can be done quickly. Other observations could take hours, days, weeks, months, years, decades and/or centuries.

Gather Data

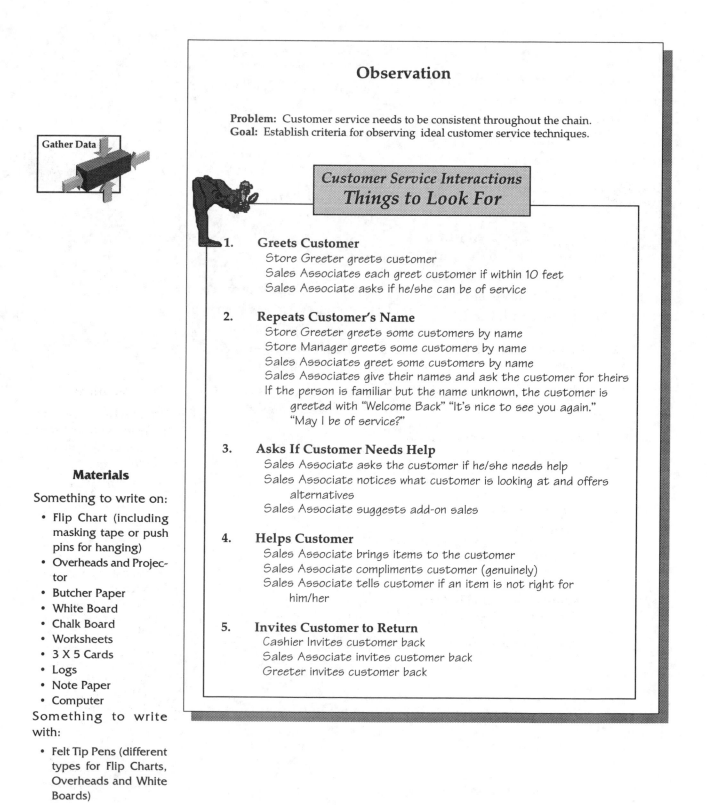

Gather Data

Observation

Problem: Customer service needs to be consistent throughout the chain.
Goal: Establish criteria for observing ideal customer service techniques.

Customer Service Interactions
Things to Look For

1. **Greets Customer**
   Store Greeter greets customer
   Sales Associates each greet customer if within 10 feet
   Sales Associate asks if he/she can be of service

2. **Repeats Customer's Name**
   Store Greeter greets some customers by name
   Store Manager greets some customers by name
   Sales Associates greet some customers by name
   Sales Associates give their names and ask the customer for theirs
   If the person is familiar but the name unknown, the customer is
       greeted with "Welcome Back" "It's nice to see you again."
       "May I be of service?"

3. **Asks If Customer Needs Help**
   Sales Associate asks the customer if he/she needs help
   Sales Associate notices what customer is looking at and offers
       alternatives
   Sales Associate suggests add-on sales

4. **Helps Customer**
   Sales Associate brings items to the customer
   Sales Associate compliments customer (genuinely)
   Sales Associate tells customer if an item is not right for
       him/her

5. **Invites Customer to Return**
   Cashier Invites customer back
   Sales Associate invites customer back
   Greeter invites customer back

Materials

Something to write on:

- Flip Chart (including masking tape or push pins for hanging)
- Overheads and Projector
- Butcher Paper
- White Board
- Chalk Board
- Worksheets
- 3 X 5 Cards
- Logs
- Note Paper
- Computer

Something to write with:

- Felt Tip Pens (different types for Flip Charts, Overheads and White Boards)
- Chalk
- Pens/Pencils

Observation

Problem: Customer service needs to be consistent throughout the chain.
Goal: Establish criteria for observing ideal customer service techniques.

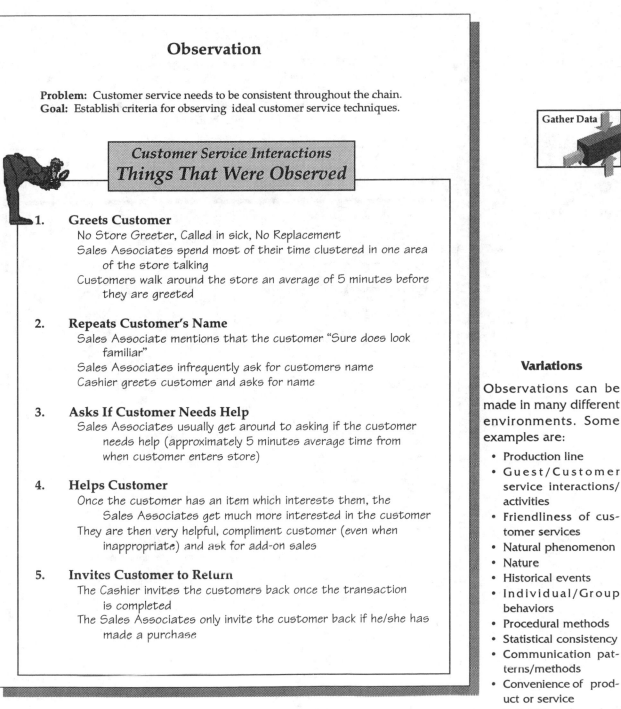

Customer Service Interactions
Things That Were Observed

1. Greets Customer
No Store Greeter, Called in sick, No Replacement
Sales Associates spend most of their time clustered in one area
of the store talking
Customers walk around the store an average of 5 minutes before
they are greeted

2. Repeats Customer's Name
Sales Associate mentions that the customer "Sure does look
familiar"
Sales Associates infrequently ask for customers name
Cashier greets customer and asks for name

3. Asks If Customer Needs Help
Sales Associates usually get around to asking if the customer
needs help (approximately 5 minutes average time from
when customer enters store)

4. Helps Customer
Once the customer has an item which interests them, the
Sales Associates get much more interested in the customer
They are then very helpful, compliment customer (even when
inappropriate) and ask for add-on sales

5. Invites Customer to Return
The Cashier invites the customers back once the transaction
is completed
The Sales Associates only invite the customer back if he/she has
made a purchase

Gather Data

Variations

Observations can be made in many different environments. Some examples are:

- Production line
- Guest/Customer service interactions/activities
- Friendliness of customer services
- Natural phenomenon
- Nature
- Historical events
- Individual/Group behaviors
- Procedural methods
- Statistical consistency
- Communication patterns/methods
- Convenience of product or service
- Reliability of product or service
- Features of product
- Error recovery process and/or time
- Prices, discounts, bonuses

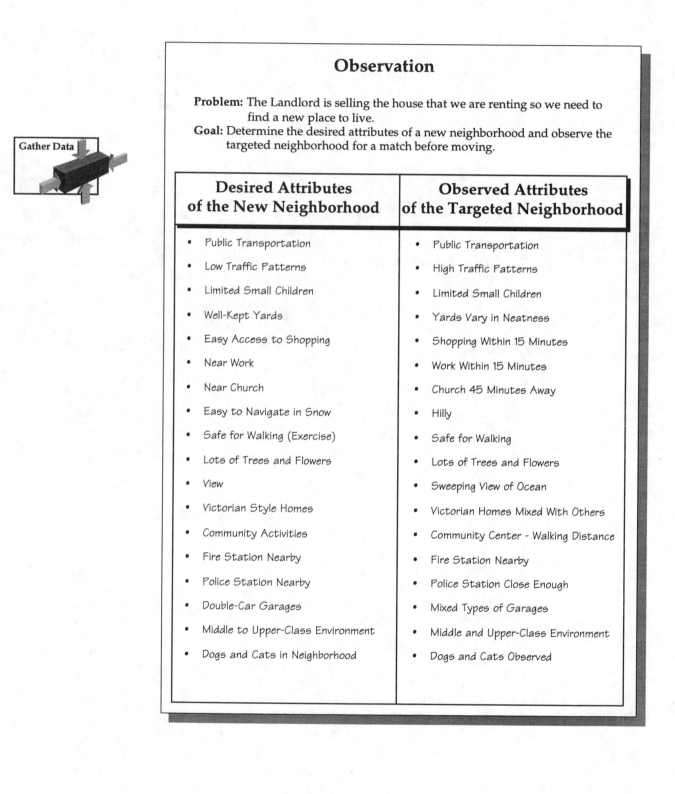

Gather Data

Observation

Problem: The Landlord is selling the house that we are renting so we need to find a new place to live.

Goal: Determine the desired attributes of a new neighborhood and observe the targeted neighborhood for a match before moving.

Desired Attributes of the New Neighborhood	Observed Attributes of the Targeted Neighborhood
• Public Transportation	• Public Transportation
• Low Traffic Patterns	• High Traffic Patterns
• Limited Small Children	• Limited Small Children
• Well-Kept Yards	• Yards Vary in Neatness
• Easy Access to Shopping	• Shopping Within 15 Minutes
• Near Work	• Work Within 15 Minutes
• Near Church	• Church 45 Minutes Away
• Easy to Navigate in Snow	• Hilly
• Safe for Walking (Exercise)	• Safe for Walking
• Lots of Trees and Flowers	• Lots of Trees and Flowers
• View	• Sweeping View of Ocean
• Victorian Style Homes	• Victorian Homes Mixed With Others
• Community Activities	• Community Center - Walking Distance
• Fire Station Nearby	• Fire Station Nearby
• Police Station Nearby	• Police Station Close Enough
• Double-Car Garages	• Mixed Types of Garages
• Middle to Upper-Class Environment	• Middle and Upper-Class Environment
• Dogs and Cats in Neighborhood	• Dogs and Cats Observed

QUESTIONS/SURVEYS

What

Asking questions is one of the most obvious ways of collecting data. A clearly asked question can yield invaluable information on any number of topics. Although sophisticated questionnaires and survey instruments are often used for information gathering and statistical compilation, the questions and survey examples discussed in this chapter are targeted for ease of use by non-professionals in a team environment.

When

Questions can be asked to generate ideas and stimulate thinking or to specifically obtain information.

Survey questions are designed to obtain specific information and come in several forms. They can be:

- given and received through the mail
- asked over the telephone
- administered during the meeting
- obtained at the point of service
- collected during an interview process or focus group meeting

How

Gather Data

1. Define the problem.
2. Set the goals of the survey or questionnaire.
3. Identify the item, activity, service, process or behavior on which you are to collect information.
4. Write/ask targeted questions that are direct and easy to answer. Some rules of thumb for effective team questions are:

   - Make sure the instructions are clear and easy to follow.
   - Limit your questions to 25 or less.
   - Ask your questions to discover information, not to prove a point.
   - Ask for demographic information when it is important to learn how different groups feel about certain issues (e.g. male/female, age, education, income bracket, etc.).
   - Ask questions in several different formats. They can be multiple choice, scaled from low to high, open-ended, force ranked, yes or no, true or false. They can also take the form of suggestions, concerns, compliments or complaints.

- Make anonymous if possible. This ensures more accurate feedback.

- Address only one thought with each question.

- If the questions are being asked through a mailing, make sure that you have a clear cover letter explaining the purpose of the survey and what will be done with the completed information.

5. Administer the survey or ask the questions.

6. Record the feedback and tabulate results.

7. Analyze information, seek solutions, verify, and/or document.

8. Feed the findings back to participants in the process.

Timing

Questionnaires and surveys should be quick and easy to use. If they take too long, people will not take the time to fill out and return them.

- If you ask pre-determined questions in a group to collect information, you may spend approximately 30 minutes.

- If the group develops survey questions to ask, they may spend several hours develop-

ing the questions and testing for consistency of interpretation.

- If a survey instrument needs to be sent out and returned, it may take days, or even weeks, to administer. In addition, you still need to tabulate and analyze the information and feed it back to the participants.

- Many different types of questionnaires and surveys can be purchased, distributed and tabulated by outside vendors. Depending on the instrument, the entire process may be done in a one hour meeting or stretched out for weeks.

Questions/Surveys

Problem: The team is meeting for the first time and needs to get to know each other quickly so that they can get down to work.

Goal: Have the participants interact in a "Getting to Know You" Icebreaker exercise.

Instructions
1. Choose someone that you do not know to be your partner.
2. Take turns asking each other the questions listed below.
3. Record each others answers.
4. Introduce your partner and share her/his answers with the rest of the class.
   You have 15 minutes to ask the questions
   We will spend 15 minutes sharing the answers

Getting to Know You Icebreaker

1. **What is your name?**

2. **What department do you work in?**

3. **What do you do there?**

4. **What is your favorite movie?**

5. **What is your favorite pastime outside of work?**

6. **What is your favorite song?**

7. **If you were to describe your feelings about today's meeting using a color, which color would you choose?**

Gather Data

Materials
Something to write on:
- Flip Chart (including masking tape or push pins for hanging)
- Overheads and Projector
- Butcher Paper
- White Board
- Chalk Board
- Questionnaires
- Survey Instruments
- Note Paper
- Computer

Something to write with:
- Felt Tip Pens (different types for Flip Charts, Overheads and White Boards)
- Chalk
- Pens/Pencils

Gather Data

Variations

There are a wide variety of questions, questionnaires and surveys that can be built, purchased and utilized. Examples of different types are:

- Guest/Customer Satisfaction Surveys
- Opinion Surveys
- Questions to help the group focus on priorities or actions
- Icebreaker questions
- Thought/idea producing questions
- Data collection questions
- Issues identification questions
- Attitude Surveys
- Point of Sale Questionnaires
- "Put yourself in someone else's place" questions
- Decision-focused questions
- Vital Statistics/Demographic questions

Questions/Surveys

Problem: Eating in the employee cafeteria has dropped off in the last year.
Goal: Find out why employees no longer eat in the employee cafeteria.

All Employee Cafeteria Survey

Complete the following and return to the Human Resources Department within the next week.

1. Do you usually eat in the employee cafeteria?   Yes   No   (Used To)

   If you *used to* eat in the employee cafeteria, but do not eat there any more, Why Not?

   The food has gotten more expensive and you get less of it.

2. How would you rate the following?

	Poor		Excellent	
Hot Dishes	1	2	③	4
Sandwiches	1	2	③	4
Salads	1	②	3	4
Beverages	1	2	3	④
Check Out	1	②	3	4
Prices	①	2	3	4
Service	1	②	3	4
Appeal of Food	1	②	3	4

3. Explain any 1 or 2 ratings.

   As I mentioned the food is too expensive. You get less salad. The cafeteria now weighs the salads and charges by the weight. The meat and cheese obviously weigh more so you get mostly lettuce. Also the service is not very good. The food centers run out of things and it takes forever to get someone to replenish them.

4. If the items that you rated a 1 or 2 were addressed as you have explained, would you eat your lunch more frequently in the employee cafeteria?

   1   2   3   4   5   ⑥   7
   No   Yes

   The prices would have to come down for me to return on a regular basis.

5. Do you have any other comments that you would like to make concerning the employee cafeteria and what would entice you to eat there?

   I'm glad someone asked these questions. It seems like the company really cares.

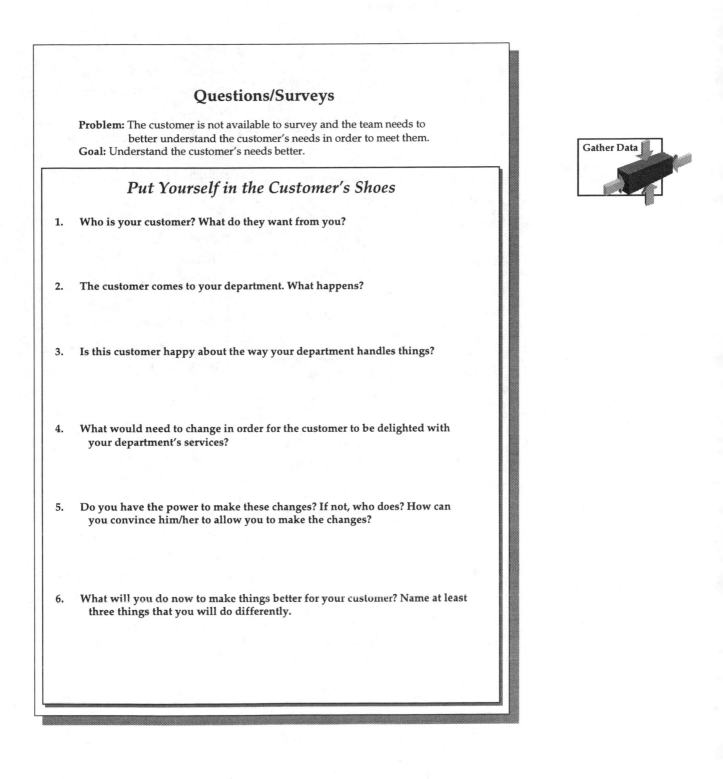

Questions/Surveys

Problem: The customer is not available to survey and the team needs to better understand the customer's needs in order to meet them.
Goal: Understand the customer's needs better.

Gather Data

Put Yourself in the Customer's Shoes

1. Who is your customer? What do they want from you?

2. The customer comes to your department. What happens?

3. Is this customer happy about the way your department handles things?

4. What would need to change in order for the customer to be delighted with your department's services?

5. Do you have the power to make these changes? If not, who does? How can you convince him/her to allow you to make the changes?

6. What will you do now to make things better for your customer? Name at least three things that you will do differently.

MYSTERY SHOPPER

What

The Mystery Shopper is someone who experiences service(s) for the express purpose of collecting information on how well the service does or does not perform. They take the role of customer or guest and are unknown to the employees as a mystery shopper.

When

Mystery Shoppers are used when the organization wants a customer point of view about its service performance. Mystery shoppers are often looking for a number of customer related services including such things as:

- consistency of product and/or service across the organization
- facilities location, appeal, access, and usability
- employee attitudes toward organization
- quality and consistency of product(s)
- attitudes of other customers

How

1. Define the problem.
2. Set the goals for the Mystery Shop.

3. Identify the item, activity, service, process or behavior on which you are collecting information.
4. Write targeted questions with which you will be collecting information during the Mystery Shop.
5. Mystery Shop and collect the targeted data as well as recording any other items of interest or concern.
6. Tabulate, analyze and feedback the results.
7. Make changes to address the identified issues.

Timing

Mystery Shopping can be done in a 1 - 2 hour segment, or in several 1 - 2 hour segments over a period of days, weeks or months, depending on the scope of the study. The Shopping might also require travel to other locations which takes additional time.

Mystery Shopper

Problem: The team does not know how its customers experience their service versus their competitor's service.

Goal: Establish some Mystery Shopper guidelines from which to evaluate ourselves against our competitor.

Gather Data

Mystery Shopper Guidelines

1. **How is the customer approached and greeted?**
   By Your Organization   By Competitor's Organization

2. **What is the sales experience the customer receives?**
   By Your Organization   By Competitor's Organization

3. **Does the customer receive accurate product knowledge?**
   By Your Organization   By Competitor's Organization

4. **Is the customer's experience friendly and helpful?**
   By Your Organization   By Competitor's Organization

5. **Does the customer experience initiative and enthusiasm when they visit?**
   By Your Organization   By Competitor's Organization

6. **Is the customer offered upselling opportunities?**
   By Your Organization   By Competitor's Organization

7. **Does the customer experience efficiency, speed and service?**
   By Your Organization   By Competitor's Organization

8. **Does the customer receive a quality product?**
   By Your Organization   By Competitor's Organization

9. **Does the customer experience a clean and organized facility?**
   By Your Organization   By Competitor's Organization

10. **Is the customer introduced to special promotions?**
    By Your Organization   By Competitor's Organization

Materials

Something to write on:

- Questionnaires
- Logs
- Note Paper
- Computer

Something to write with:

- Pens/Pencils

Variations

Types of services that often use mystery shoppers include:

- Hospitality Industry
- Insurance Industry
- Transportation Industry
- Banking Industry
- Tourist Industry
- Retail Stores
- Food Outlets
- Consumer Products Industry
- Health Care Industry

INTERVIEWS

Gather Data

What

Interviews consist of two or more people with one is asking questions of the other(s). Interviews often give the interviewer more data than the answers from questionnaires or surveys because the interviewee tells you more than he or she would typically write on a form. Probing and clarification questions can also be asked to increase or hone information.

Additional information is also obtained as the interviewer observes the non-verbal communications of the person(s) who is/are answering the questions.

When

Interviews are used to obtain information from individuals. They are used when:

- obtaining information from job applicants
- research is being conducted in the scientific and social areas
- trainers and/or organizational design and development professionals seek information regarding the needs of the organization
- Subject Matter Experts (SMEs) are asked for information in their area of expertise

- Collecting information from customers (e.g. requirements, expectations, new products/services)

How

1. Define the problem.
2. Set the goals for the interview.
3. Identify the item, activity, service, process or behavior under study.
4. Write targeted questions on your topic of study.
5. Set appointments with interviewees allowing ample time for probing and honing data collection.
6. During the interview:
   - state who you are
   - state your purpose for the interview
   - explain its importance
   - explain the confidentiality of the interview
   - explain how the interviewee was chosen
   - explain what will happen to the data
   - explain the length of the interview
   - explain any follow-up plans
   - record the answers
7. Tabulate, analyze, summarize and feed back the results.
8. Set actions based on data feedback.

Timing

Even the shortest interview should last 30 - 60 minutes. Individuals vary in their length of answers and time should be allowed for probing questions.

Group interviews can take much longer. Group interviews should include no more than 6 individuals and should allow for participants to build on each other's answers. Allow at least 2 - 4 hours for group interviews. Be aware that one of the potential problems with group interviews is that the group may begin to agree with each other on the issues since they are hearing each other's input. They may also cause more timid contributors to "clam up", especially if the input is confidential or "political" in nature. Conducting individual interviews can take longer but often bring more diverse answers and feedback.

Gather Data

Interviews

Problem: The creativity team has lost half of its members.
Goal: Identify new candidates to join the creativity team.

Creativity Team Interview Questions

CANDIDATE _____ INTERVIEWER_____

1. Do you consider yourself to be creative? Why? How?

2. Tell me about a person that you believe to be creative. How are they creative?

3. Do you dream in color? Describe one.

4. If you had to give this room a name, what would it be? Why?

5. Describe as many ways as you can think of to get home from work.

6. If you could describe the perfect creativity team, what would it look like?

7. Name 5 methods for improving creativity thinking. Why did you choose these?

8. If you could draw your feelings on a piece of paper right now, what would you draw?

9. The employee cafeteria needs a new look. What ideas do you have that would improve the look and entice more employees?

Comments

Materials

Something to write on:

- Flip Chart (including masking tape or push pins for hanging)
- Overheads and Projector
- Butcher Paper
- White Board
- Chalk Board
- Worksheets
- Note Paper
- Computer

Something to write with:

- Felt Tip Pens (different types for Flip Charts, Overheads and White Boards)
- Chalk
- Pens/Pencils

Interviews

Problem: The new team needs to know each other better.
Goal: To disclose more about themselves to each other.

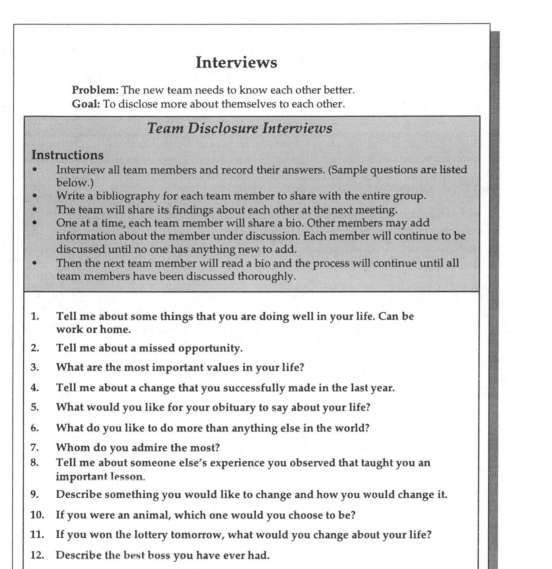

Team Disclosure Interviews

Instructions

- Interview all team members and record their answers. (Sample questions are listed below.)
- Write a bibliography for each team member to share with the entire group.
- The team will share its findings about each other at the next meeting.
- One at a time, each team member will share a bio. Other members may add information about the member under discussion. Each member will continue to be discussed until no one has anything new to add.
- Then the next team member will read a bio and the process will continue until all team members have been discussed thoroughly.

1. Tell me about some things that you are doing well in your life. Can be work or home.

2. Tell me about a missed opportunity.

3. What are the most important values in your life?

4. Tell me about a change that you successfully made in the last year.

5. What would you like for your obituary to say about your life?

6. What do you like to do more than anything else in the world?

7. Whom do you admire the most?

8. Tell me about someone else's experience you observed that taught you an important lesson.

9. Describe something you would like to change and how you would change it.

10. If you were an animal, which one would you choose to be?

11. If you won the lottery tomorrow, what would you change about your life?

12. Describe the best boss you have ever had.

13. Describe your favorite co-worker.

14. Tell me something you are learning in your life right now.

15. What is the best team experience you ever had?

16. What do you think your life will be like 15 years from now?

17. What is the one thing people most misunderstand about you?

Variations

Some of the most common interview methods are:

- Job Interviews
- Scientific or Social Research
- Needs Assessments
- Subject Matter Expert (SME) Interviews

Organize Data

T-Charts

Double T-Charts

Matrix Chart

Consensus Card Method

Paired-Choice Matrix

Multi-Voting

Force Field Analysis

Worksheet

Check/Tally Sheets

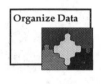

Organize Data

T-CHARTS

What

The T-Chart is one of the fundamental tools which all team facilitators should be able to use skillfully. It is easy to implement and has application in most situations. It is simply a T-shaped bar with lists or data on either side.

When

By listing information in two side-by-side columns the team can:

- point out *comparisons and differences* concerning information

- *organize relationships* of information

- show *opposite* or *opposing* thinking

- depict timing or information *shifts*

How

1. Define the problem.

2. Set the goals of the session.

3. Draw a T-shaped frame in which information can be listed on each side, leaving room for Headers at the top of each column.

4. Write the Headers at the top of each column.

5. Keeping in mind the column data relationships, the team should provide input into each list.

6. The facilitator or record keeper writes the information in the appropriate column.

7. This should continue until all ideas have been voiced and recorded.

8. Observe and analyze.

9. Set action plans for next steps.

Timing

This session can be conducted in a very short period of time, or can stretch out much longer depending on the amount of information the team is trying to bring to the surface and deal with. Ask yourself a couple of basic questions:

- Do we need a comprehensive set of data? This will take longer.

- Do we just want to get a few ideas on the chart to spur further thinking? This can be accomplished in a very short period of time.

Allow approximately 15 - 30 minutes.

Materials

Something to write on that can be seen by all participants:

- Grid-type Flip Chart (including masking tape or push pins for hanging)
- Overheads and Projector
- Butcher Paper
- White Board
- Chalk Board

Something to write with:

- Felt Tip Pens (different types for Flip Charts, Overheads and White Boards)
- Chalk

T-Chart

Opposite or Opposing

Organize Data

Problem: Need to move offices.
Goal: Identify issues affecting move.

Problem: Strategic plan may need updating.
Goal: Determine the strengths and weaknesses of the current plan.

Go	No Go
Budget Approved	Budget Delayed
Personnel Identified	Personnel Missing
Timelines are Realistic	Cannot be done in Time
Furniture Received	Furniture Delayed
Adequate Parking	Difficult Parking

Assets	Liabilities
Very Thorough	Detail Laden
Well Thought out	Technology Has Changed
Timeliness Documented	Deadlines Have Shifted
Lists All Actions	Assignments Unclear
Company Specific	Company Has Changed
Targeted Growth	Changes in Targets

Comparisons and Differences

Problem: Attendance at meetings is down.
Goal: Determine why attendance is down.

Problem: All staff need to be developed.
Goal: Identify development criteria that meets individual and organizational needs.

Theory Based	Data Based
Meetings Unfocused	No Agendas
Turnover Increasing	5 This Year/3 Last Year
Location Inconvenient	3 Members 1 Hour Drive
A Few Do All Talking	2 People Did <u>All</u> Talking
Leaders Unskilled	No Meeting Training for Leaders

Individual Career Planning	Human Resources Planning
Personal Goals	Organizational Goals
Occupational Choice	Selection Strategy
Job Choice	Job Opportunities
Performance Review	Increase Productivity

Variations

There are as many variations as there are ideas. A few are grouped and displayed here.

Comparisons and Differences

- Individual Career Planning/Human Resources Planning
- Theory Based/Data Based
- Sales/Marketing
- Mechanistic/Organic

Organize Relationships

- Behavior or Quality/Benefits
- Problem Attributes/Diagnostic Questions
- Assumptions/Questions
- Modes of Behavior/Appropriate Situations
- Target Group/Types of Interventions
- Expectations/Perceptions
- Task/Relationship

Organize Data

T-Chart

Organize Relationships

Problem: No management development has been provided.
Goal: Identify what management development is needed.

Target Group	Types of Intervention
Senior Management	Strategic Planning
	Lecture Series
	Competitive Analysis
Middle Management	Financial Planning
	Market Strategies
	Problem Performers
1st Line Supervision	Classroom Training
	Performance Management
	Time & Attendance
	Stress Management
	Professional Development

Problem: Desired organizational behaviors have not been identified.
Goal: Identify benefits of desired organizational behaviors.

Behavior or Quality	Benefits
1. Integrity	We Can Trust Each Other
	Customers Trust Us
2. Fiscal Responsibility	Resources Managed
3. Communication	No Secrets/Open System
4. Teamwork	We Support and Help Each Other

Shifts

Problem: The department is outdated.
Goal: Identify what needs to be updated.

Old	New
Computers Old	Research New Models
Functional Organization Structure	Cross-Functional Structure
Employees in Rut	Identify Development
Offices Old-fashioned	Engage Interior Designer
Motivation Lacking	Design Incentive Programs

Problem: Method of change is not effective.
Goal: Analyze current process to desired state.

Organization Transformation	Organization Development
First Stages of Change	Encompasses all Change
Accept Need for Change	Institutionalize Change
Allows/Facilitates Change	Leads/Manages Change
Individually Focused	Organizationally Focused

Variations (Continued)

Opposite or Opposing

- Likes/Dislikes
- Capable/Need Improvement
- Best/Worst
- Go/No Go
- Strengths/Weakness
- Assets/Liabilities
- Do's/Don'ts
- Old/New
- Is/Is Not

Shifts

- Organization Transformation/Organization Development
- Old Paradigm/New Paradigm
- From/To
- Old/New

DOUBLE T-CHARTS (TT-CHART)

What

The TT-Chart is an extension of the T-Chart and is also a fundamental tool for team facilitation. It adds another column to the T, allowing for three columns of information as opposed to the two found in a T-Chart.

When

Listing the information in three columns allows the information to be organized in a sequential, comparative, contrasting or phased manner. The additional first column often represents a topic, strategy, task, role, step, or phase.

How

1. Define the problem.
2. Set the goals of the session.
3. Draw a TT-shaped frame in which information can be listed in three columns. Leave room for the Headers at the top of each column.
4. Write the Headers at the top of each column.
5. Keeping in mind the column data relationships, the team should begin to provide input for each list.
6. The facilitator or record keeper writes the information in the appropriate column.
7. This should continue until all ideas have been voiced and recorded.
8. Observe and analyze.
9. Set action plans for next steps.

Timing

You should allow a minimum of 20 - 45 minutes for this exercise. The team will need time to decide on the Headers, provide the column input and discuss any differences of opinion.

Organize Data

Organize Data

TT-Chart

Problem: Teams are being formed but the organization has not changed.
Goal: Determine the things that need to change.

Organization Change Analysis

Topic	Old	New
Mission	Accomplish goals with guidelines	Explore new development/ growth
Values	Truthful, Timely, Kind, Resourceful	Ethical, Innovative, Progressive
Strategy	Meet deadlines/commitments	Continuously Improve/Progress
Customer Focus	Meet customer needs	Exceed Customer Needs
Decision Making	Top Down/Hierarchical	Team Based/Empowerment
Communications	"Grapevine", Gossip	Open, Shared

Problem: The Information Systems division has no organizational credibility.
Goal: Determine what works and what does not.

Works - Does Not Work Analysis

Task	Going Well	Needs Improvement
Programming	2 new programs this year	Project priorities unclear
System Support	Responsiveness is timely	Changes not communicated
E-Mail Installation	E-Mail is 50% installed	Project priorities unclear
Project Planning	Tools and knowledge available	Project priorities unclear
Communication	Work group shares information	Customers unclear of progress
LANS Installed	6 New LANs Installed	Project priorities unclear

Materials

Something to write on that can be seen by all participants:

- Grid-type Flip Chart (including masking tape or push pins for hanging)
- Overheads and Projector
- Butcher Paper
- White Board
- Chalk Board

Something to write with:

- Felt Tip Pens (different types for Flip Charts, Overheads and White Boards)
- Chalk

TT-Chart

Problem: Meeting leaders are confused as to their roles.
Goal: Obtain better understanding of meeting leader roles.

Organize Data

Meeting Leader Roles

Presenter	Trainer	Facilitator
Conveys information	Provides structured learning	Engages audience in learning
Content driven	Content/process driven	Process driven
Tells	Models	Guides
Inspires	Instructs	Enables

Problem: The project is floundering, going nowhere.
Goal: Get the project back on track.

Project Planning Steps

Steps	Responsible	By When
1. Convene the project team	Martha as Team Leader	Friday, January 6
2. Plan Agendas	Bill and Susan as functional leads	Have ready for Friday meeting
3. Re-establish deadlines	Martha and Frank	Have ready for Friday meeting
4. Establish project timeline	Entire Team	During Friday Meeting
5. Evaluate resources	Kevin as Financial Officer	Tuesday, January 3
6. Develop new plan	Entire Team	During Friday Meeting
7. Identify project barriers	Entire Team	During Friday Meeting

Variations

Organize Data

As with the T-Chart, there are as many variations as there are ideas. A few examples of what might be found as column headers in the Double T-Chart are displayed here. These columns can be mixed and matched to achieve other variations as well. Notice that many of the items in columns 2 and 3 are taken from the basic T-Chart.

Column 1	Column 2	Column 3
Topic	Old	New
Task	Going Well	Needs Improvement
Attribute	Formal System	Information System
Strategy	Overorganization	Underorganization
Phases	Priority Target	Implementation Target
Relationships	Do's	Don'ts
Role	Assets	Liabilities
Decision	Task	Relationship
Method	Major Advantages	Major Potential Problems
Speaker	Trainer	Facilitator
Steps	Responsible	By When

MATRIX CHART

What

The Matrix Chart organizes and displays information in interrelational columns and rows.

When

This tool can aid teams in action planning, selection of dimensions or choices, separation of issues, evaluation of data, charting information and scheduling.

How

1. Define the problem.

2. Set the goals of the session.

3. Determine the issues, dimensions and choices that need to be interrelated and create columns and rows with Headers for each.

4. List the issues, dimensions and choices in each corresponding location on the chart beneath or beside the appropriate Header.

5. Continue to fill in the matrix until completed.

6. Review the matrix and check for clarity, understanding and completeness.

7. Set action plans for next steps.

Timing

This tool can be fairly simple or very complex. It should take from 1 - 2 hours to identify, place Headers, and list all issues, dimensions and choices.

Organize Data

Organize Data

Matrix Chart

Problem: New supervisors are not prepared for the role.
Goal: Identify developmental opportunities for new supervisors.

Dimension Selection Grid

Company Training Courses

Job Dimensions	Intro. to Supervision	Disciplinary Action Basics	Behavioral Interviewing	Basic Project Management	Better Writing	Presentation Skills	Time Management	Coaching & Mentoring	Team Building	Handling Problem Performance
Supervision	X	X						X	X	X
Time and Attendance							X			
Communication					X	X				
Performance Management		X						X	X	X
Selection and Recruiting			X							
Project Management				X			X			
Scheduling				X			X			
Time Management							X			

Materials

Something to write on that can be seen by all participants:

- Grid-type Flip Chart (including masking tape or push pins for hanging)
- Overheads and Projector
- Butcher Paper
- White Board
- Chalk Board

Something to write with:

- Felt Tip Pens (different types for Flip Charts, Overheads and White Boards)
- Chalk

Matrix Chart

Problem: Responsibility for the organization's strategic initiatives is unclear.
Goal: Determine levels of responsibility by functional organization.

L-Shaped Matrix

Functional Area / Strategic Initiatives	Sales/ Marketing	Finance	Legal	Operations	Human Resources	Technical Services
Total Quality						
Service Standards						
Peer Reviews						
Product Standards						
Organization Restructuring						
Product Development						

Primary Responsibility ▲   Secondary Responsibility ❑   Need To Be Informed ○

L-Shaped Matrix

Functional Area / Strategic Initiatives	Sales/ Marketing	Finance	Legal	Operations	Human Resources	Technical Services
Total Quality	○	○	○	▲	❑	○
Service Standards	❑			▲	❑	❑
Peer Reviews				▲	❑	○
Product Standards	▲			❑	▲	▲
Organization Restructuring	❑	❑	❑	▲	▲	❑
Product Development	▲		○	▲	▲	▲

Primary Responsibility ▲   Secondary Responsibility ❑   Need To Be Informed ○

Organize Data

Variations

- Dimension Selection Grid
- Project Planning
- Project Update
- L-Shaped Matrix Simple two-dimensional representation demonstrating the intersection of related pairs of items.
- T-Shaped Matrix Relates information simultaneously to alternative applications.
- Is/Is Not Matrix
- Roles and Functions Matrix
- Meeting Decision Matrix

Organize Data

Matrix Chart

Problem: Car buyers want to match price with needs.

Goal: Examine the relationship between car buyers and their most frequent price choices.

T-Shaped Matrix

Buyers

	Station Wagon	2-Door Sedan	4-Door Sedan	Mini Van	Pick Up Truck	Convertible
Family of 4						
Contractor						
Single Person						
Married Couple						
$8,000 - $12,000						
$13,000 - $17,000						
$18,000 - $21,000						
$22,000 - $26,000						

Price Ranges

T-Shaped Matrix

Buyers

	Station Wagon	2-Door Sedan	4-Door Sedan	Mini Van	Pick Up Truck	Convertible
Family of 4	X		X	X		
Contractor					X	
Single Person		X			X	X
Married Couple		X				X
$8,000 - $12,000		X				
$13,000 - $17,000		X	X			X
$18,000 - $21,000	X		X	X	X	X
$22,000 - $26,000	X			X	X	

Price Ranges

Matrix Chart
Project Planning

Project: _Organize a one-day visit of 5 senior managers from one of the company's business units._

Project Team: _Cross-functional team representing: Marketing, Operations, Finance, Legal & Human Resources_

Project Start Time: _November, 10, 1998_

Project Finish Time: _December 3, 1998_

Organize Data

Tasks/Activities	Key Responsibility	Team Helpers	Resources	Outcome/ Deliverable	Who Needs to Know	Deadlines Start	Finish
Set a Time and Agenda to conduct 1st team meeting	Team Leader	None	E-Mail	Meeting Time and Agenda	Team Members	Nov. 11	Nov 11
Conduct 1st team meeting and develop project plan	Team Leader	Entire Team	Time	Project Plan	All Department Heads that will have a role	Nov 13	Nov 13
Establish Budget	Team Leader	Entire Team	$3,000	Budget	Budget Owner	Nov 1	Nov 13
Team members work on their personal action plans	Entire Team	Functional area contacts	Functional Contacts	Action plans working	All Department Heads that will have a role	Nov 13	Nov 26
Meet again to finalize plans and close gaps	Team Leader	Entire Team	Time	Plans Finalized	Department Heads	Nov 26	Nov 26
Host Visit	Sr. Manager	Entire Team	Time	Meeting Hosted	All Staff	Dec 3	Dec 3

Project Update

Project: _Organize a one-day visit of 5 senior managers from one of the company's business units._

Responsible Team: _Team representing: Marketing, Operations, Finance, Legal & Human Resources_

Report Date: _November 25, 1998_

Tasks/Activities	Key Responsibility	Team Helpers	Deadlines Start	Finish	Project Status to Date
Set a Time and Agenda to conduct 1st team meeting	Team Leader	None	Nov. 11	Nov 11	1st meeting held
Conduct 1st team meeting and develop project plan	Team Leader	Entire Team	Nov 13	Nov 13	Detailed action plan with assignments to all team members
Establish Budget	Team Leader	Entire Team	Nov 13	Nov 13	Budget Set
Team members work on their personal action plans	Entire Team	Functional area contacts	Nov 13	Nov 26	3 of the 5 team members are on time and budget. 2 members required extra coaching on their assignments

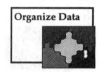
Organize Data

Matrix Chart

Problem: The hair dryer started cutting out and eventually quit.
Goal: Determine why the hair dryer quit.

Is/Is Not Matrix

	IS When does this situation occur?	IS NOT When does this situation NOT occur?	THEREFORE What could explain this situation?
Stage 1	The hair dryer works most of the time	The hair dryer does not work when the bathroom door is closed	The hair dryer coil is overheating because it is old and is not getting enough air to cool down while in the humid bathroom
Stage 2	The hair dryer stops more often	The hair dryer has to be turned on and off once during the hair drying process	The hair dryer should probably be replaced since it is old and continues to shut down when it gets hot
Stage 3	The hair dryer overheats almost immediately	The hair dryer does not work at all	The air intake filter appears to be clogged with lint. Maybe cleaning it will allow the air to flow again and the hair dryer to work
Stage 4	The hair dryer works without any problems	The hair dryer is not quitting any more	The hair dryer must have been quitting because the lint in the intake screen was preventing air from reaching the heating coil

Matrix Chart

Problem: The Total Quality lead position is new and individuals do not fully understand the scope of the role.
Goal: Identify the role and the areas for development

Organize Data

Roles and Functions Matrix

Role of TQ Lead	Training	Communication	Resources
TQ leadership at business unit	Leadership development for functional leaders	Communicate TQ strategies and obtain buy in from senior managers	Empowered to lead activity
Training and development of others on TQ process improvement and TQ tools	Train the Trainer workshop on TQ continuous improvement processes and tools	Notify employees of class dates and times. Notify employees of course content	Training course materials
Consultative services for all aspects of TQ	Coaching and mentoring workshop	Make employees aware of your abilities and availability for consulting and coaching on TQ	Integrating all activities in order to free up time for consultative services
Develop roll out of TQ strategy and facilitate ongoing efforts	Strategic Planning and Project Planning course	Communicate strategic plan for TQ roll out and ongoing efforts	Take the time to plan up front and to monitor and track process

Organize Data

Matrix Chart

Problem: Team members feel that they are attending too many meetings.
Goal: Identify the meetings that team members are attending so that meetings can be eliminated or combined.

Meeting Decision Matrix

Name of Meeting	Purpose of Meeting	Type of Meeting	Frequency of Meeting	Assessment of Meeting
Staff Meeting	Update each other on work group projects	Workgroup meeting	1/Week 2 hours	Best place to get work group information and build the team
All Staff Meeting	Share current organizational strategies and issues	All Staff in business unit	1/Month 1 hour	Feel like a part of things. Hear what is going on.
Budget Planning Meeting	Work through 5% budget reduction challenge	Budget Planning	3 mornings a week for 2 weeks	Temporary meeting -- Thank goodness!
Process Improvement Action Team	Improve the packaging process at the line	Process Action Team (PAT)	1/Week 1 Full Day with no End Date	This is going on and on and does not seem to be making progress

CONSENSUS CARD METHOD

What

This simple tool allows team members to visually demonstrate their opinions and attitudes regarding team decisions. Team members do this through the use of three-sided table cards. The sides of the card are GREEN for Agreement, RED for Disagreement and YELLOW for *I Can Live With It*. Team members use the card anytime during the course of the meeting to show their attitude toward the decision at hand. When all of the colors are showing the same by all team members, consensus is reached.

When

This technique is used when:

- you want to get decision reactions from team members on an ongoing basis because the nature of the discussion is such that opinions vary widely
- the discussion is controversial
- opinions and attitudes are blocking movement forward and the individual objections need to be addressed in real time.

How

1. Define the problem.
2. Set the goals of the session.

3. Place the 3-sided table cards on the table in front of each individual with the YELLOW (neutral) side facing out so that all can see.

4. The team then addresses the issues affecting the goal for the meeting. This is done one issue at a time.

5. Team members indicate their attitudes toward the issues as they are discussed. This is done by turning the card to the color that best fits each person's attitude toward the issue. Green or yellow can be displayed at any time during the discussion. The red side can only be displayed once the issue has been thoroughly discussed. When the majority of the cards are turned to red, the discussion continues. Once team members converge on the issue, the cards will turn to green and yellow and team consensus is then reached.

6. This process continues until all issues have been discussed to the fullest.

7. List all decisions that are made so that the entire group can see. Also make a list of the decisions that have been deadlocked.

8. Review the list of decisions and talk about next steps.

Organize Data

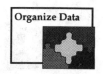

Timing

The sessions can last anywhere from 30 - 90 minutes depending on the number and complexity of issues.

Materials

Something to write on that can be seen by all participants:

- Flip Chart (including masking tape or push pins for hanging) Overheads and Projector
- Butcher Paper
- White Board
- Chalk Board

Something to write with:

- Felt Tip Pens (different types for Flip Charts, Overheads and White Boards)
- Chalk

3-Sided Table Tent Consensus Cards

RED, GREEN and YELLOW sides
Labeled *"Disagree"*, *"Agree"* and *"I can Live With It"*

Organize Data

Consensus Card Method

Problem: The company needs to change it's service strategy.

Goal: Employees need to quickly make many decisions surrounding a new service strategy direction.

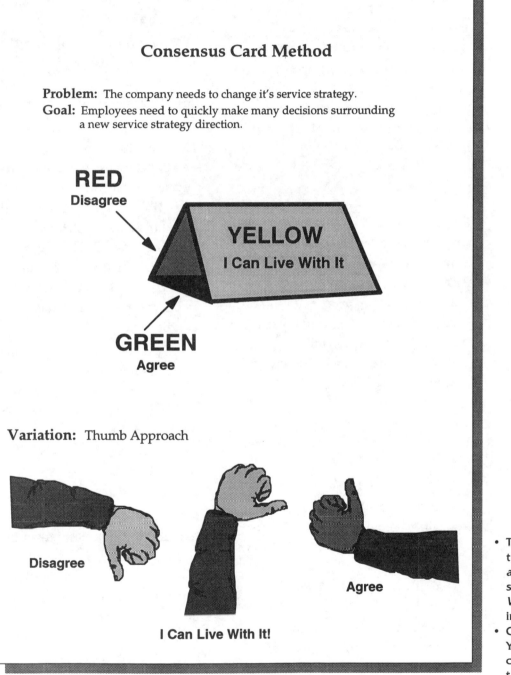

RED
Disagree

YELLOW
I Can Live With It

GREEN
Agree

Variation: Thumb Approach

Disagree

I Can Live With It!

Agree

Variations

- The thumbs up (*Agree*), thumbs down (*Disagree*), or thumbs sideways (*I Can Live With It*) method of voting on decisions.
- Colored (RED, GREEN, YELLOW) 3 X 5 cards can also be used when table tents are not available.
- Flags. Each team participant has three flags. GREEN for *It's a Go*. RED for *It's a No Go*. WHITE for *I'm Flexible to the Group Decision*.

PAIRED-CHOICE MATRIX

What

This technique enables teams to take a larger number of choices and through a paired-choice process, reduce the list systematically until only a few paired alternatives remain or until a single choice is made.

Organize Data

When

This tool is used when choices are similar and need to be reduced in number. It is also used when the team wants to use an objective decision-making process for generating alternatives and allowing for equal consideration of each issue. It is often used following a brainstorming session.

How

1. Define the problem.
2. Set the goals of the session.
3. Design a chart for comparison of each pair. The choices should be listed across the top of the chart and down the left side of the chart. The same choices should appear both vertically and horizontally. The areas of convergence between Choice A vertically and Choice A Horizontally (also Choices B, C, D, E, etc.) should be blacked out.
4. Compare each choice moving horizontally across the top with the choice listed vertically down the side.
5. Ask the team to vote for the choice that they feel most closely addresses the current problem, issue or state of affairs.
6. Record the choice that receives the most votes by placing the letter of the prevailing choice (A for choice A, B for choice B, etc.) in the converging box. This process is repeated until all boxes above the blacked out row have been compared and have received letters.
7. Tally the number of times each choice received the prevailing vote and place the totals down the vertical axis on the right and across the horizontal axis at the bottom of the chart.
8. Choose the option with the most votes. If there is a tie, ask the team to compare and choose again until one choice prevails. If a number of items have the same total scores, build another smaller matrix and ask the team members to vote on those choices again.
9. The team ends the session by making their choice as to the best solution based on the number of tallies received by the prevailing choice.

Timing

Allow approximately 30 - 40 minutes to explain the process and for the group to work through it once the chart has been drawn.

Materials

Something to write on that can be seen by all participants:

- Grid-type Flip Chart (including masking tape or push pins for hanging)
- Overheads and Projector
- Butcher Paper
- White Board
- Chalk Board

Something to write with:

- Felt Tip Pens (different types for Flip Charts, Overheads and White Boards)
- Chalk

Organize Data

Paired-Choice Matrix

Problem: Two team members have had to drop out of the team.
Goal: Select two new team members by the end of the meeting.

Team Member Replacement Analysis

	Person A	Person B	Person C	Person D	Person E	Person F	Person G	TOTAL
Person A		A	C	D	E	A	A	3
Person B	X		C	B	B	F	G	2
Person C	X	X		D	E	C	C	2
Person D	X	X	X		E	D	G	1
Person E	X	X	X	X		E	E	2
Person F	X	X	X	X	X		F	1
Person G	X	X	X	X	X	X		0
TOTAL	0	0	2	2	3	1	2	

Totals	
Person E	5
Person C	4
Person A	3
Person D	3
Person B	2
Person F	2
Person G	2

Variations

1. Although the Paired-Choice Matrix does not change much in the way that it is facilitated, it can be used for addressing various issues.

- People — Selection of candidates to replace team members
- Product — Selection of best car, house, food, clothing, etc.
- Service — Selection of best hotel, retail outlet, financial institution, etc.
- Education — Selection of best school, college, university, course, etc.
- Location — Selection of vacation place — park, beach, lake, river, resort, etc.

2. The Paired-Choice Matrix can also be handled using 3 X 5 cards. The cards can be placed on a wall or on the table and, using blank cards, the prevailing card can be assigned a letter and placed in the appropriate area for tallying.

MULTI-VOTING

What

Multi-voting is a technique that helps teams select the most important items from a large number of choices. It is a structured series of votes.

When

This technique is used when a team wants to:

- narrow a large list of options
- select a few choices to act upon
- identify the most important items from a large number of options

It often follows a brainstorming session. It is used when consensus is not necessary and all members are willing to commit to the outcomes.

How

1. Define the problem.
2. Set the goals of the session.
3. Generate a list. (The list could be items, ideas, issues, characteristics, etc.) This is done by providing a pre-determined list or through brainstorming the list during the team meeting.
4. Assess items for possible consolidations or re-groupings so that the list can be shortened where appropriate.

Organize Data

5. Give each person enough colored stick-on dots to mark approximately 1/3, but not more than 1/2, of the items on the list.
6. The participants cast their votes by either using one dot per item, or by splitting votes among a fewer number of items, thereby assigning more than one dot per item.
7. Tally the votes after the members have made their selections. If items are tied you may wish to re-vote using different colored dots (one dot per person).
8. To reduce the list, eliminate the items having the fewest votes. If the list is particularly long, you may want to continue this process until the team members have sufficiently reduced the number of items to a manageable size.
9. Observe and analyze.
10. Set action plans for next steps.

Timing

Timing is dependent on several factors. These factors include:

- whether or not you have a pre-determined list
- whether or not you are generating a list
- the size of your list
- the number of voters

This process could take as little as 1/2 hour to an hour or more depending on the above factors and team discussion.

Materials

Something to write on that can be seen by all participants:

- Flip Chart (including masking tape or push pins for hanging)
- Overheads and Projector
- Butcher Paper
- White Board
- Chalk Board

Something to write with:

- Felt Tip Pens (different types for Flip Charts, Overheads and White Boards)
- Chalk

Something to vote with:

- Colored, Stick-on Dots
- Felt Tip Pens

Multi-Voting

Problem: Sales associates do not exhibit a customer focus.
Goal: Ascertain reasons why sales associates lack customer focus.

Reasons for Lack of Customer Focus

Have not been trained in customer service

Too busy to fully address customer needs

Inexperience with customer issues

No incentive to do better

No loyalty to company or customer

Departmental conflicts

Do not understand products

Air conditioner broken

Long lines of customers

Sale items unclearly marked

Customers are a pain to deal with

Sales associates have not had time for breaks or meals

Customers blaming Sales Associates for manufacturer promises

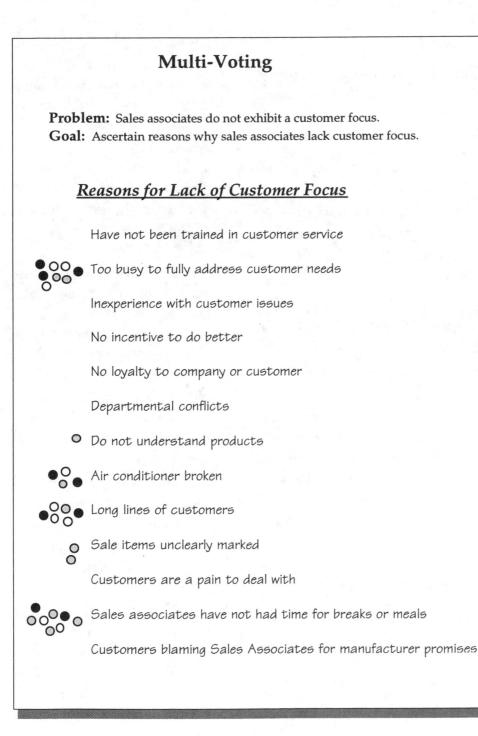

Variations

- If you wish to force a high level decision from the group, allow only one or two votes per person.
- If you want the team to categorize and identify the priority groupings, provide the participants with different colored dots. Each color will represent a different grouping.
- If you want the team to prioritize their votes, provide each person with a different colored dot representing 1st, 2nd and 3rd choices.
- If team members' votes are influenced by other team members, you may wish to have the participants vote independently on a sheet of paper. You could then take the aggregate votes and consolidate them into one master list for the entire group.

FORCE FIELD ANALYSIS

Organize Data

What

This tool aids teams in identifying those factors that are either enabling or hindering the team from moving forward in a certain area or areas. By identifying the driving and restraining forces, solutions can be developed that will shift the forces and allow for positive actionable solutions.

When

This technique is used when teams start getting bogged down or feeling immobilized and desire to develop positive, actionable solutions.

It is also used as a change model that provides teams with a technique for analysis of the current situation. Understanding the current situation enables teams to develop positive change strategies.

How

1. Define the problem.
2. Set the goals of the session.
3. Identify the forces that restrain change or present barriers for change (Restraining Forces). Place this list of Restraining Forces on the right hand side of balance sheet between the two forces.
4. Draw an arrow toward the middle of the Force Field. The

arrow should represent the size of the problem. Long arrows indicate stronger problems than short arrows.

5. Identify the forces that enable change or facilitate change (Driving Forces). Place this list of Driving Forces on the left hand side of the balance sheet between the two forces.
6. Draw arrows toward the middle of the Force Field. Again, long arrows indicate strong enabling forces while short arrows indicate weaker enablers.

   NOTE: Each individual element of a Force Field should be listed separately.
7. Rank Restraining Forces from strongest to weakest.
8. The team will want to reduce the Restraining Forces with the least resistance first since these are the easiest to resolve.
9. Next tackle the Restraining Forces with the most resistance and use the same worksheet to develop solutions.
10. Prioritize the Driving Forces and develop strategies for increasing the strongest forces to help move the Restraining Forces backward.

Timing

This exercise should take approximately 1 - 2 hours including introduction of the process, problem identification, goal identification, Force Field Analysis and solution development.

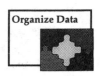

Organize Data

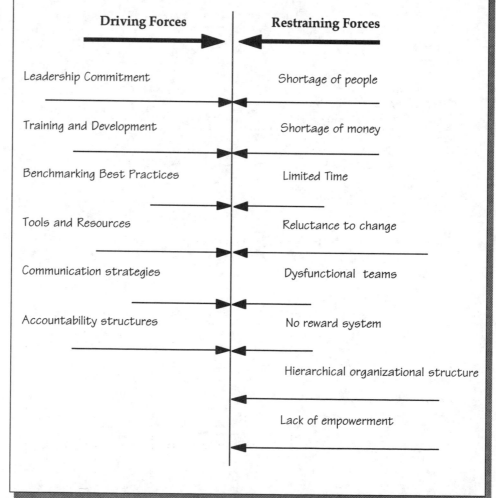

Force Field Diagram

Problem: Continuous improvement efforts are slowing down.
Goal: Refocus efforts to keep continuous improvement efforts moving forward.

Continuous Improvement Analysis

Driving Forces	Restraining Forces
Leadership Commitment	Shortage of people
Training and Development	Shortage of money
Benchmarking Best Practices	Limited Time
Tools and Resources	Reluctance to change
Communication strategies	Dysfunctional teams
Accountability structures	No reward system
	Hierarchical organizational structure
	Lack of empowerment

Materials

Something to write on that can be seen by all participants:

- Flip Chart (including masking tape or push pins for hanging)
- Overheads and Projector
- Butcher Paper
- White Board
- Chalk Board

Something to write with:

- Felt Tip Pens (different ones for Flip Charts, Overheads and White Boards)
- Chalk

Force Field Analysis Worksheet

This worksheet is an aid for developing strategies for moving the Forces in one direction or the other once they have been identified. The goal is to develop solutions for weakening the Restraining Forces and strengthening the Driving Forces so that change can take place.

As a team:

1. **Identify additional forces that might be used to help carry out the goals.**
    Reward and Recognition Programs
    Hire additional staff
    Re-organize to use cross-functional teams

2. **List the Driving Forces and Restraining Forces in rank order (per area, not in an integrated manner).**

1. Leadership commitment	1. Hierachical organizational structure
2. Training and Development	2. Lack of empowerment
3. Accountability structures	3. Reluctance to change
4. Tools and Resources	4. Shortage of people
5. Communication strategies	5. Shortage of money
6. Benchmarking Best Practices	6. Dysfunctional teams
	7. No reward system
	8. Limited Time

3. **Take each one of these ranked Forces and brainstorm ideas for increasing the Driving Forces and decreasing the Restraining Forces.**

1. Ask leaders for their commitment	1. Convince leaders to change hierachical structure
2. Schedule training & Development	2. Convince leaders to trust & empower employees
3. Build accountability structures	3. Identify & address change reluctance issues
4. Obtain tools & resources	4. Obtain additional people
5. Utilize additional communication	5. Increase budget
6. Benchmark Best Practices	6. Hold Team Building sessions
	7. Develop reward systems
	8. Examine priorities & obtain additional time

4. **Identify the forces that can be influenced by the group.**
    2, 4, 5, 6   3, 4, 6, 7, 8

5. **Identify the forces that the team has no ability to impact for change.**
    1, 3   1, 2, 5

6. **Together, develop action plan(s), assign duties and identify appropriate time frames.**

Activities/Tasks	Responsibility	Deadline
Schedule training and development	Training Manager	Roll out for Fall
Obtain tools and resources, place in a Resources Guide and Communicate	Team Leader, Public Relations Manager	Ready for Fall roll out
Begin Newsletter and Voice Mail Broadcasts	Public Relations Staff	Begin Fall
Establish Benchmarking process and Implement	Total Quality Leader	Begin Winter Next year
Hire consultant to address team building and change strategies	Team Leader, Consultant	Begin ASAP
Develop reward systems	Compensation Manager	Begin ASAP
Obtain additional resources	Total Quality Leader	Have ready for roll out

Variations

- Restraining and Driving Forces can be re-labeled to read:
  Enablers and Barriers
  Helping Forces and Hindering Forces
  Forces for Change and Forces for Maintaining the Status Quo
- The Forces can be assigned numerical weights to show the Force with which each item is associated in relation to one another.
- The traditional Force Field can be displayed either vertically or horizontally.
- Two Flip Charts can be used — one displaying the Restraining Forces and the other displaying the Driving Forces.

WORKSHEET

Organize Data

What

Worksheets are data gathering tools that look similar to forms. The user fills out the form (worksheet) which asks for information in an organized manner.

In addition to the sample worksheets that follow, there are a number of worksheets in this book designed for ease of use and planning.

When

Worksheets are used to answer questions, supply information, plan, make decisions, prioritize, audit, log, control, diagnose, learn, and work out problems.

How

1. Define the problem.
2. Set the goals for the activity.
3. Identify the item, activity, service, process or behavior under study.
4. Write targeted questions for use in collecting information. Also ask for any additional information that is pertinent to the topic.
5. Complete the form.
6. Analyze, summarize and feed back the results.
7. Make changes to address the identified issues.

Timing

If the worksheet has already been designed, the individual or team can complete the form quickly (usually within 15 - 45 minutes).

If the worksheet is being developed by the group or individual, it will often take longer (usually 2 - 4 hours depending on the complexity of the worksheet).

Worksheet

Problem: The company leadership feels they can be better leaders.
Goal: Identify ways to become better leaders.

Organize Data

Better Leader Worksheet

Name_____Title_____

Work Group_____Telephone Number_____

1. **Identify the best leader that you have ever known. This should be someone that you have either worked with or for.**

2. **What are the leadership qualities or traits that you admire in this person?**

   a.   f.
   b.   g.
   c.   h.
   d.   i.
   e.   j.

3. **How do these qualities or traits compare with your own leadership style?**

4. **List the major steps you will take to align your leadership style more closely with that of your "best leader".**

5. **Share your action plan with others in the group so you can hold each other accountable for follow-up. Identify those with whom you are sharing your plan.**

Materials

Something to write on:

- Flip Chart (including masking tape or push pins for hanging)
- Overheads and Projector
- Butcher Paper
- White Board
- Chalk Board
- Worksheets
- Note Paper
- Computer

Something to write with:

- Felt Tip Pens (different types for Flip Charts, Overheads and White Boards)
- Chalk
- Pens/Pencils

Organize Data

Worksheet

Problem: The team has not identified the customer requirements or made changes to accommodate these requirements.
Goal: Identify customer requirements and make changes.

Customer Requirements Worksheet

Describe your Product and Services	What do I need to change in order to meet the customer's requirements?	

Describe your Product and Services

Products

Ice Cream	Milk Shakes
Ice Cream Cakes	Yogurt
Ice Cream Pies	Ice Cream Cones
Banana Splits	Ice Cream Toppings
Sundaes	Yogurt Toppings
Ice Cream Floats	26 Different Flavors

Services

Cake Decorating	Convenient Hours
Hand Packed Ice Cream	Convenient Locations
Service Within 5 minutes	
Friendly Service	
Specialty Cakes to customer specifications	
Specialty Pies to customer's specifications	

Identify the specific Customer Requirements

Products

Ice Cream	Milk Shakes
Ice Cream Cakes	Yogurt
Ice Cream Pies	Ice Cream Cones
Banana Splits	Ice Cream Toppings
Sundaes	Yogurt Toppings
Ice Cream Floats	26 Different Flavors
Waffle Cones	Soda Pop
Herbal Teas	Hot Dogs
Potato Chips	Sandwiches
Coffee (Lattes, Cappuccino, etc.)	

Services

Cake Decorating	Convenient Hours
Hand Packed Ice Cream	Convenient Locations
Service Within 5 minutes	
Friendly Service	
Specialty Cakes to customer specifications	
Specialty Pies to customer's specifications	
Faster Service	Longer Hours in Summer
Gift Coupons	Party Catering
Delivery Services	Consistency
Drive Thru Window	

What do I need to change in order to meet the customer's requirements?

Products

Add a luncheon food item and see how it sells

Add waffle cones, an easy win.

Add Coffee and herbal teas. Also an easy win.

Serve soda. It is already being used for the floats.

Because of the store location, additional food and beverage service should add additional revenues. There are no other outlets in the area so these additions should add revenue to the bottom line.

Services

Time the average service to the customer.

Examine ways in which service time can be decreased.

Change the customer service standards to meet the new guidelines.

Research the cost of adding a Drive-Thru Window. (Add, if it is cost effective.)

Get some gift coupons printed. Use $5.00 increments.

Extend hours for one month in the summer only -- as a test. If it increases profits, continue.

Hire a Mystery Shopper to examine consistency of service and make recommendations for improvement.

Not ready to address Catering and Delivery Services at this time.

Having excellent service is more important than adding products. The majority of effort and money will be spent on improving services.

Variations

There are as many types of worksheets as there are ideas. Some of them are:

- Customer Requirement Definition Worksheet
- Team Meeting Feedback Worksheet
- Continuous Improvement Worksheet
- Change Strategy Worksheet
- Force Field Analysis Worksheet (See Force Field Analysis section of this book)
- Meeting planning *Agenda* located in the *Tool Selection* section of this book.

Worksheet

Problem: The team lacks the needed resources to complete its task.
Goal: Identify needed resources so they can be allowed for or obtained.

Team Resource Identification			
Resource	**Resource Necessary? Yes/No**	**Resource Available? Yes/No**	**Resource Obtainable? How?**
Money	Yes	Yes	
Time	Yes	Yes	
People	Yes	No	Do national search
Equipment	Yes	Yes	
Skill, Ability	Yes	No	Find people who already have the skills
Facilities	Yes	Yes	
Knowledge	Yes	No	Find people who already have the knowledge
Influence	Yes	Yes	
Energy	Yes	Yes	
Interest	Yes	Yes	

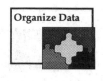

Organize Data

CHECK/TALLY SHEETS

What

The Check/Tally Sheet is a form used to collect and group data by recording and grouping the frequency with which various issues, problems, activities and processes occur. Check Sheets should be easy to use and should display the data in a format that reveals underlying patterns. Data is recorded with a simple check mark.

When

The Check/Tally Sheet is used when:

- the number of occurrences needs to be tracked over time
- the collection of information needs to be systematized
- the data has a yes or no factor (e.g. either it occurs, or it does not)
- you want to separate fact from opinion
- you want to track the type of problem that is occurring

How

1. Define the problem.
2. Set the goals of the session.
3. Agree on what is going to be observed and tracked.
4. Agree on a time period in which the data will be collected.

5. Design the form so it is easy to use. The categories for data collection should be determined by using the following method:
   - What (what happens, what are you tracking)?
   - Who (who is responsible, who does it, who receives it)?
   - Where (what location, what department, division, section, group)?
   - When (what time of day, month, quarter, year, how often)?
   - How (how does it happen, how much, how long, etc.)?

   Make sure the form has a place to indicate who the data collector is and the time frame for which the data is being collected. It should also state where, when, how, and the population for which the data is being collected. Include appropriate people in the design of the form. Those closest to the problem(s) should be able to provide the most helpful assistance.

6. Use the form to collect and group the data.
7. Develop action plans for moving forward.

Timing

The development of this tool should take a team approximately 2 hours to complete. The form should then be reviewed by others who understand what is being tracked. Modifications should then be made and the completed form readied for use.

The tracking of the data can take much longer and will be driven by the timing of the data being tracked.

Organize Data

Check/Tally Sheets

Problem: External customer satisfaction seems to be decreasing.
Goal: Track Customer Satisfaction Cards for one month.

Customer Satisfaction

This data is being collected by the General Manager's secretary and is taken from the Customer Satisfaction Cards which are completed by each customer upon receipt of merchandise.

Data Collector Name _Herman Simon_   **Time Frame** _April, 1995_

Customer Satisfaction Criteria	Unsatisfactory	Satisfactory	Above Average	World Class	Totals
Friendly Service		ⅲ ⅲ‖	ⅲ ⅲ ⅲ ⅲ‖	‖	33
Speed of Service		ⅲ ⅲ‖	‖‖		16
Order Accuracy	ⅲ‖	ⅲ‖‖			14
Product Quality		ⅲ ⅲ‖	ⅲ‖‖		18
Totals	**6**	**43**	**30**	**2**	**81**

Materials

Something to write on that can be seen by all participants:

- Grid-type Flip Chart (including masking tape or push pins for hanging)
- Overheads and Projector
- Butcher Paper
- White Board
- Chalk Board
- Note Paper (paper with quadrants is the easiest for designing forms)
- Computer

Something to write with:

- Felt Tip Pens (different types for Flip Charts, Overheads, and White Boards)
- Pens/Pencils
- Rulers
- Chalk

Check/Tally Sheets

Problem: Since the downsizing, absenteeism appears to be up.
Goal: Track employee absenteeism over the next month to determine how much and how often.

Organize Data

Absenteeism

This data is being collected by the machinist superintendent and covers all machinists in all locations throughout the facility for a period of one month.

Data Collector Name _Roberta Grange_ **Time Frame** _July, 1999_

	Anthony	Christina	Darnell	William	Michael	Jim	Jerry	Totals
How Often	‖‖ II	I	‖‖ ‖‖ II	‖‖ ‖‖ ‖‖	‖‖ ‖‖ ‖‖ ‖‖ ‖‖ I	‖‖ ‖‖ I	III	75
Totals	7	1	12	15	26	11	3	75

	Monday	Tuesday	Wednesday	Thursday	Friday	
When	‖‖ ‖‖ ‖‖ ‖‖ I	‖‖ II	‖‖ III	‖‖	‖‖ ‖‖ ‖‖ ‖‖ ‖‖ ‖‖ IIII	75
Totals	21	7	8	5	32	75

Variations

Check/Tally Sheets do not vary other than in the content. Some examples of Check Sheet usage are:

- Customer and Guest complaints
- Typing Mistakes
- Product Defects
- Telephone volume
- Customer payments
- Feedback received
- Employee absenteeism

Group Data

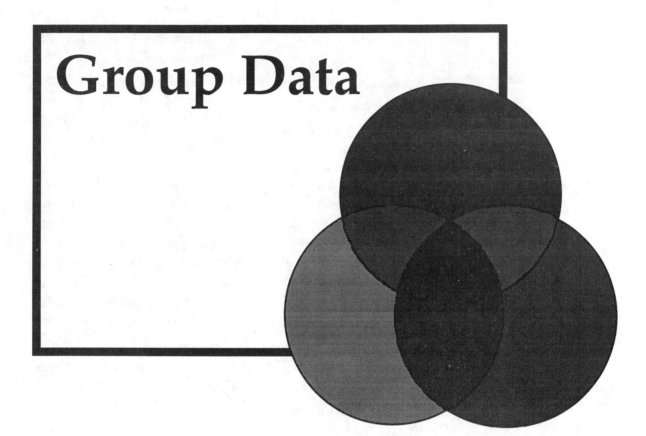

Affinity Diagram

Interrelationship Diagram

Venn Diagram

Quadrant Diagram

AFFINITY DIAGRAM

What

The Affinity Diagram allows the group to take large amounts of information, data, issues, ideas, and problems and group them into natural groupings as they relate to each other. Items are grouped as they have *affinity* to each other.

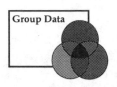

When

The Affinity Diagram is used when:

- there is a large amount of information requiring structure
- the team needs to generate creative ideas
- the team wants to expand its thinking
- a quick solution is required
- the issue is complicated and needs to be grouped

How

1. Define the problem.
2. Set the goals of the session.
3. Have each participant take a stack of 3 X 5 cards or sticky notes and record his or her ideas, issues, or problems. Participants should:
   - list only one idea per card or sticky note
   - keep the idea concise and to the point
4. The team should take the cards and place them randomly on a large table or post them on a large wall (preferably one with a large White Board or with Butcher Paper).
5. The team should then place the cards into related groupings. Sometimes there are cards which do not fit into a grouping. Just allow those cards to stand on their own. They do not require a Header card.
6. Assign Headers to each grouping. Sometimes there are subgroups within a group. Each subgroup should also be given a Header.
7. Observe and analyze the groupings. Notice repetitive input and large groupings. These could be indicators of where the group might want to begin its problem-solving efforts.
8. Set action plans for next steps.

Timing

The Affinity process takes longer than one might think. Depending on the complexity of the issue, you should allow from 1 - 2 hours for this exercise. It takes a while for the team to group and re-group data.

Affinity Diagram

1. **Problem:** Human Resources is constantly accused of not affecting the bottom line.

2. **Goal:** Identify Human Resource activities that impact the bottom line.

3. **Record** Human Resource activities that impact the bottom line on sticky notes.

4. **Place** sticky notes randomly on white board.

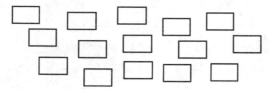

5. **Group** the notes in related groupings.

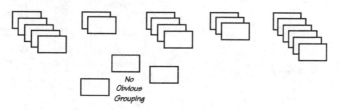

6. **Summarize** the Theme that ties each group together and give it a Header.

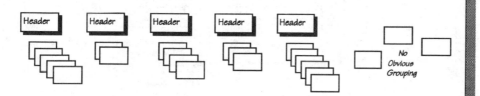

7. **Analyze** groupings for further groupings.

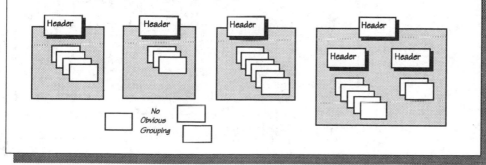

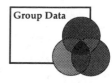

Group Data

Materials

Something to write on that can be seen by all participants:

- Grid-type Flip Chart (including masking tape or push pins for hanging)
- Butcher Paper
- White Board
- 3 X 5 Cards or Sticky Notes

Something to write with:

- Felt Tip Pens (Use black medium pens so that information can be read easily by the entire group after it has been posted.)

Group Data

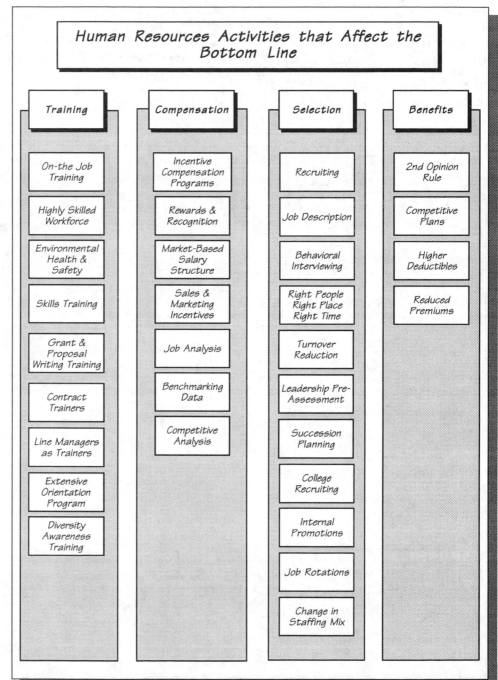

Human Resources Activities that Affect the Bottom Line

Training	Compensation	Selection	Benefits
On-the Job Training	Incentive Compensation Programs	Recruiting	2nd Opinion Rule
Highly Skilled Workforce	Rewards & Recognition	Job Description	Competitive Plans
Environmental Health & Safety	Market-Based Salary Structure	Behavioral Interviewing	Higher Deductibles
Skills Training	Sales & Marketing Incentives	Right People Right Place Right Time	Reduced Premiums
Grant & Proposal Writing Training	Job Analysis	Turnover Reduction	
Contract Trainers	Benchmarking Data	Leadership Pre-Assessment	
Line Managers as Trainers	Competitive Analysis	Succession Planning	
Extensive Orientation Program		College Recruiting	
Diversity Awareness Training		Internal Promotions	
		Job Rotations	
		Change in Staffing Mix	

Variations

The Affinity process can be modified in several different ways.

- The team can work the Affinity process together and in silence until the final analysis step.
- Each team member can contribute to the process one at a time with a recorder writing down each input. The items can be grouped as the cards start to mount up and can continue to be grouped throughout the process.
- The team can use a combination of the above two ideas. One person records all of the ideas and the team affinitizes them.

INTERRELATIONSHIP DIAGRAM

What

Allows the team to take a central idea, issue or problem and build a set of logical links between the central idea and related ideas. The Interrelationship Diagram can become very large depending on the complexity of the central issue.

When

The Interrelationship Diagram is used when:

- an issue is complex and understanding the interrelationship of the issues is difficult

- the central issue is a symptom of a bigger problem

- correctly sequencing and linking the issues is critical to the outcomes

How

1. Define the problem.
2. Set the goals of the session.
3. Create a central issue, problem or idea statement. Be concise. Place it centrally where the team is working.
4. Have each participant take a stack of 3 X 5 cards or sticky notes and record his or her ideas, issues, problems as they relate to the central issue. Participants should:

- list only one idea per card or sticky note

- keep the idea concise and to the point

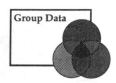

Group Data

5. The team should take the cards and place them randomly on a large table or post them on a wall (with White Board or Butcher Paper).

6. The team should then take the card(s) that is/are most closely linked to the central issue and place them next to it. Natural groupings, causal relationships and interrelationships will start to surface.

7. The placement of the cards should continue in a sequential order from the central source. Cards will be moved and regrouped throughout the entire process.

8. Next draw lines or arrows between the groupings to show causal interrelationships.

9. Analyze the trends that have emerged in the diagram.

10. Build action plans or decide on the next tool.

Timing

The Interrelationship Diagram process takes a minimum of 2 hours. Since the team is dealing with complex issues, they should more realistically allow 3 - 4 hours to complete this exercise.

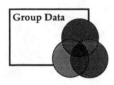

Group Data

Interrelationship Diagram

1. **Problem:** Family vacation plans have not been established.
2. **Goal:** Establish family vacation plans.
3. **Create** the central issue: *Family Vacation Plans*
4. **Record** all issues that affect the planning of the family vacation.
5. **Place** sticky notes randomly on white board.

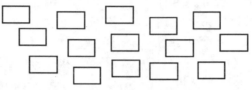

6. **Group** the notes in related groupings with the most closely linked placed next to the central issue.

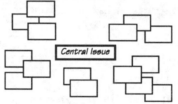

7. **Continue** to place cards in sequential order from the central source.

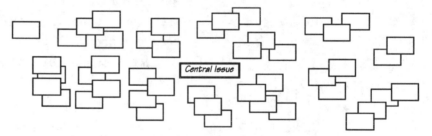

8. **Draw** arrows between groupings to show causal interrelationships.

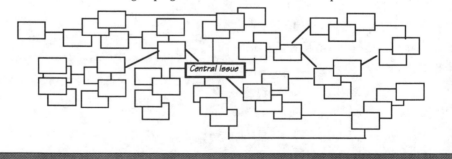

Materials

Something to write on that can be seen by all participants:

- Grid-type Flip Chart (including masking tape or push pins for hanging)
- Butcher Paper
- White Board
- 3 X 5 Cards or Sticky Notes

Something to write with:

- Felt Tip Pens (Use black medium pens so that information can be read more easily by the entire group after it has been posted.)

Interrelationship Diagram

Problem: Family vacation plans have not been established.
Goal: Establish family vacation plans.

Family Vacation

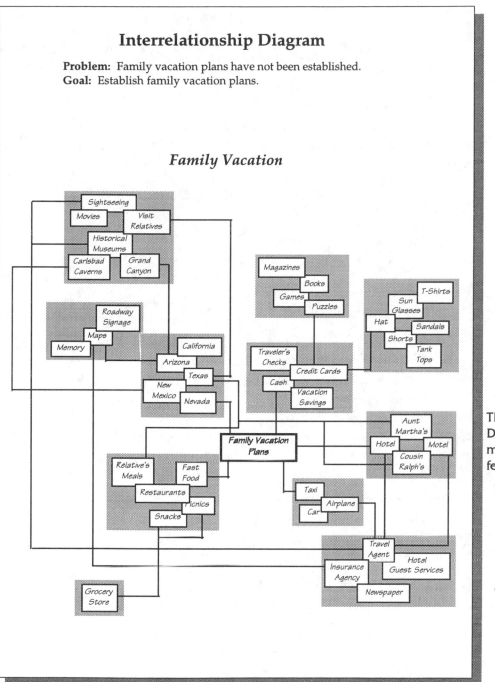

Variations

The Interrelationship Diagram process can be modified in several different ways:

- Instead of working from a central spot and moving in all directions, the clusters could move out in only one direction from the Issue Statement.

- Each team member can contribute to the process one at a time with a recorder writing down each input. The cards can then be placed next to appropriate cluster as they are given.

- The team could use a combination of the above two ideas. One person records all of the ideas and the team clusters them.

VENN DIAGRAM
(OVERLAPPING ISSUES)

What

Venn Diagrams visually show how elements, issues and problems overlap each other. The Diagram consists of overlapping circles that are often shaded or crosshatched to show relationships between sets.

When

The Venn Diagram is used when:

- issues overlap
- interrelationships need to be visually demonstrated
- size and type of overlapping issues need to be examined
- the problem is simple and easy to address

How

1. Define the problem.
2. Set the goals of the session.
3. Identify the issues that are involved in addressing the problem.
4. Determine the number, size and relationship of each issue and draw interconnecting circles demonstrating the relationships.
5. Examine the interrelationships and set plans.

Timing

This session should take no more than 45 minutes to complete.

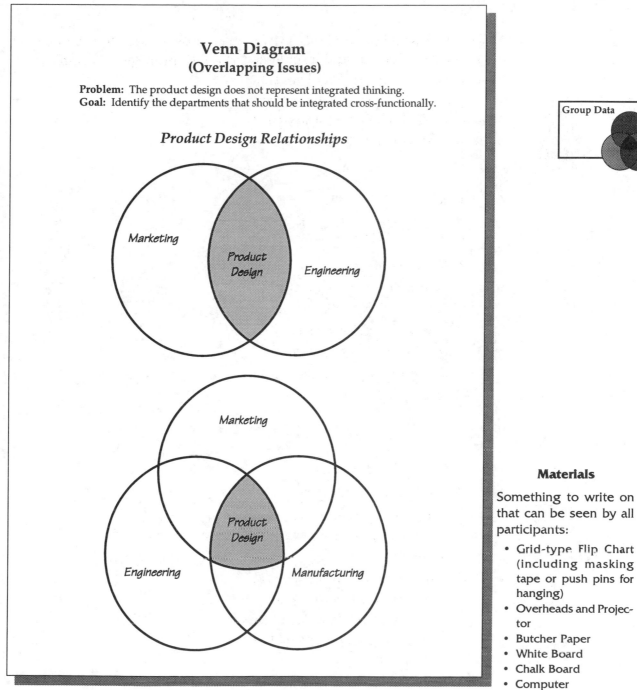

Venn Diagram
(Overlapping Issues)

Problem: The product design does not represent integrated thinking.
Goal: Identify the departments that should be integrated cross-functionally.

Product Design Relationships

Marketing

Product Design

Engineering

Marketing

Product Design

Engineering   Manufacturing

Group Data

Materials

Something to write on that can be seen by all participants:

- Grid-type Flip Chart (including masking tape or push pins for hanging)
- Overheads and Projector
- Butcher Paper
- White Board
- Chalk Board
- Computer

Something to write with:

- Felt Tip Pens (different types for Flip Charts, Overheads and White Boards)
- Chalk

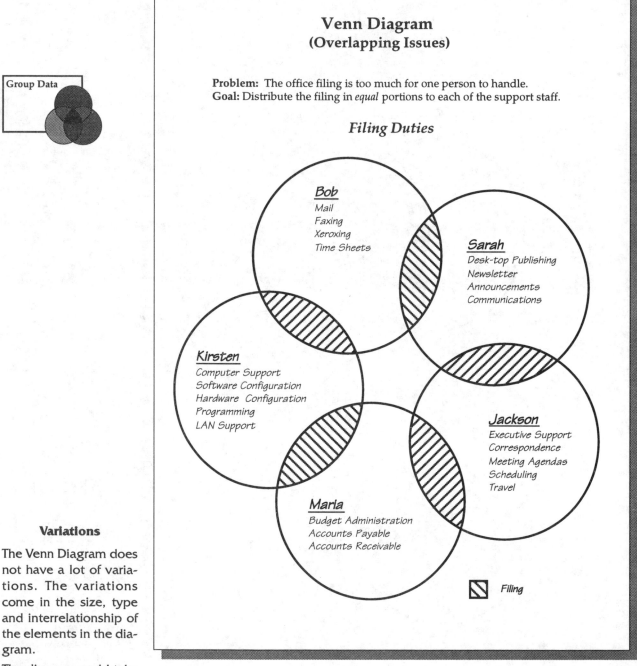

Group Data

Venn Diagram
(Overlapping Issues)

Problem: The office filing is too much for one person to handle.
Goal: Distribute the filing in *equal* portions to each of the support staff.

Filing Duties

Bob
Mail
Faxing
Xeroxing
Time Sheets

Sarah
Desk-top Publishing
Newsletter
Announcements
Communications

Kirsten
Computer Support
Software Configuration
Hardware Configuration
Programming
LAN Support

Jackson
Executive Support
Correspondence
Meeting Agendas
Scheduling
Travel

Maria
Budget Administration
Accounts Payable
Accounts Receivable

Filing

Variations

The Venn Diagram does not have a lot of variations. The variations come in the size, type and interrelationship of the elements in the diagram.

The diagram could take on other shapes such as overlapping boxes, rectangles, triangles and ovals. This would add variety to the look but little else.

Venn Diagram
(Overlapping Issues)

Problem: In an effort to build a leadership development program, the team was
not clear what the differences and common attributes of leaders and managers
should be.

Goal: Agree on the difference between leader and manager attributes as well as the
similarities.

Group Data

Attributes of Leaders
and Managers

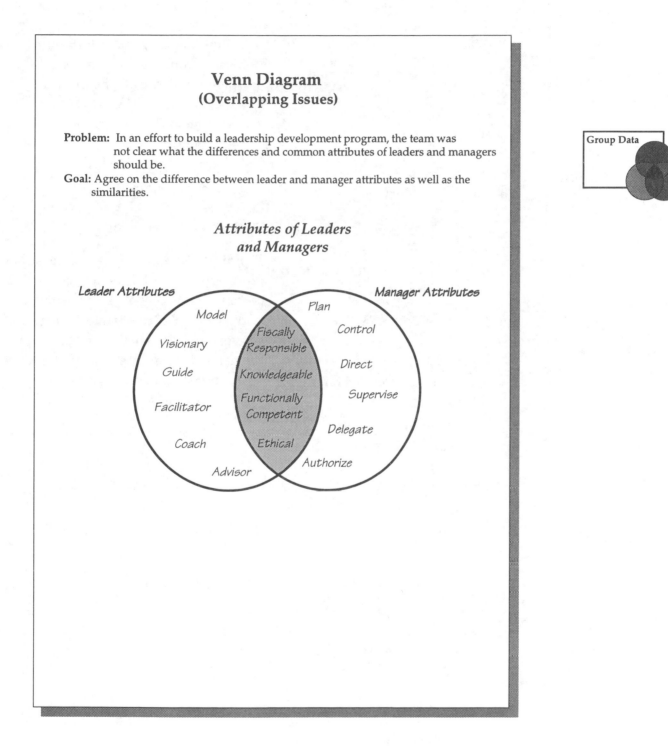

Leader Attributes   Manager Attributes

Model   Plan

Visionary   Fiscally   Control
                   Responsible

Guide   Knowledgeable   Direct

Facilitator   Functionally   Supervise
                   Competent

                                     Delegate

Coach   Ethical

Advisor   Authorize

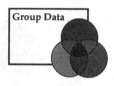

Group Data

QUADRANT DIAGRAM

What

A Quadrant Diagram is made up of four cells or quads. The cells are interrelational and usually represent a continuum from high to low with high being in the top right corner and low being in the bottom left corner.

When

The Quadrant Diagram is used when it is important to:

- show how factors impact each other
- demonstrate how interrelated factors are grouped on a continuum
- focus efforts on the factors that have the highest chance for success
- identify areas for improvement

How

1. Define the problem.
2. Set the goals of the session.
3. Identify the issues involved in addressing the problem.
4. Draw a box (or lines) with four quadrants/cells.
5. Label the cells. Two across the top and two down the left side of the box.
6. Plot the data as it falls into each cell. The top right cell should contain the highest factors while the left bottom cell should contain the lowest factors.
7. Analyze the data and build an action plan.

Timing

Building a quadrant can take a group from 1 - 2 hours depending on the complexity of the information. Allow plenty of time for discussion of the issues and where they should be plotted, as well as the implications of the data once it has been plotted.

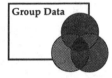

Group Data

Quadrant Diagram

Problem: Communication is difficult with the current E-Mail system.
Goal: Examine the cost/benefit of changing to a new E-Mail system..

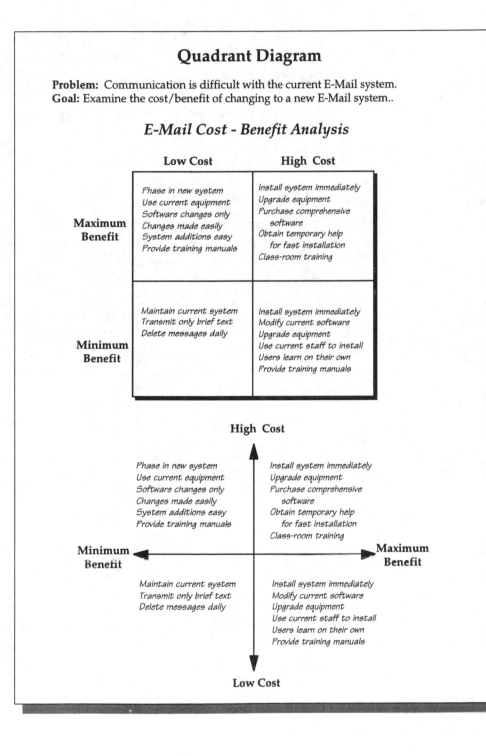

E-Mail Cost - Benefit Analysis

	Low Cost	High Cost
Maximum Benefit	*Phase in new system* *Use current equipment* *Software changes only* *Changes made easily* *System additions easy* *Provide training manuals*	*Install system immediately* *Upgrade equipment* *Purchase comprehensive* * software* *Obtain temporary help* * for fast installation* *Class-room training*
Minimum Benefit	*Maintain current system* *Transmit only brief text* *Delete messages daily*	*Install system immediately* *Modify current software* *Upgrade equipment* *Use current staff to install* *Users learn on their own* *Provide training manuals*

High Cost

Phase in new system
Use current equipment
Software changes only
Changes made easily
System additions easy
Provide training manuals

Install system immediately
Upgrade equipment
Purchase comprehensive
*   software*
Obtain temporary help
*   for fast installation*
Class-room training

Minimum Benefit ← → **Maximum Benefit**

Maintain current system
Transmit only brief text
Delete messages daily

Install system immediately
Modify current software
Upgrade equipment
Use current staff to install
Users learn on their own
Provide training manuals

Low Cost

Materials

Something to write on that can be seen by all participants:

- Grid-type Flip Chart (including masking tape or push pins for hanging)
- Overheads and Projector
- Butcher Paper
- White Board
- Chalk Board
- Computer

Something to write with:

- Felt Tip Pens (different types for Flip Charts, Overheads and White Boards)
- Chalk

Group Data

Variations

Quadrants can be drawn in several different ways but they always have four corners in which data is plotted.

- Quadrants can be drawn with two lines. One going straight up and down with the other one going from left to right and crossing the middle.
- Quadrants can be drawn using circles.
- Quadrants can contain grids within each cell or be open cells.
- The sides of the quadrant and cells themselves can have additional labels which add further clarification to the plotted data.

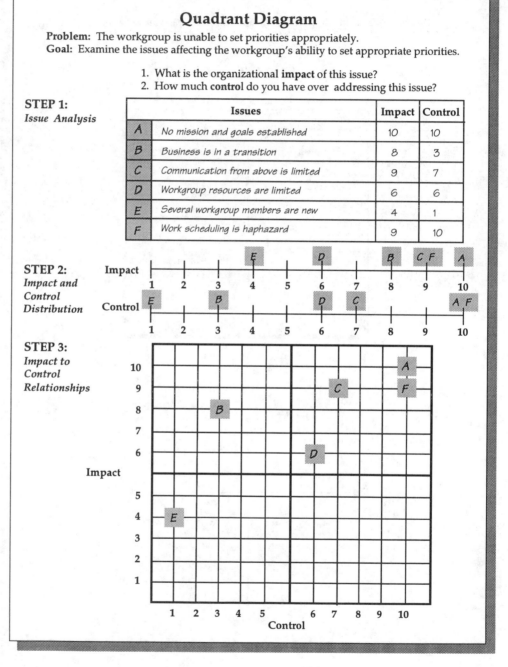

Quadrant Diagram

Problem: The workgroup is unable to set priorities appropriately.
Goal: Examine the issues affecting the workgroup's ability to set appropriate priorities.

1. What is the organizational **impact** of this issue?
2. How much **control** do you have over addressing this issue?

STEP 1:
Issue Analysis

	Issues	Impact	Control
A	No mission and goals established	10	10
B	Business is in a transition	8	3
C	Communication from above is limited	9	7
D	Workgroup resources are limited	6	6
E	Several workgroup members are new	4	1
F	Work scheduling is haphazard	9	10

STEP 2:
Impact and Control Distribution

STEP 3:
Impact to Control Relationships

Sequence Data

Continuums

Stages

Levels

Gantt Chart

CONTINUUMS

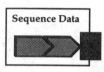

Sequence Data

What

The continuum allows the group to organize information, data, issues, ideas and problems in a sequential manner. Information is displayed sequentially in steps, phases, scales, levels, rank order and timelines.

When

The Continuum is used when:

- there is a need to examine information in a sequential manner
- the team needs to examine the factors leading up to a certain event
- the team needs to identify errors in the process
- the team needs to look at historical events in order to predict the future
- understanding the order of events is important
- understanding priorities, preferences or perceptions (scales) is important
- showing linkages between events and activities is important

How

1. Define the problem.
2. Set the goals of the session.
3. Using butcher paper, draw a long, horizontal, straight line across one wall of the room.
4. Write the *beginning* of the process on the left side of the line and the *end* of the process on the right side of the line.
5. Place short vertical lines along the horizontal line. These lines represent various points along the continuum.
6. Assign Headers to each short vertical line. These Headers can take the form of numbers, dates, events, phases, steps, etc.
7. Observe and analyze the sequence. Look for ways to identify errors, areas of emphasis, historical events, ranking, order of things, and factors leading up to certain events. These could be indicators of where the group might want to begin its problem-solving efforts.
8. Set action plans for next steps.

Timing

Building a continuum should take approximately 60 - 90 minutes. This includes analyzing the information and building action plans.

Continuums

Problem: Managers do not understand the needs of their international subsidiaries.

Goal: Organize a trip to each international subsidiary with learning criteria for each visit.

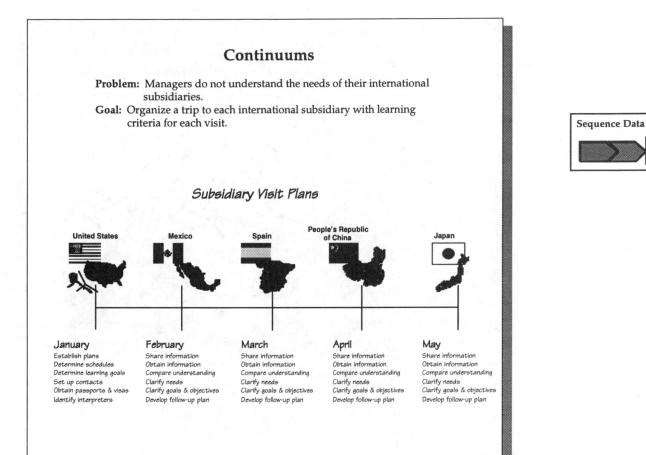

Subsidiary Visit Plans

United States	Mexico	Spain	People's Republic of China	Japan
January	**February**	**March**	**April**	**May**
Establish plans	Share information	Share information	Share information	Share information
Determine schedules	Obtain information	Obtain information	Obtain information	Obtain information
Determine learning goals	Compare understanding	Compare understanding	Compare understanding	Compare understanding
Set up contacts	Clarify needs	Clarify needs	Clarify needs	Clarify needs
Obtain passports & visas	Clarify goals & objectives	Clarify goals & objectives	Clarify goals & objectives	Clarify goals & objectives
Identify interpreters	Develop follow-up plan	Develop follow-up plan	Develop follow-up plan	Develop follow-up plan

Sequence Data

Materials

Something to write on that can be seen by all participants:

- Butcher Paper
- White Board
- Chalk Board
- 3 X 5 Cards or Sticky Notes

Something to write with:

Felt Tip Pens (different types for Flip Charts, Overheads and White Boards)

Chalk

Sequence Data

Variations

The Continuum can be modified in several different ways.

- Pictures can be drawn along the continuum denoting historical events, activities, work processes, phases, stages, steps and significant events.

- The entire team can work on the continuum together, or individuals can tell the facilitator or recorder what should be indicated at each point along the continuum.

- Team members can write their input on 3 X 5 cards or sticky notes which are then placed on the continuum at the appropriate point.

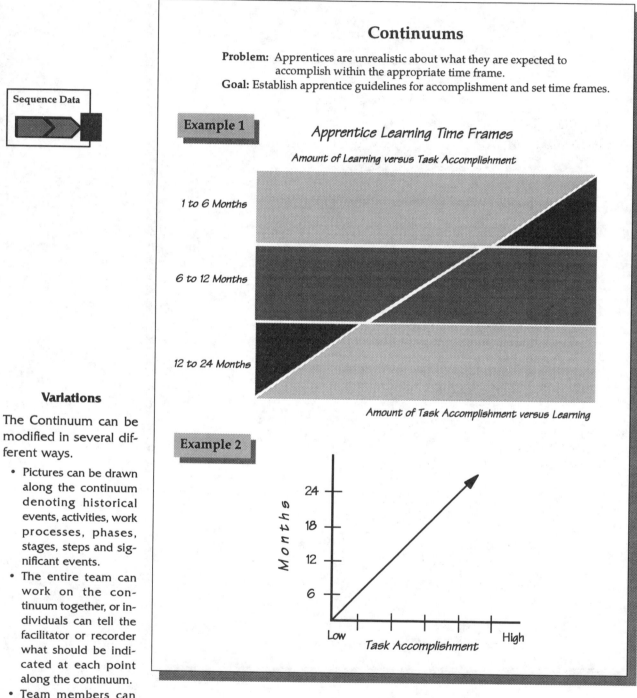

Continuums

Problem: Apprentices are unrealistic about what they are expected to accomplish within the appropriate time frame.

Goal: Establish apprentice guidelines for accomplishment and set time frames.

Example 1

Apprentice Learning Time Frames

Amount of Learning versus Task Accomplishment

1 to 6 Months

6 to 12 Months

12 to 24 Months

Amount of Task Accomplishment versus Learning

Example 2

Months

24
18
12
6

Low   *Task Accomplishment*   High

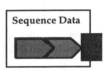

Continuums

Problem: A hiring system does not exist for the new company.
Goal: Identify an overall process for hiring.

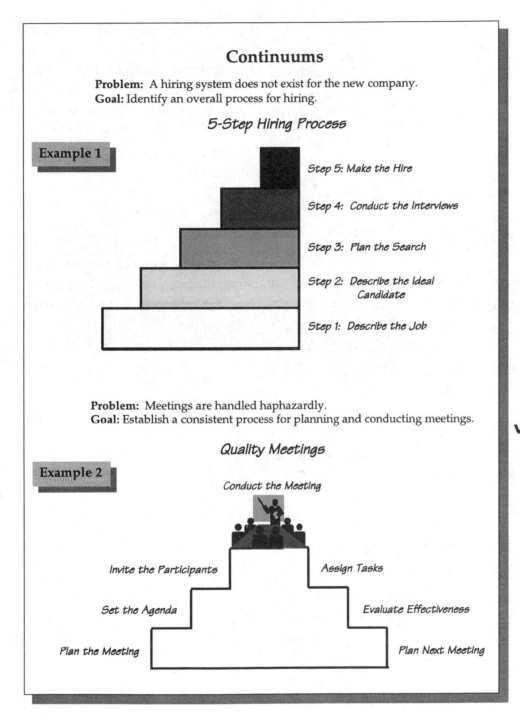

5-Step Hiring Process

Example 1

Step 5: Make the Hire

Step 4: Conduct the Interviews

Step 3: Plan the Search

Step 2: Describe the Ideal Candidate

Step 1: Describe the Job

Problem: Meetings are handled haphazardly.
Goal: Establish a consistent process for planning and conducting meetings.

Quality Meetings

Example 2

Conduct the Meeting

Invite the Participants   Assign Tasks

Set the Agenda   Evaluate Effectiveness

Plan the Meeting   Plan Next Meeting

Variations (Continued)

- The continuum can be drawn at a slant denoting a movement upward or downward.
- For showing comparative data, information can be recorded above the line as well as below the line.
- The continuum can be segmented in various ways:
  - Even distribution along the line.
  - Quadrants denoting phases or quarters in a year. Events can be recorded within each quadrant to provide further detail.
  - Various other larger groupings with the detailed events displayed within each grouping.

STAGES

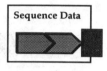

What

Sometimes data needs to be examined by the stages in which it occurs. The integration of sequence and grouping occurs by staging the data or events on a continuum.

When

Staging data is used when there is a need to:

- examine information in stages

- display and analyze the various stages of a process

- show a progression from beginning to end

- clarify groupings of information

- systematically examine information

How

1. Define the problem.

2. Set the goals of the session.

3. List the major stages in the process, event or timeline.

4. Write the processes, events or timelines within each stage.

5. Observe and analyze the sequence that emerges. Look for activities or information that will help identify errors, target areas for emphasis, clarify historical events, sug-

gest an order of things, and determine factors leading up to certain events. These could be indicators of where the group might want to begin its problem-solving efforts.

6. Set action plans for next steps.

Timing

Building a Stages continuum should take approximately 60 - 90 minutes. This includes analyzing the information and building action plans.

Stages

Problem: A *How To* book needs to be written to explain the operation of new machinery.
Goal: Determine methodology for writing the workbook.

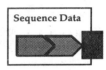

Sequence Data

Manual Design Project

Stage	Activity
Collect Information	Review manufacturer's information
	Review other similar manuals
	Talk with current operators
Determine Outcomes	Define learning outcomes
	Examine Safety issues
	Identify skills, knowledge & abilities for success
Develop Outline	Organize information
	Develop detailed outline
	Include Appendices
Write Manuscript	Follow Outline
	Write manual
	Edit manuscript
Identify Media	Examine text
	Evaluate various multi-media
	Choose appropriate delivery methods
Prepare Visuals	Examine opportunities for use of visuals
	Organize presentation of visuals
	Prepare visuals
Set-up Evaluation	Develop instrument to measure pre-determined outcomes
	Evaluate
	Fine tune manual and complete for distribution

Materials

Something to write on that can be seen by all participants:

- Grid-type Flip Chart (including masking tape or push pins for hanging)
- Overheads and Projector
- Butcher Paper
- White Board
- Chalk Board
- Computer
- 3 X 5 Cards or Sticky Notes

Something to write with:

- Felt Tip Pens (different types for Flip Charts, Overheads and White Boards)
- Chalk

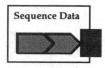

Sequence Data

Stages

Problem: The salary structure does not reflect career stages for engineers.
Goal: Identify and describe the career stages for engineers.

Career Stages of Engineers

Novice →	Growth →	Competent →	Sponsor/Mentor
Beginner	Increase	Qualified	Advisor
Learner	Learn	Grounded	Guide
Student	Develop	Trained	Counselor
Pupil	Stretch	Ready	Master
Protege	Advance	Capable	Guru
Disciple	Expand	Efficient	Coach
Intern	Reinforce	Prepared	Teacher
Apprentice	Supplement	Effective	Instructor
Trainee	Deepen	Knowledgeable	Educator
Probationer	Amplify	Practiced	Tutor
Newcomer	Produce	Polished	Trainer
Rookie	Specialize	Accomplished	Sage
		Skilled	Pundit
		Savvy	Expert
			Authority
			Luminary

Variations

The Stages diagram can be modified in several different ways.

- Pictures can be drawn denoting the stages and events contained within each stage.
- Team members can write their input on 3 X 5 cards or sticky notes which are then placed on the continuum at the appropriate stage.
- For showing comparative data, information can be recorded above the line as well as below the line.
- Stages can vary in content and length on the continuum.

LEVELS

What

Displaying data by Levels demonstrates the hierarchy of events, activities, processes, issues or timing.

When

A Level diagram is used when:

- understanding hierarchy is important

- setting priorities needs to be established

- analyzing a spectrum of information is important (e.g., high to low, low to high, good to bad, bad to good)

- examining the progression or regression of events, activities, processes, issues or timing

How

1. Define the problem.

2. Set the goals of the session.

3. List the major Levels in the process, event or timeline.

4. Write the issues, processes, events or timelines within each level.

5. Observe and analyze the sequence that emerges. Look for activities or information that will help identify errors, target areas for emphasis, clarify historical events, suggest an order of things, and determine factors leading up to certain events. These could be indicators of where the group might want to begin its problem-solving efforts.

6. Set action plans for next steps.

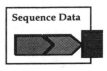

Sequence Data

Timing

Building a Levels continuum should take approximately 60 - 90 minutes. This includes analyzing the information and building action plans.

Sequence Data

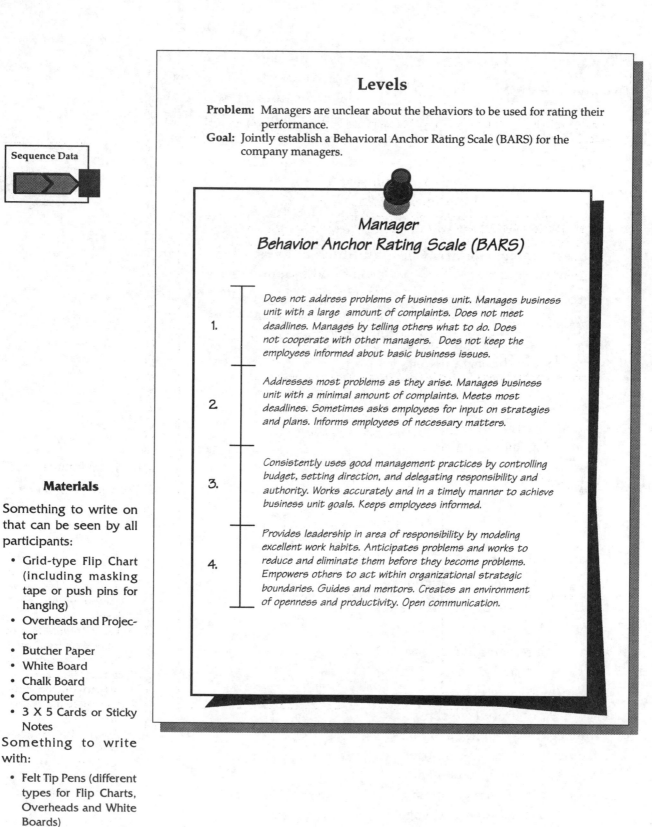

Levels

Problem: Managers are unclear about the behaviors to be used for rating their performance.

Goal: Jointly establish a Behavioral Anchor Rating Scale (BARS) for the company managers.

Manager
Behavior Anchor Rating Scale (BARS)

1. Does not address problems of business unit. Manages business unit with a large amount of complaints. Does not meet deadlines. Manages by telling others what to do. Does not cooperate with other managers. Does not keep the employees informed about basic business issues.

2 Addresses most problems as they arise. Manages business unit with a minimal amount of complaints. Meets most deadlines. Sometimes asks employees for input on strategies and plans. Informs employees of necessary matters.

3. Consistently uses good management practices by controlling budget, setting direction, and delegating responsibility and authority. Works accurately and in a timely manner to achieve business unit goals. Keeps employees informed.

4. Provides leadership in area of responsibility by modeling excellent work habits. Anticipates problems and works to reduce and eliminate them before they become problems. Empowers others to act within organizational strategic boundaries. Guides and mentors. Creates an environment of openness and productivity. Open communication.

Materials

Something to write on that can be seen by all participants:

- Grid-type Flip Chart (including masking tape or push pins for hanging)
- Overheads and Projector
- Butcher Paper
- White Board
- Chalk Board
- Computer
- 3 X 5 Cards or Sticky Notes

Something to write with:

- Felt Tip Pens (different types for Flip Charts, Overheads and White Boards)
- Chalk

Levels

Problem: The candidates for Shop Manager are evaluated without criteria.
Goal: Establish consistent criteria for evaluating candidates for Shop Manager.

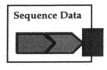

Sequence Data

Shop Manager
Candidate Evaluation

Level of Importance	Skills/Knowledge/Abilities
Primary Importance	*Technical Skills to do the job* *Management experience* *Proven leadership ability* *Integrity and Ethics* *Excellent work habits* *Role Model*
Secondary Importance	*Understands and operates computers* *High Technology industry experience* *Knowledge of operations* *Managed large budgets* *Experience with large projects*
Important	*Local candidate* *Available in 3 months* *Experience in training new hires* *Good communication skills* *Makes decisions easily and able to take risks* *Ability to travel*
Would be Nice	*Fluent Spanish language skills*

Variations

The Levels diagram can be modified in several different ways.

- Pictures can be drawn denoting the issues, events, processes and/or activities contained within each level.
- Team members can write their input on 3 X 5 cards or sticky notes which are then placed on the continuum at the appropriate level.
- For showing comparative data, information can be recorded above the line as well as below the continuum.
- Levels can vary in content and length on the continuum.

GANTT CHART

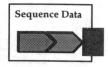

Sequence Data

What

The Gantt Chart is a project planning and scheduling tool. It entails a sequence of steps that are necessary for completion of a project. The Gantt Chart consists of a scale divided into units of time (e.g., hours, days, weeks, months, or years) across the top and a listing of the project elements down the left-hand side. Bars, lines, or other symbols are used to indicate the schedule and status of each element in relation to the time scale.

When

The Gantt Chart is used when:

- meeting project planning timelines are important

- a visual display of project timeframes is necessary

- planning timeframes overlap or are reliant on one another

- time is a primary element needing tracking

- numerous deadlines need to be coordinated and tracked

- the plan, schedule and progress of a plan need to be graphically displayed

How

1. Define the problem.
2. Set the goals of the session.
3. Break the project down into elements to be scheduled.

4. Estimate the time required to complete each element.
5. List the elements down the left-hand side in sequence of time, considering those which must be performed sequentially as well as those which can be performed simultaneously. (The easiest method is to sequence backward from the project completion date.)
6. For each element, extend a bar or line from the starting time to the necessary completion date.
7. Develop an action plan for tracking the progress of the project and adjusting the timeframes as necessary.

Timing

The development of this tool should take a team at least 2 - 4 hours to complete. If the project is really large and detailed, it can take many days and involve numerous people to develop.

If a project team is developing the chart, it should be reviewed by others who understand what is being tracked and are affected by the timeframes. Modifications should then be made and the completed chart ready for use.

The continuous tracking of the project can take much longer and will be driven by the overall project plan.

Materials

Something to write on that can be seen by all participants:

- Note Paper (paper with quadrants is the easiest for designing forms)
- Computer
- Grid-type Flip Chart (including masking tape or push pins for hanging)
- Overheads and Projector
- Butcher Paper
- White Board
- Chalk Board

Something to write with:

- Felt Tip Pens (different types for Flip Charts, Overheads and White Boards)
- Chalk
- Pencils, Pens
- Rulers

Gantt Chart

Problem: The Information System project has many deadlines and timeframes that have not been accounted for.

Goal: Establish a Project Plan with timeframes.

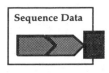

Sequence Data

New Information System Project Plan

Months / Activities	January	February	March	April	May	June
Appoint Project Planning Team	▬					
Establish Mission and Goals	▬					
Determine Project Plan	▬▬					
Estimate Costs/ Identify Resources	▬		✎			
Phase 1 of Project		▬▬				
Mid-term Budget Adjustments			▬			
Materials ordered			▬	✎		
Phase 2 of Project			▬▬			
Phase 3 of Project				▬▬		
Final Budget Adjustments					▬	✎
Phase 4 of Project						▬

✎ *Check Points to Review Process*

Variations

Gantt Charts are typically organized the same way each time they are built. The detail, graphics, timeframe variables and timeframes vary per project.

Very large projects can contain several Gantt Charts that track the various large elements of the project.

Breakdown Data

Tree Diagram

Work Breakdown
Structure (WBS)

Link Pin Diagram

Circles (Relationship)

Iceberg Diagram

TREE DIAGRAM

What

In order for the primary goals and related sub-goals of the team to be accomplished, the Tree Diagram provides a systematic map of the tasks that need to be completed. It looks like an organization chart or family tree turned sideways. The information expands as it moves from left to right.

When

The Tree Diagram is a planning tool used when:

- all the possible causes of a problem need to be explored
- the sequence of tasks for implementation need to be arranged
- identification of possible gaps in the process is important

How

1. Define the problem or goal.
2. Set the goals of the session.
3. Place the problem statement (or goal) on the left side of your work space.
4. Ask the question, "What needs to happen, be addressed, be resolved, or achieved in order to support the goal (problem) statement?"

5. Using 3 X 5 cards or sticky notes, brainstorm the tasks, methods or causes most closely related to the problem statement or goal.
6. Identify the cards or sticky notes that most closely relate to the problem statement or goal and place them to the immediate right of the problem statement or goal. These become the major Tree Headers.
7. Identify the cards or sticky notes that most closely relate to the Tree Headers and place them to the right of the Tree Headers. These become the tasks, methods or causes leading up to the problem or goal. These tasks, methods or causes should become more specific as you move from left to right. Each branch of the tree should have a direct cause and effect relationship, and should become more detailed as you move from left to right.
8. Continue this process until all of the completed 3 X 5 cards or sticky notes have been exhausted.
9. Place Headers at the top indicating what each row represents.
10. Review the Tree Diagram to ensure that there are no ob-

vious gaps in the sequence or logic. Ask the question, "Will these actions actually lead to these results?" This checks the specific to general (right to left) logic. Also ask the question, "If I want to accomplish these results do I really need to do these tasks?" This confirms the general to specific (left to right) logic.

11. Set action plans for next steps.

Timing

This session should take 2 - 4 hours.

Breakdown Data

Tree Diagram

Problem: There are many activities within the Guest Check-In Process during which mistakes can be made.
Goal: Breakdown the Guest Check-In Process into activities.

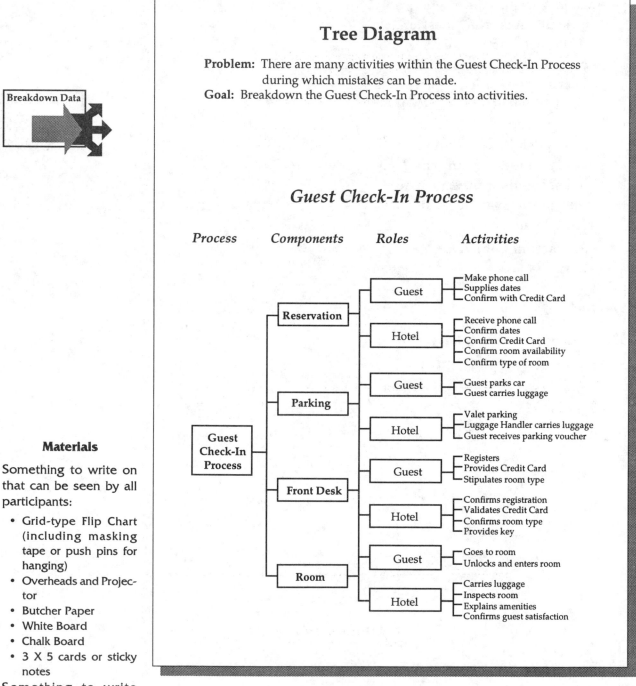

Guest Check-In Process

Materials

Something to write on that can be seen by all participants:

- Grid-type Flip Chart (including masking tape or push pins for hanging)
- Overheads and Projector
- Butcher Paper
- White Board
- Chalk Board
- 3 X 5 cards or sticky notes

Something to write with:

- Felt Tip Pens (different types for Flip Charts, Overheads and White Boards)
- Chalk

Tree Diagram

Problem: The organizational mission statements are not linked.
Goal: Show the linkage between mission statements throughout the organization.

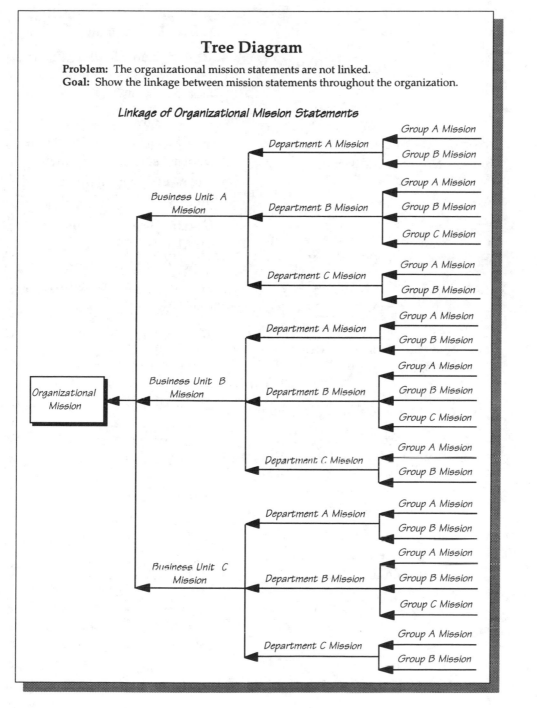

Linkage of Organizational Mission Statements

Variations

- If the problem or goal is not clear, the group can brainstorm issues, methods or tasks and start working from right to left.

WORK BREAKDOWN STRUCTURE (WBS)

What

The Work Breakdown Structure (WBS) divides the overall process into elements that represent assignable work activities. These work activities then become the common denominator around which the process is built.

When

The Work Breakdown Structure is used when the team:

- wants to identify where it may have gone off track
- wants to make sure that no tasks or activities are overlooked
- wants to identify the steps that are necessary versus those that are not
- wants to keep the entire process in mind while examining the ways in which the work gets done
- breaks the work down into "work packages" which are assignable and for which accountability is expected

How

1. Define the problem.
2. Set the goals of the session.
3. Divide the process into major groupings and write them on 3 X 5 cards or sticky notes and place them in sequence from left to right across your work surface. These will become your Headers.
4. Under each Header, list the major Groupings which break down into Tasks.
5. Break down the Tasks into Subtasks, then into further Subtasks, and so on, until the work is broken down completely.
6. Give each element a distinct identifier. This is usually done using the numbering system which is shown below.

  1.0

     1.1

       1.1.1

         1.1.1.1

         1.1.1.2

       1.1.2. etc.

7. This should continue until all ideas have been voiced and recorded.
8. Review and rework the WBS. Look for gaps and inconsistencies in the sequence of activities.
9. Set action plans for next steps.

Timing

You should allow 2 - 3 hours for this exercise.

Work Breakdown Structure (WBS)

Problem: There are no recommended procedures to provide to people who are being laid off.

Goal: Provide a breakdown of the work processes for finding a new job.

Breakdown Data

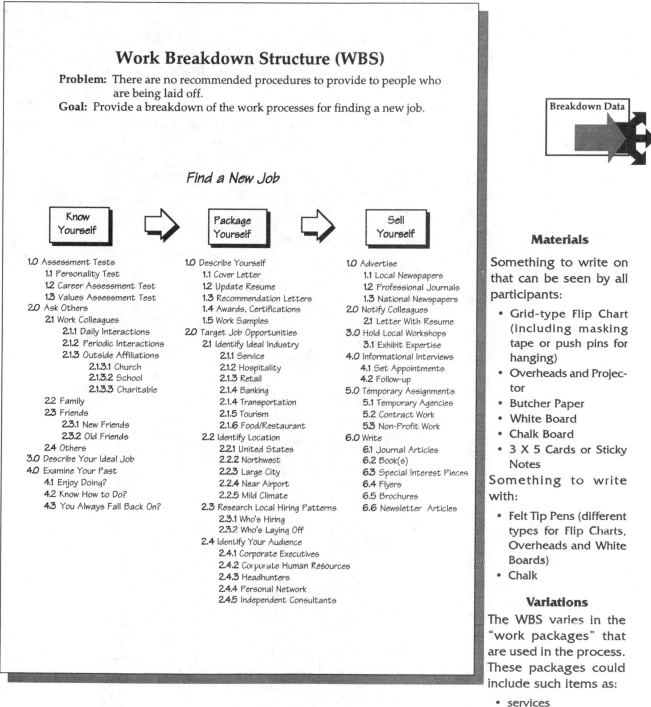

Find a New Job

Know Yourself

1.0 Assessment Tests
   1.1 Personality Test
   1.2 Career Assessment Test
   1.3 Values Assessment Test
2.0 Ask Others
   2.1 Work Colleagues
      2.1.1 Daily Interactions
      2.1.2 Periodic Interactions
      2.1.3 Outside Affiliations
         2.1.3.1 Church
         2.1.3.2 School
         2.1.3.3 Charitable
   2.2 Family
   2.3 Friends
      2.3.1 New Friends
      2.3.2 Old Friends
   2.4 Others
3.0 Describe Your Ideal Job
4.0 Examine Your Past
   4.1 Enjoy Doing?
   4.2 Know How to Do?
   4.3 You Always Fall Back On?

Package Yourself

1.0 Describe Yourself
   1.1 Cover Letter
   1.2 Update Resume
   1.3 Recommendation Letters
   1.4 Awards, Certifications
   1.5 Work Samples
2.0 Target Job Opportunities
   2.1 Identify Ideal Industry
      2.1.1 Service
      2.1.2 Hospitality
      2.1.3 Retail
      2.1.4 Banking
      2.1.4 Transportation
      2.1.5 Tourism
      2.1.6 Food/Restaurant
   2.2 Identify Location
      2.2.1 United States
      2.2.2 Northwest
      2.2.3 Large City
      2.2.4 Near Airport
      2.2.5 Mild Climate
   2.3 Research Local Hiring Patterns
      2.3.1 Who's Hiring
      2.3.2 Who's Laying Off
   2.4 Identify Your Audience
      2.4.1 Corporate Executives
      2.4.2 Corporate Human Resources
      2.4.3 Headhunters
      2.4.4 Personal Network
      2.4.5 Independent Consultants

Sell Yourself

1.0 Advertise
   1.1 Local Newspapers
   1.2 Professional Journals
   1.3 National Newspapers
2.0 Notify Colleagues
   2.1 Letter With Resume
3.0 Hold Local Workshops
   3.1 Exhibit Expertise
4.0 Informational Interviews
   4.1 Set Appointments
   4.2 Follow-up
5.0 Temporary Assignments
   5.1 Temporary Agencies
   5.2 Contract Work
   5.3 Non-Profit Work
6.0 Write
   6.1 Journal Articles
   6.2 Book(s)
   6.3 Special Interest Pieces
   6.4 Flyers
   6.5 Brochures
   6.6 Newsletter Articles

Materials

Something to write on that can be seen by all participants:

- Grid-type Flip Chart (including masking tape or push pins for hanging)
- Overheads and Projector
- Butcher Paper
- White Board
- Chalk Board
- 3 X 5 Cards or Sticky Notes

Something to write with:

- Felt Tip Pens (different types for Flip Charts, Overheads and White Boards)
- Chalk

Variations

The WBS varies in the "work packages" that are used in the process. These packages could include such items as:

- services
- activities
- tasks
- subtasks
- types of products
- communications methods

LINK PIN DIAGRAM

What

The Link Pin Diagram joins the Breakdown Structure together through a series of linkages. The process is linked from problem or goal to methods, issues, activities or tasks.

When

This tool is used to visually show the linkages between the elements of the process.

How

1. Define the problem or goal.

2. Set the goals of the session.

3. Write the problem statement or goal at the top of your work surface. Draw the *link pin* below the statement.

4. Identify the issues, methods, activities or tasks that link directly to the problem statement. Write them under the problem or goal statement and draw the *link pins* that connect the two.

5. Continue to identify issues, methods, activities or tasks that link directly to the next level until the entire Link Pin Diagram is completed. Draw the linkages.

6. Review the diagram and check for sequence, logic and completeness.

7. Establish action plans for next steps.

Timing

This process should take approximately 1 - 2 hours to complete.

Link Pin Diagram

Problem: The business units do not feel linked to the corporate organization.
Goal: Visually depict the linked relationship of the business units to corporate so that planning can begin for better communication.

Breakdown Data

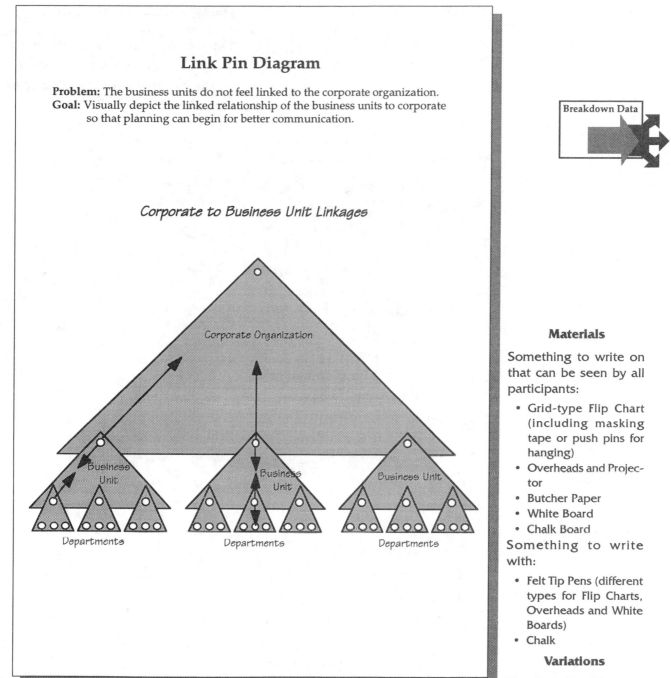

Corporate to Business Unit Linkages

Materials

Something to write on that can be seen by all participants:

- Grid-type Flip Chart (including masking tape or push pins for hanging)
- Overheads and Projector
- Butcher Paper
- White Board
- Chalk Board

Something to write with:

- Felt Tip Pens (different types for Flip Charts, Overheads and White Boards)
- Chalk

Variations

The Link Pin Diagram varies in what is being linked.

- organization structure
- work breakdown
- hierarchy of projects or tasks
- steps, phases, stages

CIRCLES (RELATIONSHIPS)

What

Circle Diagrams visually show how elements, issues, problems relate to each other.

When

This technique is used when:

- related issues need to be graphically displayed for clarification and understanding

- the team wants to visually show the expansion of ideas, processes, elements or issues

- issues, ideas, processes or elements begin and end at the same point or continue in a circular fashion

- issues, ideas, processes or elements can be divided into individual parts but are still part of a whole

How

1. Define the problem.
2. Set the goals of the session.
3. Identify the issues, processes, elements or ideas that need to be graphically displayed.
4. Determine the number, size and relationship of each issue and draw the circle representing these relationships.
5. Examine the relationships and set plans.

Timing

The session can last anywhere from 60 - 90 minutes depending on the number and complexity of issues.

Circles (Relationships)

Problem: The Human Resources Organization has never looked at itself
as a Customer-focused Organization.
Goal: Visually depict the relationship of the Internal Customer and the External
Customer to the service strategy of Human Resources.

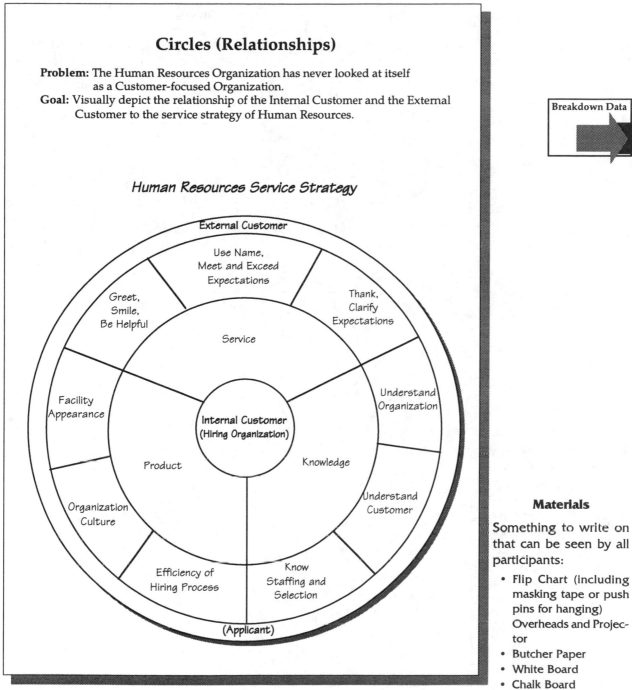

Human Resources Service Strategy

Breakdown Data →

Materials

Something to write on
that can be seen by all
participants:

- Flip Chart (including
  masking tape or push
  pins for hanging)
  Overheads and Projec-
  tor
- Butcher Paper
- White Board
- Chalk Board

Something to write
with:

- Felt Tip Pens (different
  types for Flip Charts,
  Overheads and White
  Boards)
- Chalk

Variations

The variations depend on the purpose of the information being displayed. The relational circle can vary in several ways. The information can:

- progress in a circular fashion beginning and ending at the same place
- have a core issue, process, element or idea that expands, adding data rings to the circle
- be displayed as a pie with various sized pieces representing the portion sizes
- be displayed with interconnecting links, or lines, between the outer and inner data

Circles (Relationships)

Problem: The company has grown so fast that employees no longer understand where they fit into the larger organization.

Goal: The team not only wants to visually show the employee where he/she fits into the organization, but also to emphasize the importance of the individual as the core of the organization.

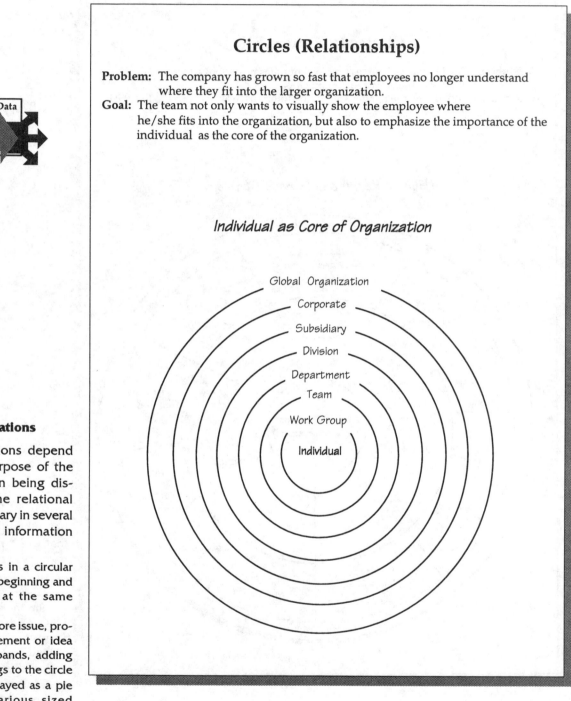

Individual as Core of Organization

Global Organization
Corporate
Subsidiary
Division
Department
Team
Work Group
Individual

Circles (Relationships)

Problem: The team does not have a clear understanding of the interrelationships of the business requirements.

Goal: Map the interrelationships of the business requirements so that relationships can be better understood.

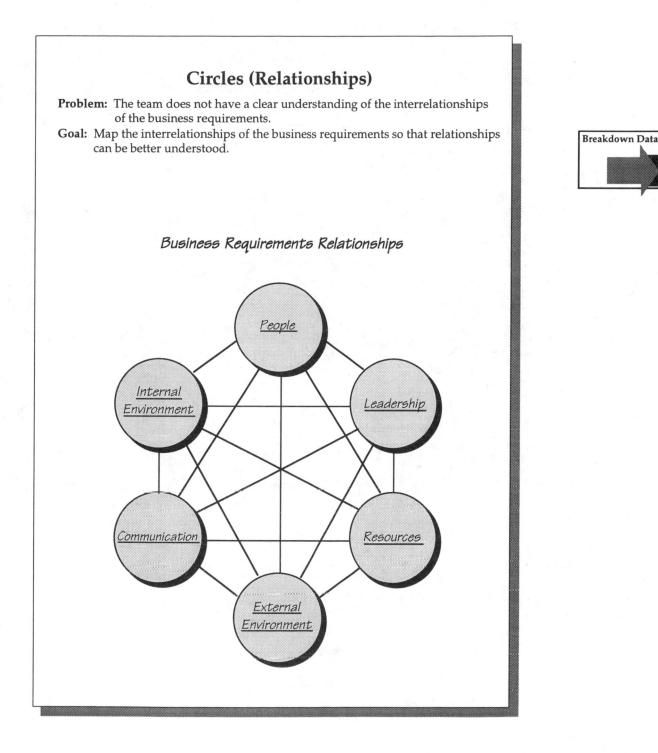

Business Requirements Relationships

Breakdown Data

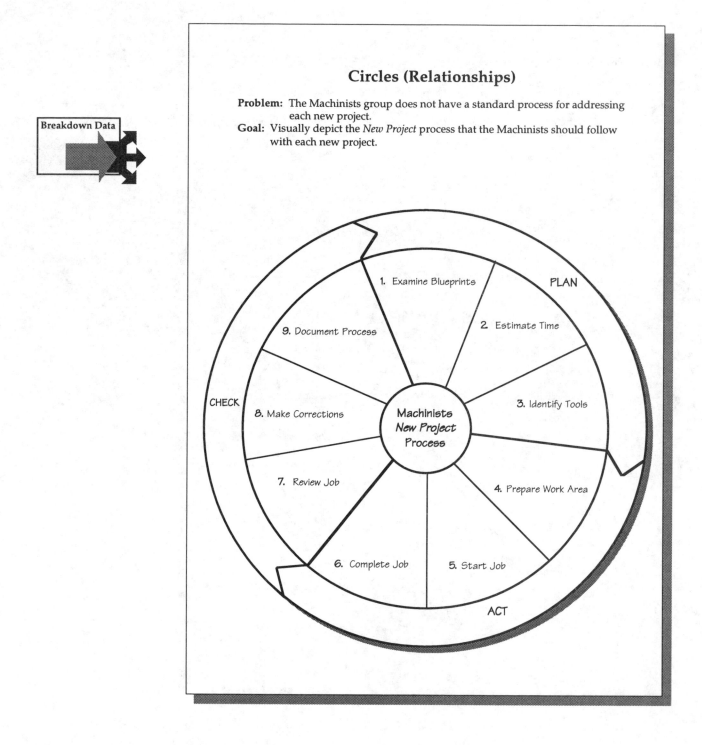

Circles (Relationships)

Problem: The Machinists group does not have a standard process for addressing each new project.

Goal: Visually depict the *New Project* process that the Machinists should follow with each new project.

PLAN

1. Examine Blueprints

2. Estimate Time

9. Document Process

3. Identify Tools

CHECK

8. Make Corrections

Machinists
New Project
Process

7. Review Job

4. Prepare Work Area

6. Complete Job

5. Start Job

ACT

ICEBERG DIAGRAM

What

The Iceberg Diagram visually depicts an iceberg with a small top showing above the water line and a much larger area hidden under the surface of the water.

When

This tool is used when the team wants to focus on the easily recognizable issues above the surface, as well as underlying issues beneath the surface for the stated problem or goal.

How

1. Define the problem.
2. Set the goals of the session.
3. Draw an Iceberg with a horizontal water line across the center of the iceberg.
4. Record the surface issues above the line and the hidden issues below the line.
5. Review the diagram and check for completeness.
6. Establish action plans for next steps.

Timing

Allow approximately 30 - 40 minutes to explain the process and for the group to work through it once the chart has been drawn.

Breakdown Data

Iceberg Diagram

Problem: The team feels that they are immobilized because of organizational barriers.

Goal: Examine how the organization gets things done so that barriers can be reduced or eliminated.

How Things Get Done

Formal Organization

Mission
Chain of Command
Goals & Objectives
Proposals
Organization Charts
Requests
Policies & Procedures
"Just Do It"

Leadership

Networks

Negotiation

"I'll scratch your back if you scratch mine"

Power Politics

Pecking Order

Relationships

Information Sharing

"Working the System"

Informal Organization

Materials

Something to write on that can be seen by all participants:

- Flip Chart (including masking tape or push pins for hanging)
- Overheads and Projector
- Butcher Paper
- White Board
- Chalk Board

Something to write with:

- Felt Tip Pens (different types for Flip Charts, Overheads and White Boards)
- Chalk

Iceberg Diagram

Problem: The long-term success of the organization is in jeopardy.
Goal: Identify the critical success factors for long-term survival.

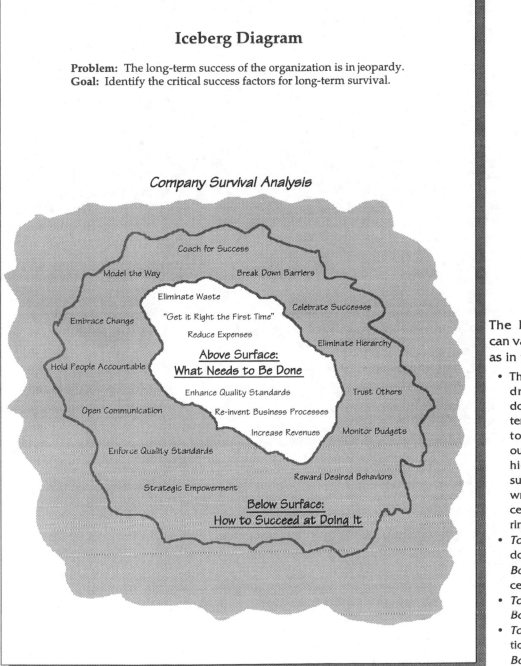

Company Survival Analysis

Coach for Success

Model the Way   Break Down Barriers

Eliminate Waste

Embrace Change   "Get it Right the First Time"   Celebrate Successes

Reduce Expenses

Eliminate Hierarchy

Above Surface:
What Needs to Be Done

Hold People Accountable

Enhance Quality Standards   Trust Others

Open Communication   Re-invent Business Processes

Increase Revenues   Monitor Budgets

Enforce Quality Standards

Reward Desired Behaviors

Strategic Empowerment

Below Surface:
How to Succeed at Doing It

Variations

The Iceberg Diagram can vary visually as well as in terms of content.

- The Iceberg can be drawn from a top-down view. The center of the iceberg is the top and the larger, outer surface is what is hidden beneath the surface. The issues are written either in the center or on the outer ring.

- *Top:* What needs to be done.
  Bottom: How to succeed.

- *Top:* Organization
  Bottom: Environment

- *Top:* Formal Organization
  Bottom: Informal Organization

- *Top:* Formal Communication
  Bottom: Informal Communication

- *Top:* Assumptions
  Bottom: Data-based information

Map Data

Storyboard

Process Flow Chart

Deployment Process
Flow Chart

Work Flow Diagram

Map Data

STORYBOARD

What

Storyboarding helps you organize ideas, methods, issues or elements into logical categories. These categories of grouped information are sequenced into a logical flow.

When

The Storyboard is used when:

- there is a need to examine information in a sequential manner
- the team needs to examine the factors leading up to a certain event
- the team needs to identify errors in the process
- the team needs to look at historical events in order to predict the future
- understanding the order of events is important
- understanding priorities, preferences or perceptions (scales) is important
- showing linkages between events and activities is important

Materials

Something to write on that can be seen by all participants:

- Grid-type Flip Chart (including masking tape or push pins for hanging)
- Butcher Paper
- White Board
- Chalk Board
- 3 X 5 Cards or Sticky Notes

Something to write with:

- Felt Tip Pens (different types for Flip Charts, Overheads and White Boards)
- Chalk

How

1. Define the problem.
2. Set the goals of the session.
3. Using 3 X 5 cards or sticky notes, write the *beginning* of the process on the left side of the work surface and the *end* of the process on the right side of the work surface.
4. Using 3 X 5 cards or sticky notes, brainstorm the categories of ideas, methods, issues or elements.
5. Align the categories in a sequence within the pre-determined boundaries. They should move from left to right across the work surface.
6. Using 3 X 5 cards or sticky notes, brainstorm the ideas, methods, issues or elements associated with each category and place under the category heading.
7. Observe and analyze the sequence. Look for ways to identify errors, areas of emphasis, historical events, order of things, and factors leading up to certain events. These could be indicators of where the group might want to begin its problem-solving efforts.
8. Set action plans for next steps.

Timing

Building a Storyboard should take approximately 60 - 90 minutes. This includes analyzing the information and building action plans.

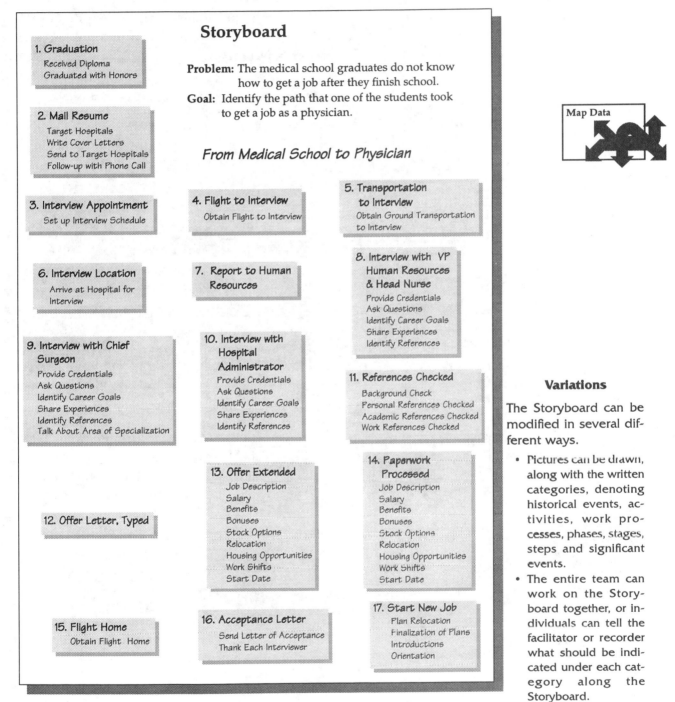

Storyboard

Problem: The medical school graduates do not know how to get a job after they finish school.

Goal: Identify the path that one of the students took to get a job as a physician.

From Medical School to Physician

Map Data

1. Graduation
Received Diploma
Graduated with Honors

2. Mail Resume
Target Hospitals
Write Cover Letters
Send to Target Hospitals
Follow-up with Phone Call

3. Interview Appointment
Set up Interview Schedule

4. Flight to Interview
Obtain Flight to Interview

5. Transportation to Interview
Obtain Ground Transportation to Interview

6. Interview Location
Arrive at Hospital for Interview

7. Report to Human Resources

8. Interview with VP Human Resources & Head Nurse
Provide Credentials
Ask Questions
Identify Career Goals
Share Experiences
Identify References

9. Interview with Chief Surgeon
Provide Credentials
Ask Questions
Identify Career Goals
Share Experiences
Identify References
Talk About Area of Specialization

10. Interview with Hospital Administrator
Provide Credentials
Ask Questions
Identify Career Goals
Share Experiences
Identify References

11. References Checked
Background Check
Personal References Checked
Academic References Checked
Work References Checked

12. Offer Letter, Typed

13. Offer Extended
Job Description
Salary
Benefits
Bonuses
Stock Options
Relocation
Housing Opportunities
Work Shifts
Start Date

14. Paperwork Processed
Job Description
Salary
Benefits
Bonuses
Stock Options
Relocation
Housing Opportunities
Work Shifts
Start Date

15. Flight Home
Obtain Flight Home

16. Acceptance Letter
Send Letter of Acceptance
Thank Each Interviewer

17. Start New Job
Plan Relocation
Finalization of Plans
Introductions
Orientation

Variations

The Storyboard can be modified in several different ways.

- Pictures can be drawn, along with the written categories, denoting historical events, activities, work processes, phases, stages, steps and significant events.

- The entire team can work on the Storyboard together, or individuals can tell the facilitator or recorder what should be indicated under each category along the Storyboard.

- Team members can write their input on 3 X 5 cards or sticky notes which are then included in the Storyboard at the appropriate point.

Map Data

Variations (Continued)

- The team can Storyboard the current method process and then Storyboard the proposed process. This allows for comparisons and revisions.
- The Storyboard can be segmented in various ways:
  - even distribution along a straight path with quadrants denoting phases or quarters in a year and events recorded within each quadrant to provide further detail
  - various other larger groupings with the detailed events displayed within each grouping

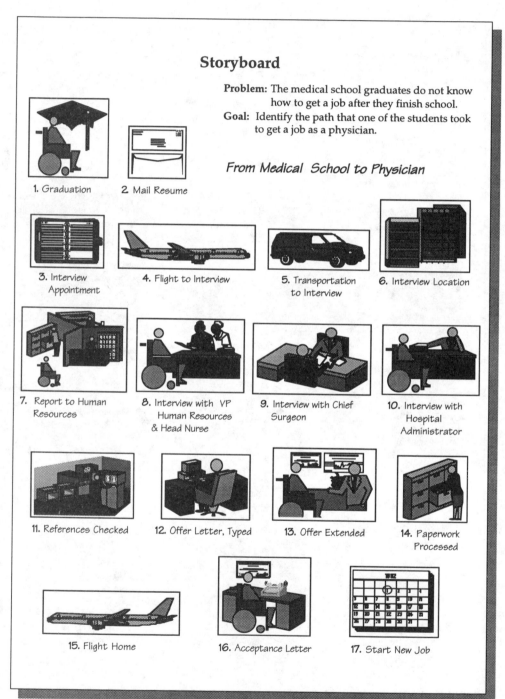

Storyboard

Problem: The medical school graduates do not know how to get a job after they finish school.
Goal: Identify the path that one of the students took to get a job as a physician.

From Medical School to Physician

1. Graduation
2. Mail Resume
3. Interview Appointment
4. Flight to Interview
5. Transportation to Interview
6. Interview Location
7. Report to Human Resources
8. Interview with VP Human Resources & Head Nurse
9. Interview with Chief Surgeon
10. Interview with Hospital Administrator
11. References Checked
12. Offer Letter, Typed
13. Offer Extended
14. Paperwork Processed
15. Flight Home
16. Acceptance Letter
17. Start New Job

PROCESS FLOW CHART

What

The Process Flow Chart is a visual representation showing all the steps in a process. It uses a set of recognizable symbols to document these steps.

When

The Process Flow Chart is used when:

- there is a need to examine information in a sequential manner
- the team needs to examine the factors leading up to a certain event
- the team needs to identify errors in the process
- the team needs to look at historical processes in order to predict the future
- understanding the order of a process is important
- showing linkages between decisions and activities is important
- eliminating unnecessary or duplicative tasks is important
- improving work flow and reducing paperwork is important

How

1. Define the problem.
2. Set the goals of the session.

3. Using 3 X 5 cards or sticky notes, write the process *beginning* on the left side of the work surface and *end* of the process on the right side of the work surface.
4. Using 3 X 5 cards or sticky notes, list all of the steps in the process.
5. Align the categories in a sequence within the pre-determined boundaries. They should move from left to right across the work surface.
6. Attach the appropriate symbol (see symbol key on graphic) for each process step.
7. Observe and analyze the sequence. Look for ways to identify errors, areas to emphasize, duplication of work, missing steps, unnecessary steps, order of things, and simplification opportunities. These could be indicators of where the group might want to begin its problem-solving efforts.
8. Set action plans for next steps.

Timing

The Process Flow Chart session should take approximately 2 - 4 hours. This includes building the Process Flow Chart, analyzing the information and building action plans.

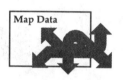

Map Data

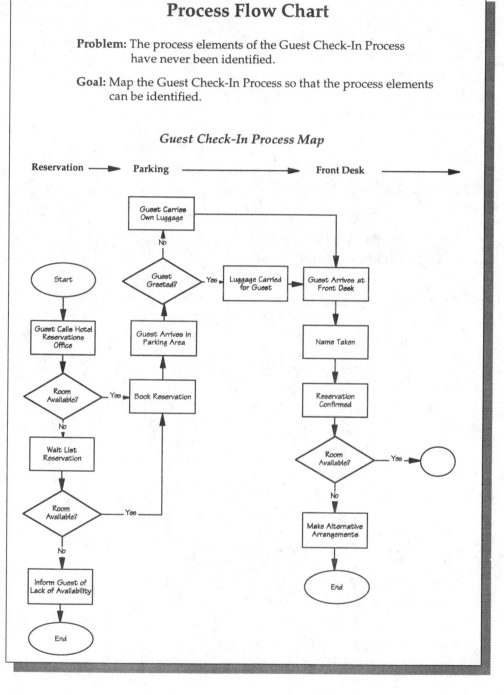

Process Flow Chart

Problem: The process elements of the Guest Check-In Process have never been identified.

Goal: Map the Guest Check-In Process so that the process elements can be identified.

Guest Check-In Process Map

Reservation ➝ Parking ——————➝ Front Desk ——————➝

Materials

Something to write on that can be seen by all participants:

- Grid-type Flip Chart (including masking tape or push pins for hanging)
- Overheads and Projector
- Butcher Paper
- White Board
- Chalk Board
- Computer
- 3 X 5 Cards or Sticky Notes

Something to write with:

- Felt Tip Pens (different types for flip charts, overheads and white boards)
- Chalk

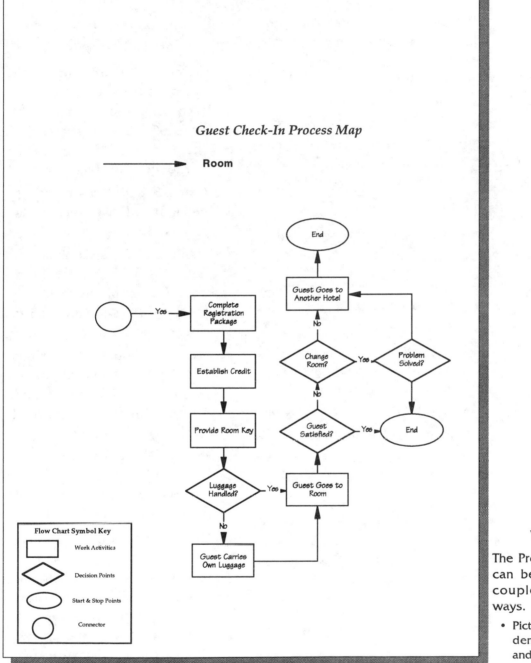

Guest Check-In Process Map

Room

Variations

The Process Flow Chart can be modified in a couple of different ways.

- Pictures can be drawn denoting the stages and events contained within each stage.
- The current and future processes can be flow charted and compared. This would allow the team to identify and target areas for improvement.

DEPLOYMENT PROCESS FLOW CHART

What

The Deployment Process Flow Chart is a visual representation showing all the steps in a process and also indicating the job function that is responsible for each activity. It uses a set of recognizable symbols to document these various process steps.

When

The Deployment Process Flow Chart is used when:

- there is a need to examine information in a sequential manner

- the team needs to identify the job function that is responsible for each action

- the team needs to identify errors in the process

- the team needs to look at historical processes in order to predict the future

- understanding the sequence of a process and assigning responsibility for each activity is important

- showing linkages between decisions and activities is important

- eliminating unnecessary or duplicative tasks is important

- improving work flow and reducing paperwork is important

How

1. Define the problem.

2. Set the goals of the session.

3. Using 3 X 5 cards or sticky notes, write the process *beginning* on the left side of the work surface and the *end* of the process on the right side of the work surface.

4. Using 3 X 5 cards or sticky notes, list all the steps in the process.

5. Using 3 X 5 cards or sticky notes, identify the job function responsible for each activity. Different color cards can be used for each function.

6. Working from left to right and top to bottom, align the process steps sequentially within the pre-determined boundaries while also aligning to each job function responsibility.

7. Attach the appropriate symbol to each process step.

8. Observe and analyze the sequence. Look for ways to identify errors, areas to emphasize, duplication of work, missing steps, unnecessary steps, order of things, and simplification opportunities. These could be indicators of where the group might begin its problem-solving efforts.

9. Set action plans for next steps.

Timing

Building a Deployment Process
Flow Chart should take approximately 2 - 4 hours. This includes
creating the Deployment Process
Flow Chart, analyzing the information and building action plans.

Map Data

Deployment Process Flow Chart

Problem: Downsizing may be imminent. There is no transition plan for employees.

Goal: Map an employee transition plan that will allow employees the opportunity to develop toward other positions.

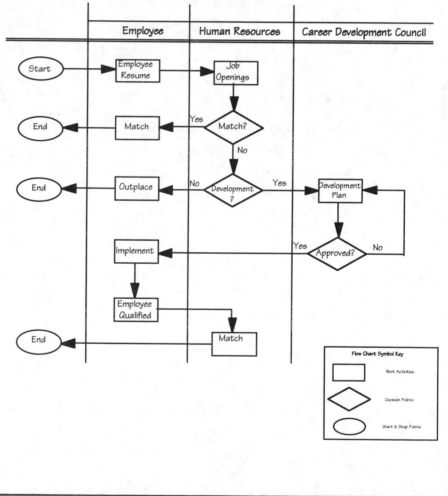

Materials

Something to write on that can be seen by all participants:

- Grid-type Flip Chart (including masking tape or push pins for hanging)
- Overheads and Projector
- Butcher Paper
- White Board
- Chalk Board
- Computer
- 3 X 5 Cards or Sticky Notes

Something to write with:

- Felt Tip Pens (different types for Flip Charts, Overheads and White Boards)
- Chalk

Map Data

Deployment Process Flow Chart

Problem: The mail seems to take up a lot of time each day.

Goal: Examine the sequence in which the mail is handled. Identify the supplier and the customer. Look for possible short-cuts or role elimination.

Mail Distribution Sequence Flow Chart

Task \ Who	Mail Attendant	Secretary	Manager A	Manager B	Time
1. Pick Up Mail	▼				5 mins.
2 Open Mail	●				20 mins.
3. Sort Mail	●				10 mins.
4. Date Stamp Mail		▼			15 mins.
5. Distribute Mail		●			10 mins.
6. Read Mail			▼		30 mins.
7. Throw Away Mail			●		5 mins.
8. Answer Mail			●		10 mins.
9. Re-route Mail			●		5 mins.
10. File Letters		▼			10 mins.
11. Receive Re-routed				▼	5 mins.
12. Generate Mail				●	30 mins.
13. Address Mail		▼			20 mins.
14. Post Mail		●			3 mins.
15. Pick Up Mail		▼			5 mins.

Symbol Key

▼ Supplier

● Customer

Variations

The Deployment Process Flow Chart can be modified in a couple of different ways.

- Pictures can be drawn denoting the issues, events, processes and/or activities contained within the Flow Chart.
- A Sequence Flow Chart can be used to indicate the process flow in relation to the *person* who is responsible for each activity. A designation of supplier or customer is given at each step in the process.
- The current and future processes can be flow charted and compared. This would allow the team to identify and target areas for improvement.

WORK FLOW DIAGRAM

What

The Work Flow Diagram is a visual presentation of the movement of people, materials, information or documents in a process.

When

The Work Flow Diagram is used when:

- there is a need to visually examine information in a sequential manner
- the team needs to identify errors in the process
- the team needs to look at historical processes in order to predict the future
- understanding the sequence of a process is important
- visually showing linkages between activities is important
- eliminating unnecessary or duplicative tasks is important
- improving work flow and reducing paperwork is important

How

1. Define the problem.
2. Set the goals of the session.
3. Using a large work surface, write the *beginning* of the process on the left side of the work surface and the *end* of the process on the right side of the work surface.
4. Draw or illustrate the area, place or layout in which the people, materials, information or documents are processed.
5. Draw arrows or lines, or attach string or yarn, to show the flow of each element.
6. Observe and analyze the sequence. Look for ways to identify errors, areas to emphasize, duplication of work, missing steps, unnecessary steps, order of things, and simplification opportunities. These could be indicators of where the group might want to begin its problem-solving efforts.
7. Set action plans for next steps.

Timing

The development of this tool should take a team approximately 2 - 3 hours to complete. This includes analysis and action planning.

Work Flow Diagram

Problem: The machinists want to improve the amount of time spent machining.
Goal: Examine the traffic patterns of a typical machinist and eliminate wasted movements.

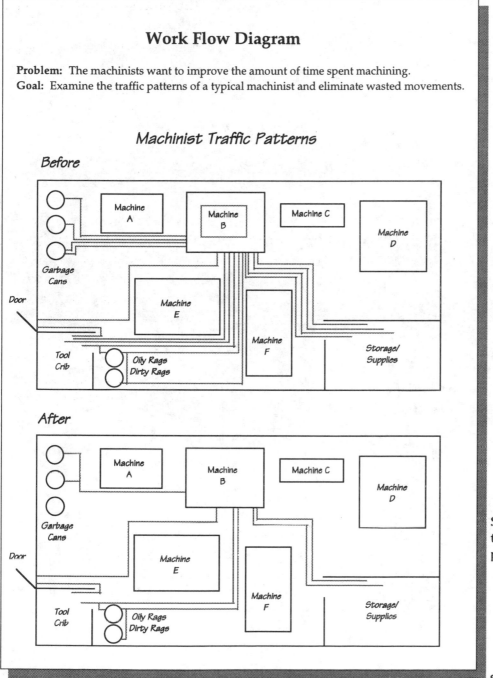

Machinist Traffic Patterns

Before

After

Materials

Something to write on that can be seen by all participants:

- Grid-type Flip Chart (including masking tape or push pins for hanging)
- Butcher Paper
- White Board
- Chalk Board

Something to write with:

- Felt Tip Pens (different types for Flip Charts, Overheads and White Boards)
- Chalk
- Yarn

Map Data

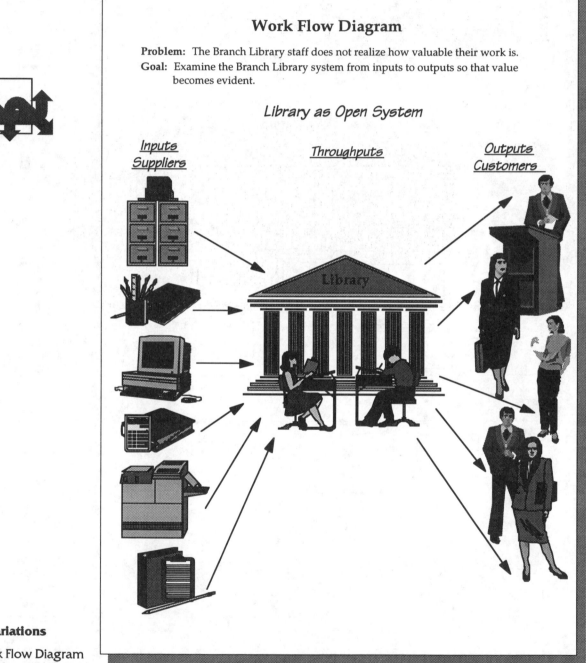

Work Flow Diagram

Problem: The Branch Library staff does not realize how valuable their work is.
Goal: Examine the Branch Library system from inputs to outputs so that value becomes evident.

Library as Open System

Inputs
Suppliers

Throughputs

Outputs
Customers

Library

Variations

The Work Flow Diagram can be modified by visually showing the connection between people, materials, information or documents and their flow throughout the organization.

Display Data

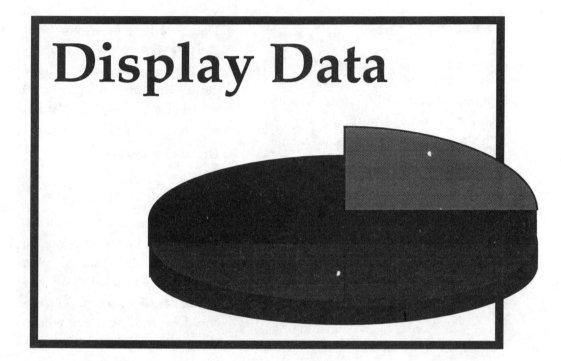

Area Graph

Bar Graph

Line Graph/Run Chart

AREA GRAPH

What

The Area Graph shows the relative importance of values over a period of time. It visually displays the amount of change as opposed to the rate of change. Ideal for use in quality control, forecasting and marketing.

When

The Area Graph is used when:

- there is a need to show the amount of change

- the team needs to show the relative importance of values over a period of time

- the team needs to visually see what is happening in the process under examination

- the team needs to find patterns in the process over time

- there is a need to visually compare data over the same time period

- the team needs to plot the information gathered from the Check Sheet

How

1. Define the problem.

2. Set the goals of the session.

3. Identify the information you are measuring.

4. Decide what the X axis (horizontal) and the Y axis (vertical) will contain. These could be time periods and numbers in various incremental patterns.

5. Draw the graph.

6. Plot the information you are measuring on the chart.

7. Observe and analyze the sequence. Look for ways to identify errors in the process, change over time, and the amount of change. These could be indicators of where the group might want to begin its problem-solving efforts.

8. Set action plans for next steps.

Timing

Building an Area Graph should take approximately 60 minutes. This assumes that the information is readily available for plotting and includes analyzing the information and building action plans.

Materials

Something to write on that can be seen by all participants:

- Grid-type Flip Chart (including masking tape or push pins for hanging)
- Overheads and Projector
- Butcher Paper
- White Board
- Chalk Board
- Computer

Something to write with:

- Felt Tip Pens (different types for Flip Charts, Overheads and White Boards)
- Chalk
- Computer Software Graphic Packages

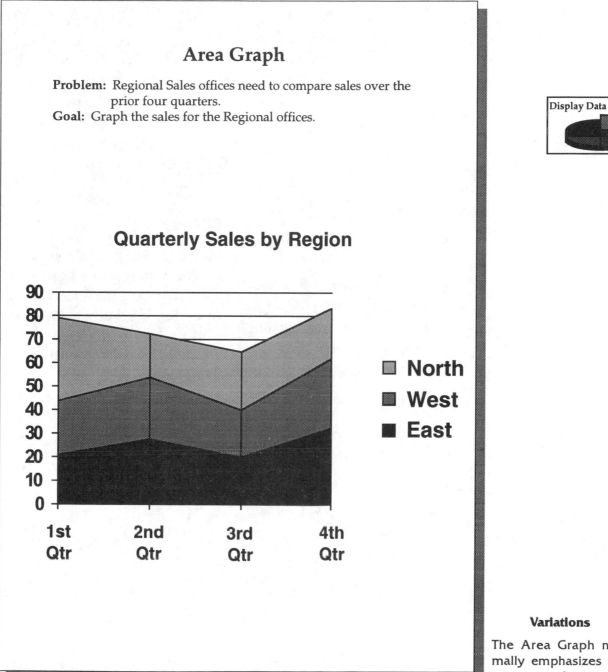

Area Graph

Problem: Regional Sales offices need to compare sales over the
prior four quarters.
Goal: Graph the sales for the Regional offices.

Display Data

Quarterly Sales by Region

◻ **North**
◼ **West**
■ **East**

Variations

The Area Graph nor-
mally emphasizes the
amount of change,
rather than rate of
change, over time. The
Area Chart can also be
used to plot several dif-
ferent sets of informa-
tion over time. This al-
lows for comparisons

BAR GRAPH

Display Data

What

The Bar Graph is a visual representation showing comparisons of quantities of data. It uses horizontal and vertical bars of varying length or height and uniform width.

When

The Bar Graph is used when:

- there is a need to compare and contrast data
- the team needs to examine trends over time
- the team needs to identify errors in the process
- the team needs to visually communicate variable process information

How

1. Define the problem.
2. Set the goals of the session.
3. Identify the information you are measuring.
4. Decide what the X axis (horizontal) and the Y axis (vertical) will contain. These could be time periods, percentages and numbers in various incremental patterns.
5. Draw the graph.
6. Draw bars of uniform width and variable length or height to equal the quantity of items or frequency of happenings.
7. Compare and contrast the data. Look for ways to identify errors, areas to emphasize and simplification opportunities. These could be indicators of where the group might want to begin its problem-solving efforts.
8. Set action plans for next steps.

Timing

Making a Bar Graph should take approximately 30 minutes to 1 hour. This assumes that the information is readily available for plotting and includes analyzing the information and building action plans.

Bar Graph

Problem: Regional Sales offices need to compare sales over the prior four quarters.
Goal: Graph the sales for the Regional offices.

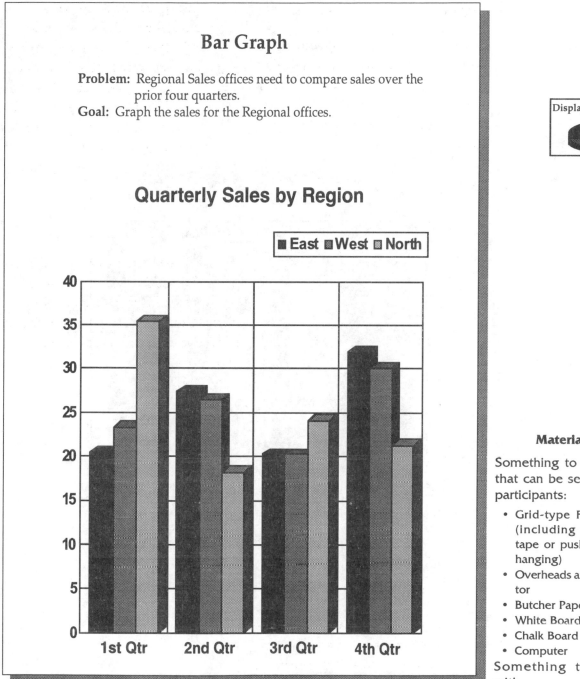

Quarterly Sales by Region

■ East ■ West ■ North

Display Data

Materials

Something to write on that can be seen by all participants:

- Grid-type Flip Chart (including masking tape or push pins for hanging)
- Overheads and Projector
- Butcher Paper
- White Board
- Chalk Board
- Computer

Something to write with:

- Felt Tip Pens (different types for Flip Charts, Overheads and White Boards)
- Chalk
- Computer Software Graphic Packages

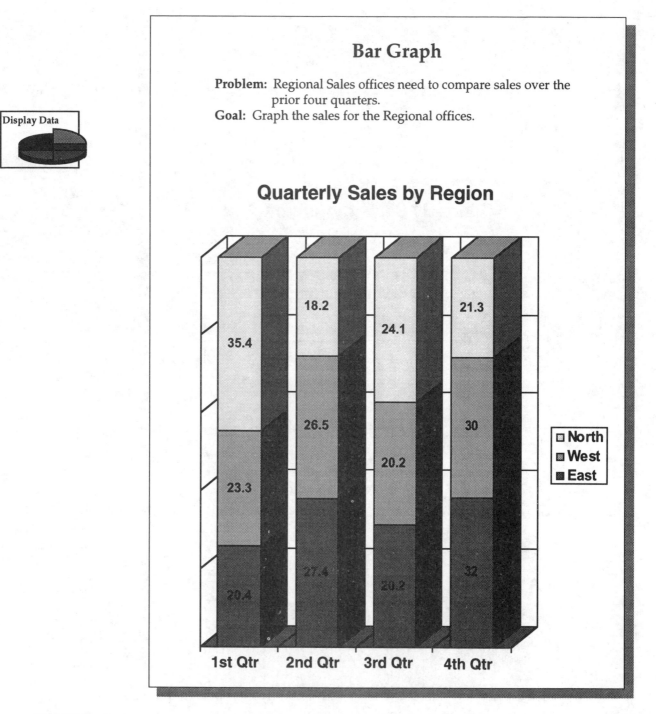

Bar Graph

Problem: Regional Sales offices need to compare sales over the prior four quarters.
Goal: Graph the sales for the Regional offices.

Quarterly Sales by Region

Display Data

□ North
▨ West
■ East

Variations

The most common Bar Graphs are Histograms and Column Graphs. Bar Graphs can also be stacked.

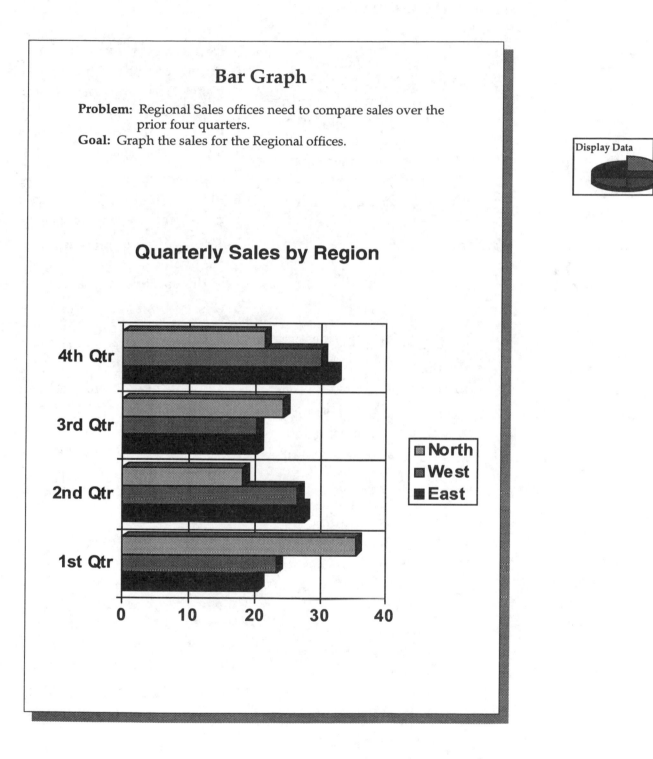

Bar Graph

Problem: Regional Sales offices need to compare sales over the prior four quarters.

Goal: Graph the sales for the Regional offices.

Display Data

Quarterly Sales by Region

Legend:
- North
- West
- East

LINE GRAPH/RUN CHART

What

The Line Graph/Run Chart is a visual representation showing trends or changes in data over a period of time. It is similar to an Area Graph but emphasizes the time flow and rate of change as opposed to the amount of change.

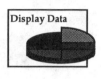

When

The Line Graph/Run Chart is used when:

- there is a need to show change over time
- the team needs to track more than one set of data at a time
- the team needs to identify errors in the process
- the team needs to visually see what is happening in the process
- the team needs to find patterns in the process over time
- there is a need to visually compare data over the same time period
- the team needs to plot the information gathered from the Check Sheet

How

1. Define the problem.
2. Set the goals of the session.
3. Identify the information you are measuring.
4. Decide what the X axis (horizontal) and the Y axis (vertical) will contain. These could be time periods and numbers in various incremental patterns.
5. Draw the graph.
6. Plot the information you are measuring on the chart.
7. Draw a line connecting the quantities observed on each of the successive intervals.
8. Observe and analyze the sequence. Look for ways to identify errors in the process, change over time and the amount of change. These could be indicators of where the group might want to begin its problem-solving efforts.
9. Set action plans for next steps.

Timing

Building a Line Graph/Run Chart should take approximately 1 hour. This assumes that the information is readily available for plotting and includes analyzing the information and building action plans.

Line Graph/Run Chart

Problem: Regional Sales offices need to compare sales over the
prior four quarters.
Goal: Graph the sales for the Regional offices.

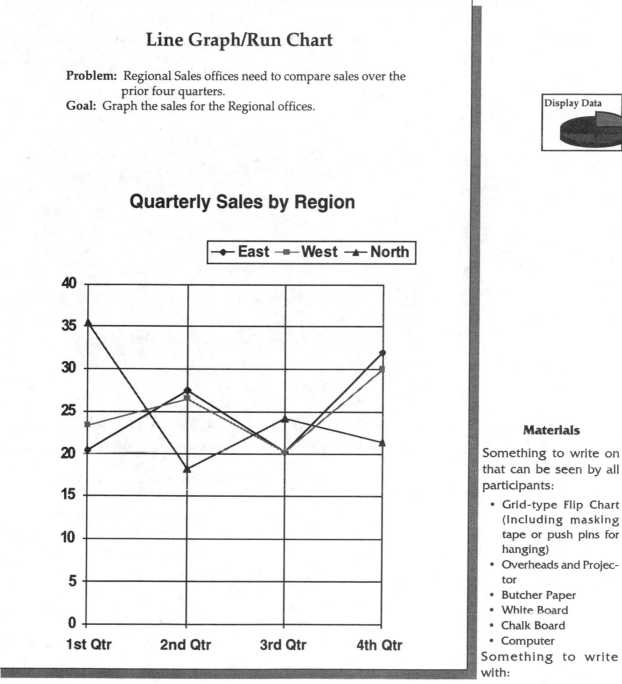

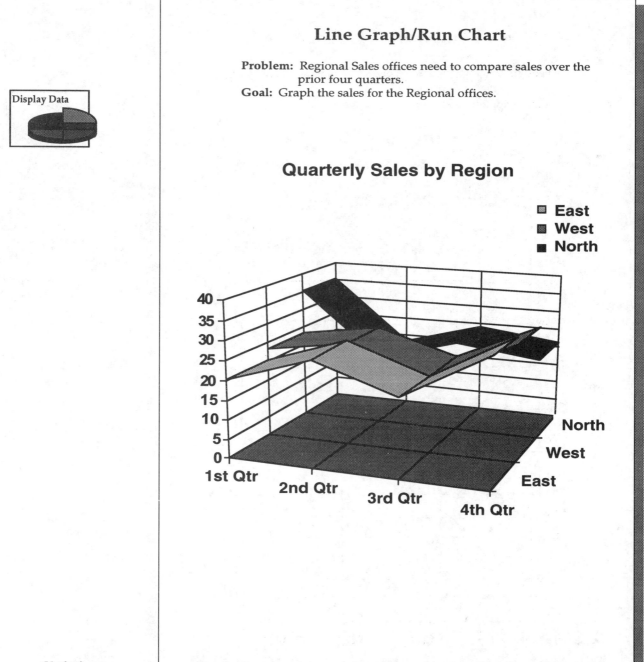

Line Graph/Run Chart

Problem: Regional Sales offices need to compare sales over the prior four quarters.

Goal: Graph the sales for the Regional offices.

Quarterly Sales by Region

- East
- West
- North

Variations

The Line Graph/Run Chart emphasizes time flow and rate of change. Variations exist in the incremental measurements of time and change.

Line Graph/Run Chart

Problem: Regional Sales offices need to compare sales over the
            prior four quarters.
Goal: Graph the sales for the Regional offices.

Display Data

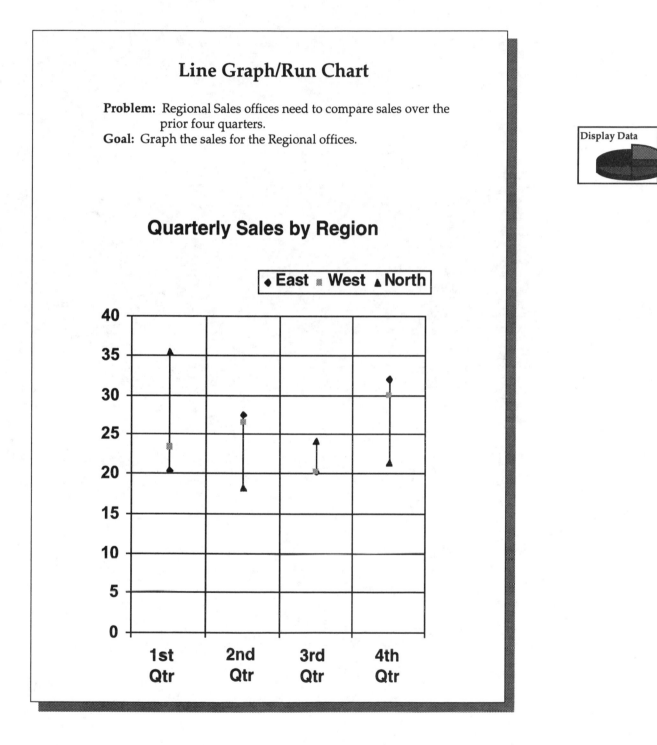

III

Case
Studies

SERVICE

◆

FINANCE

◆

MANUFACTURING

Overview

The case studies follow the *15 Steps to Facilitating a Successful Meeting.* The meeting planning *Agenda,* the *Process and Tool Selection Questions,* as well as various meeting facilitation tools, are completed and incorporated into each case study.

The cases and team compilation vary in order to show the uses of facilitation tools in different work environments. The process decision making varies, showing that the leader and the team can both contribute to process decisions. Meeting time frames also differ in order to accommodate team availability and urgency for action.

The *Case Studies* section should be used as a reference for utilizing the 15 step integrated system of **planning**, **organizing**, **conducting** and **evaluating** a meeting.

Case Study

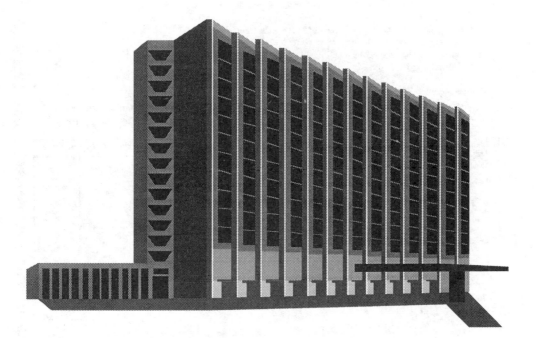

Service

Hotel Company
Guest Check-In Process Action Plan

SERVICE

HOTEL COMPANY

GUEST CHECK-IN PROCESS ACTION TEAM

Organize Data

Worksheet

Agenda

1. Meeting Purpose/Outcome(s):
The Guest Check-In Process takes too long and has too many errors.

2. Boundaries (Beginning and Ending):
The Guest Check-In Process **begins** when the customer makes a reservation and **ends** when the customer is safely inside the room of their choice.

3. Meeting Objectives (These become the Agenda Item(s) below.):

Establish Overall Agenda	Identify Problem Areas
Examine the Guest Check-In Process	Develop Solution Alternatives
Break Down each Process Component Area	Develop Action Plan

4. Owner(s):
The General Manager owns the process since the problem is cross-functional and affects the entire operation. As owner, the General Manager will ensure that the team's decisions will be acted upon.

5. Agenda Item(s)	6. Process	7. Tool(s)	8. Responsibility	9. Time
Establish Overall Agenda	None	Agenda	Team	2 hours
Examine Guest Check-In Process	Map Data	Process Flow Chart	Team	2 hours
Break Down Process Component	Breakdown Data	Tree Diagram	Team	2 hours
Identify Problem Areas	Group Data	Affinity Diagram	Team	2 hours
Develop Solution Alternatives	Organize Data	Paired-Choice Matrix	Team	2 hours
Develop Action Plan	Organize Data	Matrix (Planning)	Team	2 hours

9a. Total Time Needed: 6 weeks, 2 hours per week -- Total of 12 hours

10. Roles:

Leader: General Manager   **Facilitator:** Front Desk Manager   **Recorder:** Concierge
Presenter(s): None
Participants:

1. Operations Manager	**5.** Front Desk Agent	**9.**
2. Director or Rooms	**6.** Housekeeping Supervisor	**10.**
3. Front Desk Manager	**7.** Concierge	**11.**
4. Reservations Agent	**8.**	**12.**

11. Logistics:

Date: 6 Thurs. Mornings   **Time:** 8:30 a.m. - 10:30 a.m.   **Location:** Large Conference Room

12. Materials Needed: Flip Charts (2), Felt Tip Pens, Masking Tape, Pins, Pencils, 3 X 5 Sticky Notes, Colored Sticky Dots, Notepads

Background

A cross-functional team from a major hotel chain gathered to examine the front desk check-in process. Although the feeling is that, in general, the check-in process works well, the team is convinced that improvements can be made and that these improvements will give their organization a competitive advantage in the industry.

Pre-Meeting Preparation

Refer to the *Agenda,* and the *Process and Tool Selection Questions* at the end of this case study for clarification.

1. **MEETING PURPOSE/OUTCOME(S)**

   The Leader defined the problem as:

   The Guest Check-In Process takes too long and has too many errors.

2. **BOUNDARIES (BEGINNINGS AND ENDINGS)**

   The team first listed all of the possible boundaries that they could think of. They then voted (Multi-voting), using sticky dots, as to where they thought the boundaries should be.

Multi-Voting

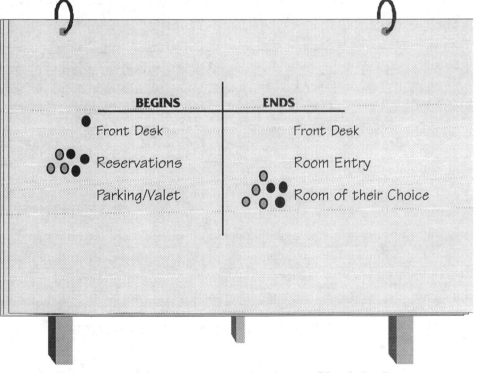

The voting determined that the Guest Check-In Process **begins** *when the customer makes a reservation and* **ends** *when the customer is safely inside the room of their choice.*

3.   **MEETING OBJECTIVES (THESE BECOME THE AGENDA ITEM(S) BELOW.)**

The team determined the meeting objectives to be:

Meeting 1:   Establish Overall Agenda

Meeting 2:   Examine the Guest Check-In Process

Meeting 3:   Break Down each Process Component Area

Meeting 4:   Identify Problem Areas

Meeting 5:   Develop Solution Alternatives

Meeting 6:   Develop Action Plan

4.   **OWNER(S)**

The General Manager owns the process since the problem is cross-functional and affects the entire operation. As owner, the General Manager will ensure that the team's decisions will be acted upon.

5.   **AGENDA ITEM(S) (THESE ARE TAKEN FROM THE MEETING OBJECTIVES ABOVE.)**

Based on the objectives and agenda, questions 6 - 9 were handled together.

6. PROCESS

7. TOOL(S) (SEE *PROCESS AND TOOL SELECTION QUESTIONS* **AT THE END OF THIS CASE STUDY.)**

8. RESPONSIBILITY

9. TIME

9A. TOTAL TIME NEEDED

The team agreed that weekly two-hour meetings should be adequate. Their business schedules and need to gather and process data between meetings drove the scheduling decision. It was anticipated that the entire process would take no more than three months using this schedule.

The graph in the Agenda was used to determine the Agenda Items, Process, Tools, Responsibility and Time needed. This was done with the entire team at the first meeting. The Process and Tool Selection Questions were also used to complete the Process and Tools columns of the graph.

5. Agenda Items	6. Process	7. Tools	8. Responsibility	9. Time
Meeting 1: Establish Overall Agenda	None	Agenda	Team	2 hours
Meeting 2: Examine Guest Check-in Process	Map Data	Process Flow Chart	Team	2 hours
Meeting 3: Break Down Process Component Areas	Breakdown	DataTree Diagram	Team	2 hours
Meeting 4: Identify Problem Areas	Group Data	Affinity Diagram	Team	2 hours
Meeting 5: Develop Solution Alternatives	Organize Data	Paired-Choice Matrix	Team	2 hours
Meeting 6: Develop Action Plan	Organize Data	Matrix (Planning)	Team	2 hours

Matrix Chart

10. ROLES

Leader

The General Manager was the Leader. The General Manager initiated the meetings and directed the outcomes.

Facilitator

The Front Desk Manager had taken facilitator classes and had experience, so the team chose him to facilitate.

Recorder

The Concierge volunteered to be the team recorder. This commitment meant that she would record team activities during the meetings and give the notes to the General Manager's secretary for typing and dissemination to the team.

Participants

The team was comprised of a General Manager, an Operations Manager, a Director of Rooms, a Front Desk Manager, a Reservations Agent, a Front Desk Agent, a Housekeeping Supervisor and a Concierge. These eight individuals represented a cross-section of the functions that have direct impact on Guest Check In. The team agreed that this was a good number for identifying and working with the issues. If additional information was needed, the appropriate individuals would be invited to share or participate at that time.

11. LOGISTICS

Date

Every other Thursday morning for 2 hours beginning the following week and ending after 6 meetings (3 months) was the time frame that the team established.

Time

Every two weeks for two hours from 8:30 a.m. - 10:30 a.m. was the time that the team set.

Location

The large conference room was centrally located and the right size for this group. Many of the necessary materials for conducting the meeting were also available in this meeting room.

12. MATERIALS NEEDED

The Facilitator created a facilitation kit that was taken to each meeting. The kit contained a number of items, including: felt tip pens, masking tape, pins, pencils, 3 X 5 sticky notes, colored sticky dots, notepads, and flip charts.

13. GROUND RULES

They initiated and agreed to the following Meeting Ground Rules:

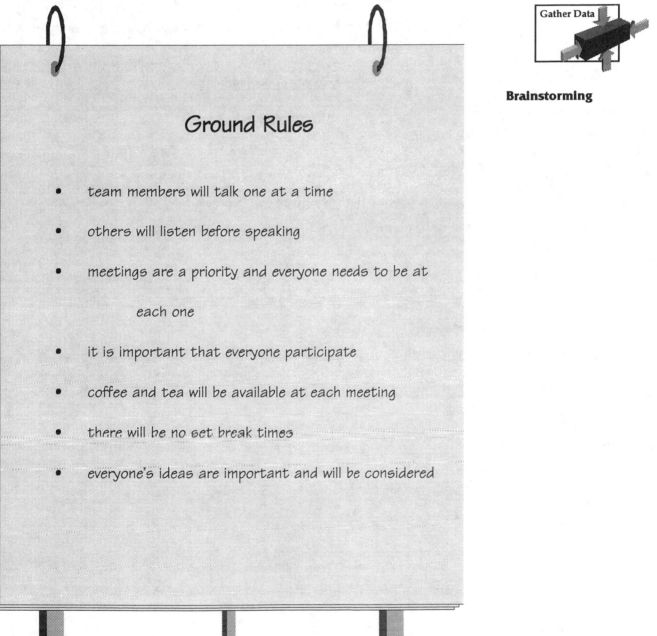

Gather Data

Brainstorming

Ground Rules

- team members will talk one at a time

- others will listen before speaking

- meetings are a priority and everyone needs to be at

  each one

- it is important that everyone participate

- coffee and tea will be available at each meeting

- there will be no set break times

- everyone's ideas are important and will be considered

14. ACTIONS

At the first meeting, the team established the purpose, boundaries, ownership, objectives, agenda, roles and responsibilities, location, date and time, and ground rules. Thereafter, the meetings followed the Agenda that had been established for the upcoming meetings.

The team spent the last part of each meeting assessing progress and re-affirming the upcoming meeting agenda. The secretary typed and distributed this agenda with the prior meeting's notes.

At the end of the First Meeting, the agenda was set for the Second Meeting.

Second Meeting Agenda

- Review team goals
- Map the Guest Check-In Process

  Tool: Process Flow Chart

- Summarize Process
- Plan next Agenda

Second Meeting

Since the meeting Agenda had been established at the last team meeting, the members first reviewed their previous week's work. With no changes, the team proceeded to identify the problem and goal of the meeting and to map *(see following pages)* the Guest Check-In Process.

> **Problem:** The elements of the Guest Check-In Process have never been identified.
>
> **Goal:** Map the Guest Check-In Process so that the elements can be identified.

Upon completion of the process map, the findings were discussed. The team learned that the Guest Check-In Process consists of four major components. These components include: making the reservation, parking, front desk check-in, and the guest room. Within each of these four components exist numerous activities in which anything could go wrong. In addition, each one of these four components contain activities that could be streamlined or eliminated. The tree diagram planned for the next meeting should be just the tool to help them further breakdown the process.

The agenda for the next meeting was planned.

Third Meeting Agenda

- Review team accomplishments so far
- Develop Tree Diagram from Process Flow Chart

  Tool: Tree Diagram
- Summarize Process
- Plan next Agenda

Process Flow Chart

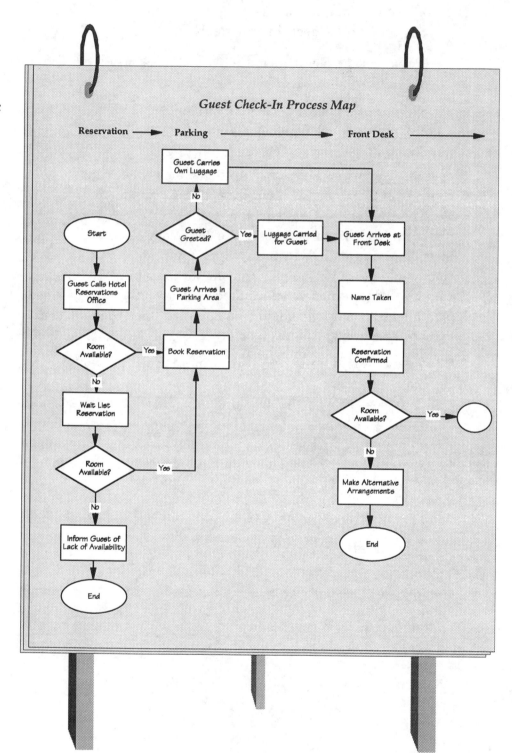

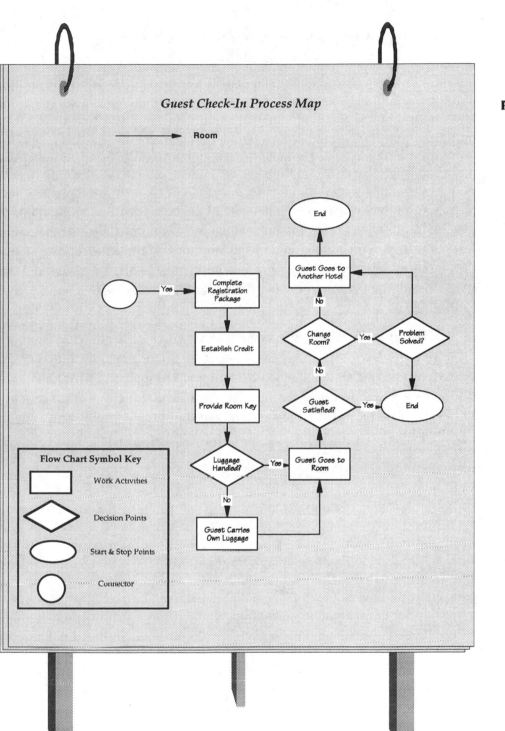

Map Data

Process Flow Chart

Guest Check-In Process Map

→ Room

Flow Chart Symbol Key

☐ Work Activities

◇ Decision Points

⬭ Start & Stop Points

○ Connector

Third Meeting

Since the meeting Agenda was established at the last team meeting, the members reviewed the previous week's work. With no changes, the group was ready to break down the process components.

> **Problem:** There are many activities within the Guest Check-In Process where mistakes can be made.
>
> **Goal:** Breakdown the Guest Check-In Process into activities.

Now that the process had been broken down, the team could better understand all of the activities involved in the Guest Check-In Process. One of the things that became very clear during the building of the Tree Diagram, was that there were different roles in the process. The guest had a role and the hotel had a role. Once these roles were identified, the activities were grouped around the two roles. This allowed the team to examine the hotel-specific activities so that process issues could be directed toward activities that were within their control.

Having identified the components, roles and activities of the Guest Check-In Process, the team next needed to identify the issues surrounding the efficiency of the process. The Affinity Diagram planned for session four was confirmed to be the perfect tool to identify these issues.

The agenda for the next meeting was planned.

Fourth Meeting Agenda

- Review team accomplishments so far
- Identify Process Issues

    Tool: Affinity Diagram

- Summarize Process
- Plan next Agenda

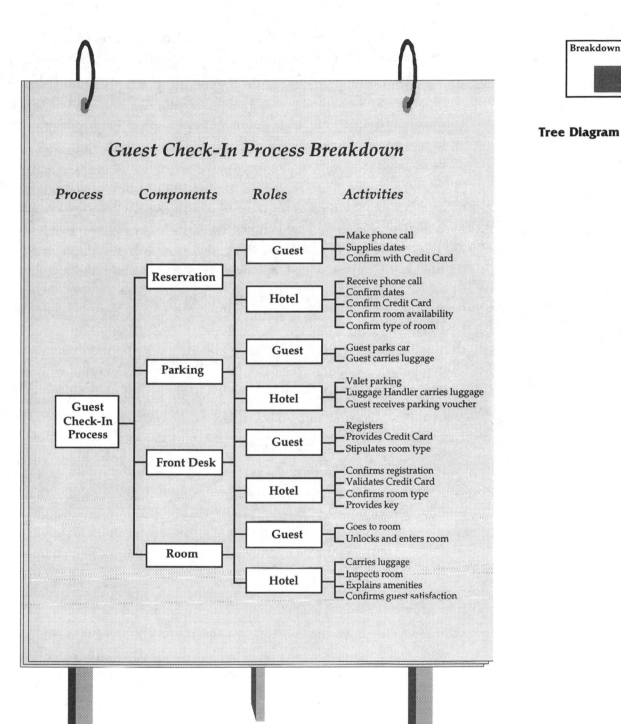

Breakdown Data

Tree Diagram

Guest Check-In Process Breakdown

Process	Components	Roles	Activities

Guest Check-In Process

Reservation
- **Guest**
  - Make phone call
  - Supplies dates
  - Confirm with Credit Card
- **Hotel**
  - Receive phone call
  - Confirm dates
  - Confirm Credit Card
  - Confirm room availability
  - Confirm type of room

Parking
- **Guest**
  - Guest parks car
  - Guest carries luggage
- **Hotel**
  - Valet parking
  - Luggage Handler carries luggage
  - Guest receives parking voucher

Front Desk
- **Guest**
  - Registers
  - Provides Credit Card
  - Stipulates room type
- **Hotel**
  - Confirms registration
  - Validates Credit Card
  - Confirms room type
  - Provides key

Room
- **Guest**
  - Goes to room
  - Unlocks and enters room
- **Hotel**
  - Carries luggage
  - Inspects room
  - Explains amenities
  - Confirms guest satisfaction

Fourth Meeting

The members reviewed the previous meeting's minutes. With no changes to the minutes, the group was now ready to identify the process issues.

> **Problem:** The issues surrounding efficient Guest Check-In had not been examined.

> **Goal:** Identify the issues surrounding an efficient Guest Check-In.

The team learned that the Guest Check-In Process had a number of process issues needing attention. As they examined the Affinity Diagram, they identified certain areas for improvement. The areas that they felt needed further attention were: **staffing, room type availability, reservations accuracy, billing complications, and room maintenance**. These five issues would be the target for next week's meeting and would be used in the Paired-Choice Matrix.

The agenda for the next meeting was planned.

Agenda

- Review team accomplishments so far
- Identify Solution Alternatives

  Tool: Paired-Choice Matrix
- Summarize Process
- Plan next Agenda

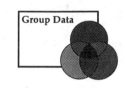

Affinity Diagram

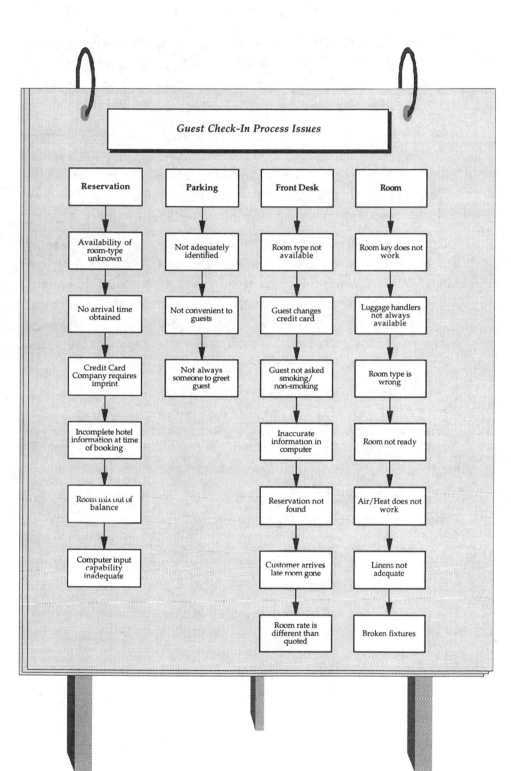

Guest Check-In Process Issues

Reservation	Parking	Front Desk	Room
Availability of room-type unknown	Not adequately identified	Room type not available	Room key does not work
No arrival time obtained	Not convenient to guests	Guest changes credit card	Luggage handlers not always available
Credit Card Company requires imprint	Not always someone to greet guest	Guest not asked smoking/ non-smoking	Room type is wrong
Incomplete hotel information at time of booking		Inaccurate information in computer	Room not ready
Room mix out of balance		Reservation not found	Air/Heat does not work
Computer input capability inadequate		Customer arrives late room gone	Linens not adequate
		Room rate is different than quoted	Broken fixtures

Fifth Meeting

The process team reviewed the previous meeting's work. With no changes to the minutes, the group was now ready to develop solution alternatives.

> **Problem:** The issues needing immediate attention in the Guest Check-In Process have not been prioritized.
>
> **Goal:** Identify the issues in the Guest Check-In Process in order of priority.

By comparing the areas needing further attention, the team was able to prioritize their interventions. They decided to look for a linkage between the reservation and the room type availability since these were the two items with the highest totals.

They discussed the process and the linkages. *When making the reservation, the room type availability is often unknown. It is not usually determined until the day of the guest's arrival. The confirmation number given when making the reservation simply confirms that the guest has a room — not what type of room. The Reservations Agent takes the request, but room type is still subject to availability.*

Room assignments are made when the guest arrives at the hotel. It is at this time that the guest is expecting to receive the requested room — after all, the guest has made a request and has a confirmation number.

The team recognized that it would not be able to properly address this issue in the time frame remaining and decided to build this into the planning process.

The agenda for the next meeting was planned.

Sixth Meeting Agenda

- Review team accomplishments so far
- Summarize Process
- Develop Action Plan

  Tool: Action Planning Matrix
- Set accountability process

  Progress reports

  Updated plans

Organize Data

Paired-Choice Matrix

Guest Check-In Process Paired-Choice Matrix

	Staffing	Room Type Availability	Reservations Accuracy	Billing Complications	Room Maintenance	TOTAL
Staffing		Room Type Availability	Reservations Accuracy	Billing Complications	Room Maintenance	0
Room Type Availability	X		Room Type Availability	Room Type Availability	Room Type Availability	3
Reservations Accuracy	X	X		Reservations Accuracy	Reservations Accuracy	2
Billing Complications	X	X	X		Billing Complications	1
Room Maintenance	X	X	X	X		0
TOTAL	0	1	1	1	1	

Totals	
Room Type Availability	4
Reservations Accuracy	3
Billing Complications	2
Room Maintenance	1
Staffing	0

Sixth Meeting

This was the final scheduled meeting, so the team had to take all of the information that they had gathered so far and create a plan. The plan needed to include a method for keeping each other updated and holding each other accountable.

Problem: There are no more scheduled team meetings and the Reservations and Room-Type linkage still need to be addressed so that the Guest Check-In Process can become more efficient.

Goal: Create a plan for a cross-functional team to address the linkages between Reservations and Room Type.

Matrix Chart

Guest Check-In Planning Matrix

Project: Fix the Guest Check-In Process by providing accurate reservations with room type availability linkages.

Project Team: Cross-functional team representing: Front Desk, Reservations, Housekeeping, MIS, Operations

Project Start Time: April 1, 1999

Project Finish Time: June 30, 1999

Tasks/Activities	Key Responsibility	Team Helpers	Resources	Outcome/ Deliverable	Who Needs to Knows	Deadlines Start	Finish
Set a Time and Agenda to conduct 1st team meeting	Team Leader	None	E-Mail	Meeting Time and Agenda	Team Members	April 1	April 1
Conduct 1st team meeting and develop project plan	Team Leader	Entire Team	Time	Project Plan	Team Members	April 5	April 5
Establish Ongoing Meetings	Team Leader	Entire Team	Time	Meetings	Team Members	April 5	April 5
Team members Process Issues	Entire Team	None	Time	Action Meetings	Team Members	April 5	June 30
Meet again to review progress and close gaps	Team Leader	Entire Team	Time	Plans Finalized	Team Members	July 30	July 30

15. EVALUATION

At the last meeting, the team completed a Meeting Evaluation form and submitted it to the Recorder. The Recorder agreed to summarize the input and return to the team within the week. All team members agreed to review the summarized data and work toward continuous improvement.

Observation

Team Meeting Evaluation Form

Please complete and return to the Facilitator within one week of the meeting. Place a check mark (✔)next to each observation that applies to you, the Team, the Leader, the Facilitator, the Process and the Outcomes.

Participation	Myself	Team	Leader	Facilitator
Listened to others	❑	❑	❑	❑
Participated generously	❑	❑	❑	❑
Sought additional facts	❑	❑	❑	❑
Encouraged others	❑	❑	❑	❑
Came prepared	❑	❑	❑	❑
Explored alternatives	❑	❑	❑	❑
Problem solved effectively	❑	❑	❑	❑
Suggested solutions	❑	❑	❑	❑
Agreed to actions	❑	❑	❑	❑
Agreed to accountability	❑	❑	❑	❑

Process & Outcomes	Yes	No
Meeting notice helpful	❑	❑
Agenda followed	❑	❑
Tools used appropriately	❑	❑
Entire team participated	❑	❑
Actions clear and targeted	❑	❑
Outcomes useful and targeted	❑	❑

What were the most positive aspects of this meeting?_____

_____

What needs improving?_____

_____

_____

The Guest Check-In Process team finished its goals within the designated time frame. They were able to examine the check-in process and conclude that the primary problem areas were in Reservations and Room-Type. Since there is a linkage between these two areas, the team agreed that a follow-up cross-functional team should be established to further examine the problem and recommend solutions for reducing errors in the process. This was done and a new project plan was established.

Tool Selection

These process and tool selection worksheets were used during Steps 6 and 7. The team reviewed the *Agenda* items and completed the worksheets in order to focus the process and select tools.

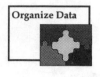

Worksheet

Tool Selection Questions

Use this set of questions to identify appropriate tools for your meeting facilitation. (Designed to be used with the *Tool Selection Worksheet*.)

<u>Gather Data</u>

- ❑   Do you have data?
- ❑   Do you have enough data?
- ❑   Does it represent all areas of concern?
- ❑   Should the team be collecting more data?

What data should the team be collecting?

What would this data collection tell you?

What method(s) should the team use to collect the data?

<u>Organize Data</u>

- ❑   Is the data organized?
- ❑   Is it organized in a manner that is usable for the team?
- ☑   Should the team better organize the data?

How could the team better organize the data?

The data could be be better organized by prioritizing solution alternatives and creating an action plan.

What would this organized data tell you?

The organized data would help the team identify and target priority actions for planning purposes.

What method(s) should the team use to organize the data?

Paired-Choice Matrix
Matrix (Action Plan)

Worksheet

<u>Group Data</u>

❑   Is the data grouped?

❑   Is it grouped in a manner that is usable for the team?

☑   Does the data need to be grouped?

How could the data be grouped in order to facilitate clarity around the issues?

The data could show check-in process issue groupings.

What would this grouped data tell you?

The grouped data would tell the team where to focus it's efforts.

What method(s) should the team use to group the data?

Affinity Diagram

<u>Sequence Data</u>

❑   Is there a sequence implied by the data?

❑   Are there steps, phases, levels, stages, timelines associated with the data?

❑   Should the team sequence the data?

How could the team better sequence the data?

What would this sequenced data tell you?

What method(s) should the team use to sequence the data?

Worksheet

<u>Breakdown Data</u>

- ❏   Is the data in manageable chunks?
- ☑   Should it be broken down so that the various parts become evident?
- ❏   Are the components and relationships among the data in their simplest form?
- ❏   Is the data broken down in a manner that is usable?

How could the data be broken down in order to facilitate clarity around the issues?

The data could be broken down to visually show the activities that are involved in the Guest Check-In Process.

What would this broken down data tell you?

The broken down data would show the Guest Check-In activities.

What method(s) should the team use to break down the data?

Tree Diagram

<u>Map Data</u>

- ☑   Is it important to understand the flow of the data and/or process being addressed?
- ☑   Can the data and/or processes be mapped to visually show the flow?
- ☑   Should the team map the data?

How could the data be mapped in order to facilitate clarity around the issues?

The data could be mapped to show the process elements.

What would this mapped data tell you?

The mapped data would visually show the elements of the process.

What method(s) should the team use to map the data?

Process Flow Chart

Worksheet

Display Data

❑   Is the data easy to understand in its current form?
❑   Should it be displayed so that the various parts become evident?
❑   Are the components and relationships among the data evident?
❑   Is the data displayed in a manner that is usable?

How could the data be displayed in order to facilitate clarity around the issues?

What would this displayed data tell you?

What method(s) should the team use to display the data?

Case Study

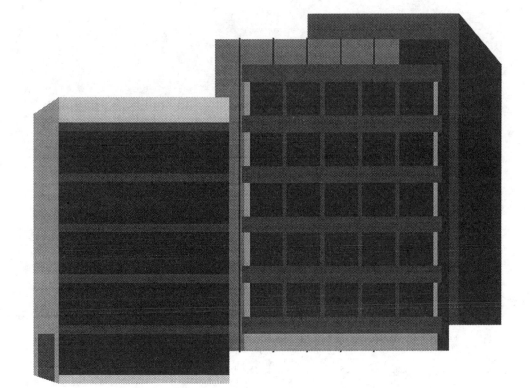

FINANCE

INVESTMENT BANKING

SALES AND MARKETING STRATEGIC PLANNING

Organize Data

Worksheet

Agenda

1. Meeting Purpose/Outcome(s):
The new sales office does not have a current strategic sales and marketing process in place and is not as prepared for the upcoming year as they should be.

2. Boundaries (Beginning and Ending):
The Boundaries **begin** with research and market analysis and **end** when the accountability and control structures are put in place.

3. Meeting Objectives *(These become the Agenda Item(s) below.):*

Analyze Current Situation	Develop Market Strategies
Research & Analyze Market	Develop Market Tactics
Identify Market Opportunities	Establish Accountability and Controls

4. Owner(s):
The problem is owned by all participants. All have a personal stake in a successful outcome.

5. Agenda Item(s)	6. Process	7. Tool(s)	8. Responsibility	9. Time
Analyze Current Situation	Gather Data	Questions/Surveys	Facilitator/Team	1 week
Research & Analyze Market	Display Data	Bar Graph	Sales & Marketing	2 hours
Identify Market Opportunities	Group Data	Quadrant Diagram	Team	4 hours
Develop Market Strategies	Breakdown Data	Circle Diagram	Team	2 hours
Develop Market Tactics	Organize Data	Matrix (L-Shaped)	Team	2 hours
Establish Accountability & Controls	Organize Data	Matrix (L-Shaped)	Team	4 hours

9a. Total Time Needed: 2 days

10. Roles:

Leader: Branch Manager   **Facilitator:** V.P. HR   **Recorder:** Exec. Secretary
Presenter(s): Sales & Marketing
Participants:

1. President	**5.** Marketing Representative	**9.** Sales Associate
2. VP Sales & Marketing	**6.** Marketing Representative	**10.** Sales Associate
3. Controller	**7.** Sales Associate	**11.**
4. Branch Manager	**8.** Sales Associate	**12.**

11. Logistics:

Date: January   **Time:** 8:30 a.m. - 5:00 p.m.   **.Location:** Country Club

12. Materials Needed:.
Flip Charts (2), Felt Tip Pens, Multi-Colored Sticky Dots, Pens/Pencils, Notepads

Background

A regional Investment Banker recently added a 6th sales office. The sales office, located in a new metropolitan West Coast market, needed a sales and marketing strategy directed toward the unique local markets. It had been relying only on its exceptional reputation, highly qualified sales personnel, and local advertising for the past 3 months and it was felt that sales could be significantly increased with a strategic plan in place.

Pre-Meeting Preparation

Refer to the *Agenda* and the *Process and Tool Selection Questions* at the end of this case study for clarification.

1. **MEETING PURPOSE/OUTCOME(S)**

   Prior to the meeting, the Leader and the Facilitator determined the team problem to be:

   The new sales office does not have a current strategic sales and marketing process in place and is not as prepared for the upcoming year as they should be.

2. **BOUNDARIES (BEGINNINGS AND ENDINGS)**

   The Leader and the Facilitator also pre-determined the problem Boundaries that would provide the meeting framework. *The Boundaries begin with research and market analysis and end when the accountability and control structures are put in place.*

3. **MEETING OBJECTIVES (THESE BECOME THE AGENDA ITEM(S) BELOW.)**

   The Leader and Facilitator agreed to the following objectives:

   Analyze the Current Situation

   Research and Analyze the Market

   Identify Market Opportunities

   Develop Market Strategies

   Develop Market Tactics

   Establish Accountability & Controls

4.   **OWNER(S)**

The Leader and Facilitator agreed that the problem was owned by all participants. Because of the nature of the business, all members of the planning team had a personal stake in the outcome and achievement of the strategic planning.

The President of the Company was the primary owner, however, since the meeting was initiated, planned and directed at that level. The V.P. of Sales and Marketing was also a primary stakeholder for a successful outcome.

5.   **AGENDA ITEM(S)**

The agenda was planned based on the pre-work input, local market research, and the sales and marketing strategic management process traditionally followed by the Regional office. The Leader, Facilitator and V.P. of Sales and Marketing planned the Agenda Items.

1st Day

- Analyze Current Situation
- Research & Analyze Market
- Identify Market Opportunities
- Develop Market Strategies

2nd Day

- Continue Market Strategies
- Develop Strategy Tactics
- Establish Accountability & Controls

Based on the objectives and agenda, questions 6 - 9 were handled together.

6. PROCESS

7. TOOL(S) (SEE *PROCESS AND TOOL SELECTION QUESTIONS* **AT THE END OF THIS CASE STUDY.)**

8. RESPONSIBILITY

9. TIME

9A. TOTAL TIME NEEDED

One two-day meeting was planned. It was agreed that the development of a sales and marketing strategy could be accomplished in this two-day period. In order to keep the team on track and accountable, quarterly update meetings were also planned.

The graph in the Agenda was used to determine the Process, Tools, Responsibility and Time needed. This was done prior to the meeting by the Leader and the Facilitator. The *Process and Tool Selection Questions* were also used to complete the Process and Tools columns of the graph.

5. Agenda Item(s)	6. Process	7. Tool(s)	8. Responsibility	9. Time
Analyze Current Situation	Gather Data	Questions/Surveys	Facilitator/Team	1 hour
Research & Analyze Market	Display Data	Bar Graph	Sales/Marketing	2 hours
Identify Market Opportunities	Group Data	Quadrant Diagram	Team	4 hours
Develop Market Strategies	Breakdown Data	Venn Diagram	Team	2 hours
Develop Market Tactics	Organize Data	Matrix (L-Shaped)	Team	2 hours
Establish Accountability & Controls	Organize Data	Matrix (L-Shaped)	Team	4 hours

Matrix Chart

10. ROLES

Leader

The President was the Leader. The meeting was initiated, planned and directed by the President.

Facilitator

The President asked the Regional V.P. of Human Resources to facilitate. This individual was chosen because of a broad-based knowledge of the business and of the participants. The V.P. of Human Resources had been considered to be a strategic partner in the organization and had been highly regarded as an organizational strategic thinker.

The Facilitator sent out a pre-work questionnaire to each of the participants before the meeting. The pre-work provided individual, as well as team information, from which the group could make decisions.

Recorder

The Executive Secretary from the regional office provided the meeting documentation and record keeping. The Secretary was chosen because of business familiarity and ability to quickly record and feed back meeting information, as well as document decisions.

Presenter(s)

The only presenters were those from the group. Outside presenters were not needed. The President presented the pre-work summaries and the V.P. of Sales and Marketing presented the market data.

Participants

Since this was the initial sales and marketing strategy meeting, several key regional managers participated in the meeting, including the company President, the V.P. of Sales and Marketing, and the Controller. In addition, the Branch Manager and the entire sales and marketing staff of the new office participated. Their contributions were valuable since several had worked for local competitors and were familiar with the local markets. In addition, it was important for all staff to have the same information and strategy. This enhanced closure of targeted sales and reduced duplication of efforts. There were 15 participants.

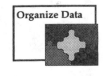

Questions/Surveys

Sales and Marketing
Strategic Planning Session
Pre-Work Questionnaire

In preparation for the upcoming strategic planning session, please complete the following questions and return to Human Resources by Friday. Do not sign your name. All information will be consolidated and reported in a confidential manner.

Organization

1. If you were planning this strategic planning session, what would you hope to accomplish by the end of the meeting?

2. What do you think are our 3 most important strategic priorities.

3. What should be our accomplishments over the next 12 months?

1 - 3 Months
4 - 6 Months
7 - 12 Months

Personal

4. What skills, knowledge and abilities do you contribute to this organization?

5. Based on the above, what will you personally contribute to this organization?

11. LOGISTICS

Date

The meeting was planned for January since it had traditionally been the lowest sales month for this region. The January date was also two months before the company's fiscal year end which allowed time for refinement of organizational plans in preparation for the upcoming year.

Time

The meeting was scheduled from 8:30 a.m. to 5:00 p.m. each day with continental breakfast available in the morning and lunch served in the adjoining restaurant.

Location

The local Country Club, at which the Corporation held a membership, was chosen as the location for the meeting because of its superior meeting facilities. In addition, this location was chosen because it provided an excellent opportunity for the Sales and Marketing staff to experience the facilities and evaluate them for future customer entertainment.

12. MATERIALS NEEDED

The Facilitator obtained flip charts (2), felt tip pens, multi-colored sticky dots, pens, pencils and notepads. The tables and chairs were organized in a U shape so that participants could easily see the presentation materials, the work-in-progress, and each other.

During the Meeting Activities

13. GROUND RULES

The team contributed to, and agreed to, the following Meeting Ground Rules:

Gather Data

Brainstorming

Ground Rules

- 100% Attendance

- 100% Participation

- Think Big but Be Practical

- 100% Commitment to Outcomes

- Start and End on Time

- Listen to Others

- Straight Talk

- Have Fun

- Work Hard

14. ACTIONS

The team took these actions during the meeting.

Analyze Current Situation

The President shared the summarized findings from the Pre-Work Questionnaire, but he first noted the problem and goals of the activity.

> **Problem:** This group had never worked together and had not articulated priorities, strategies and talents.

> **Goal:**   Identify group priorities, strategies and talents.

The entire team was energized by the ideas, commitment and qualifications of the staff. It was obvious that they had the right people with the right ideas and methods to do the job. They were eager to develop a plan from this foundation. The Facilitator reminded them that there was another piece of data to be considered and analyzed before the actual planning process could begin.

The overall process took one week to distribute, collect and summarize. One hour was spent reviewing the summarized information during the meeting.

Questions/Surveys

Sales and Marketing
Strategic Planning Session
Pre-Work Questionnaire

In preparation for the upcoming strategic planning session, please complete the following questions and return to Human Resources by Friday. Do not sign your name. All information will be consolidated and reported in a confidential manner.

Organization

1. **If you were planning this strategic planning session, what would you hope to accomplish by the end of the meeting?**

   A strategic plan (ha! ha!)   Targeted markets   Understanding of work flow
   A Team Spirit   Common Goals   Agreement on direction
   Understanding of each other   Roles & Responsibilities   Timeframes

2. **What do you think are our 3 most important strategic priorities.**
   1. Target the market and aggressively go after it.
   2. Learn and understand products
   3. Cold Call. Cold Call. Cold Call.
   4. Continuously improve sales techniques.
   5. Create -- and buy sales leads.

3. **What should be our accomplishments over the next 12 months?**

1 - 3 Months	
Combine learning and doing.	Beat the Competition!!
Go after targets as if our lives depend on them.	

4 - 6 Months	
Service our customers.	Add-on sales to existing customers.
Build up sales leads by purchasing or creating.	Specialize where possible.

7 - 12 Months	
Examine what worked -- and do it again!	Identify new targets and go after them
Increase sales to existing customers.	Continue to learn new products.

Personal

4. **What skills, knowledge and abilities do you contribute to this organization?**

   Understanding of local market   Significant Sales Training
   5 - 10 years of sales experience   Awards and recognition for highest sales
   Competitive, energetic, enthusiastic, tenacious, hard working, smart, tireless

5. **Based on the above, what will you personally contribute to this organization?**

   Hard Work   Knowledge   Existing Customer Base
   Connections/Network   Quick Study   Long Hours
   Years of Experience   Credibility in Community   Financial Prowess

Research and Analyze Market

The Vice President of Sales and Marketing presented the group with a *Stacked Bar Graph* displaying information on the local market. The problem and goal of this activity was also presented.

Problem: The team had no local market data from which to target efforts.

Goal: Display local market data on High-Income Earners as a target group.

It was explained that the Graph was built around the High-Income Earners as demonstrated by those who:

- own high end homes
- invest in tax shelter investments
- maintain Country Club memberships
- own luxury boats
- drive luxury cars

Each of these high-income earners were examined in four areas.

- **Nos.** - The percentage of high-income earners compared by group?
- **$s** - The percentage of money each group makes compared by group?
- **Avg. Inc.** - The percentage of individual average income compared by group?
- **Inv. $s** - The percentage of money that individuals invest by group?

He noted from the displayed data that each group would be likely to purchase services from the new office. He also suggested that the team think about which groups would be most likely to purchase which services or products. Since the new sales office would be offering stocks and bonds, insurance and annuities, tax sheltered investments, mutual funds, options trading, precious metals purchases, and commodities trading, there would be numerous opportunities for increased sales.

This information was researched and compiled during the previous week, and 2 hours were spent analyzing the market during the meeting.

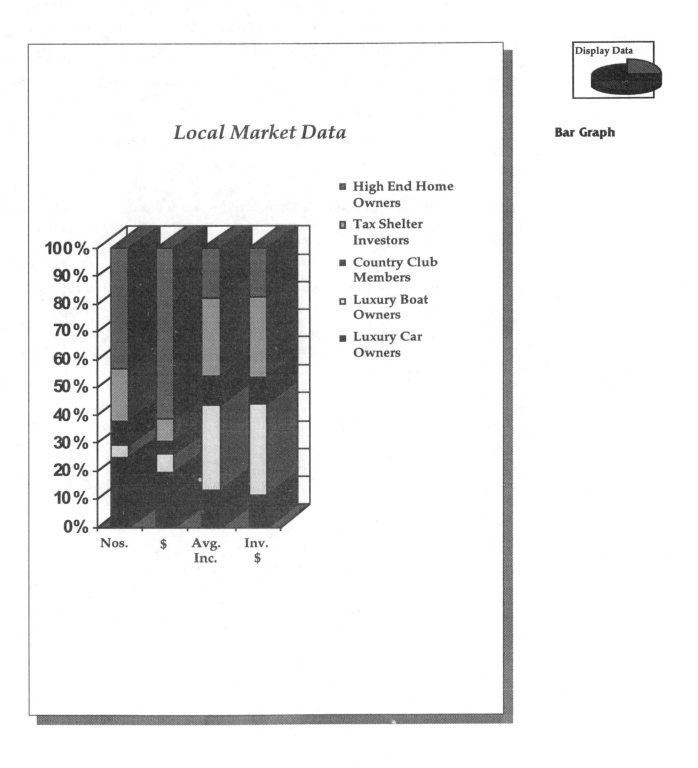

Display Data

Bar Graph

Local Market Data

- High End Home Owners
- Tax Shelter Investors
- Country Club Members
- Luxury Boat Owners
- Luxury Car Owners

100%
90%
80%
70%
60%
50%
40%
30%
20%
10%
0%

Nos. $ Avg. Inc.   Inv. $

Identify Market Opportunities

Now that the group had examined both the pre-work summary data and the research data, the Facilitator led them toward targeting sales and marketing opportunities. This was done through the use of a *Quadrant Diagram*. The team identified the current problem and goals, then proceeded in the process.

Problem: Local market opportunities have not been strategically targeted.

Goal: Strategically target local market opportunities.

As a first step, the team listed the top six strategies to target over the next year and then assigned a rating to each based upon the potential cost and benefit to the organization. A 1 to 10 scale was used to determine each rating. They next plotted the cost and benefit assignments to see the distribution. In the final step, the costs and benefits were plotted on the graph to show the cost and benefit relationships. This activity helped the team to visually see how to prioritize the strategies.

The Team spent 4 hours on this exercise. There was a lot of discussion and review of data that had previously been presented.

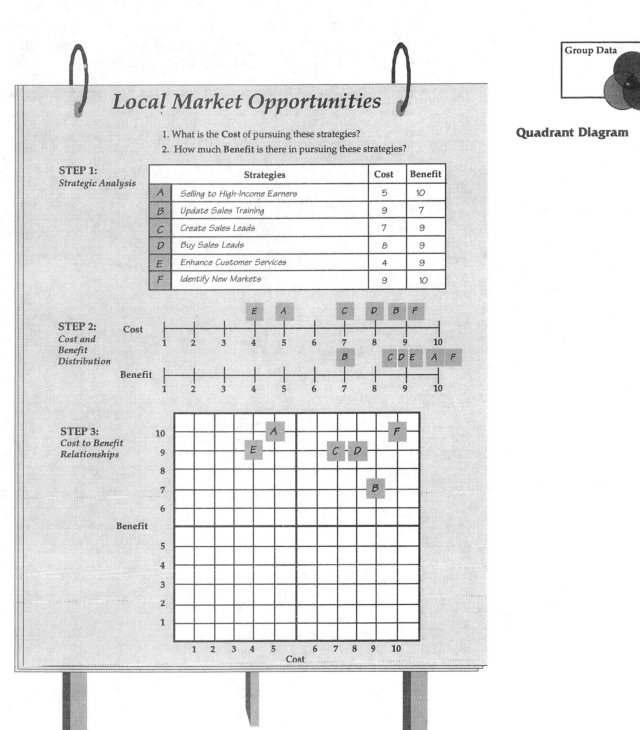

Local Market Opportunities

1. What is the **Cost** of pursuing these strategies?
2. How much **Benefit** is there in pursuing these strategies?

STEP 1:
Strategic Analysis

	Strategies	Cost	Benefit
A	Selling to High-Income Earners	5	10
B	Update Sales Training	9	7
C	Create Sales Leads	7	9
D	Buy Sales Leads	8	9
E	Enhance Customer Services	4	9
F	Identify New Markets	9	10

STEP 2:
Cost and Benefit Distribution

STEP 3:
Cost to Benefit Relationships

Develop Market Strategies

All top six strategies were adopted as priorities to pursue. They were visually displayed on a Circle Diagram (Relationships). Three more strategies were added to provide accountability and control to the process. This made a total of 9 Strategic Initiatives. The circle included arrows to show the circular flow of priorities and controls.

> **Problem:** The relationships of local market strategic initiatives are unclear.

> **Goal:** Identify the relationships of the local market strategic initiatives.

It took the team 2 hours to develop their strategies. A lengthy discussion was held regarding the 3 additional strategies. Originally 5 additional strategies had been proposed, while only 3 were confirmed.

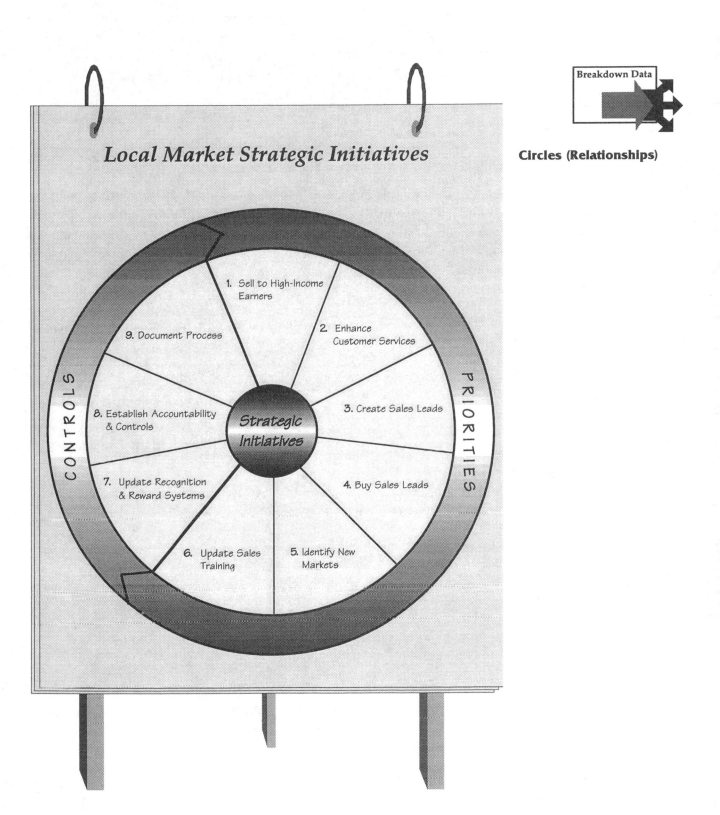

Local Market Strategic Initiatives

Circles (Relationships)

Develop Market Tactics -

Establish Accountability and Controls

The nine Strategic Initiatives were then listed down the left side of an L-Shaped Matrix Diagram and tactics were added under each. The accountable persons or groups were then listed across the top. In order to assign responsibility, the team decided on three factors:

▲   Primary Responsibility

❑   Secondary Responsibility

○   Need To Be Informed

These responsibility factors were then assigned symbols and plotted on the chart. These plotted symbols made it easy to identify responsible persons or groups and to visually see the actions to be taken over the next 12 months.

> **Problem:** There are no tactics and accountabilities for the strategic initiatives.

> **Goal:** Develop tactics and assign accountabilities for accomplishment of strategic initiatives.

6 hours were spent on these 2 activities.

At the end of the meeting the team agreed on these actions.

Individual and group actions were agreed to upon completion of the L-Shaped Matrix. Each participant committed to accomplishing their assigned tasks.

The **Recorder** agreed to have the meeting documentation to each of the participants within a week's time.

The **entire team** agreed to meet again in 3 months to review progress and make any necessary adjustments to the plan.

Tactics and Accountabilities

Strategic Initiatives & Tactics / Functional Area	Local Sales Office	Adm. Support Staff	Regional V.P. Sales & Mktg.	Regional Human Resources	Regional Research Dept.
1. Sell to High-Income Earners					
Call 8 new prospects a day	▲		○		
Call 4 old prospects a day	▲		○		
Call 4 current clients a day	▲		○		
2. Enhance Customer Services					
Answer all calls by 3rd ring	▲	▲	▲	▲	▲
Keep deadlines & promises	▲	▲	▲	▲	▲
Greet Walk-ins enthusiastically	▲	▲	▲	▲	▲
3. Create Sales Leads					
Place Ads in newspapers	❑	▲	○		
Distribute targeted mailings	❑	▲	○		
Place Ads on radio news shows	❑	▲	○		
4. Buy Sales Leads					
Buy *High-Income Earner* lists	❑		▲		
5. Identify New Markets					
Research economic trends	○		○		▲
Research labor market trends	○		○		▲
Research investment spending	○		○		▲
Research earnings trends	○		○		▲
6. Update Sales Training					
Assess current training needs	○		○	▲	
Buy or Build sales training	○		○	▲	
Customize local market training	○		○	▲	
Establish minimum standards	○		○	▲	
7. Update Recognition & Rewards					
Examine goals of current systems	○		○	▲	
Develop goals for future systems	○		○	▲	
Modify to meet future directions	○		○	▲	
8. Establish Acctblty. & Controls					
Examine current systems	○		○	▲	
Adapt Performance Mgt. process	○		○	▲	
Communicate consequences	○		○	▲	
9. Document Process					
Establish recording process	▲	❑	▲	○	

Primary Responsibility ▲   Secondary Responsibility ❑   Need To Be Informed ○

Organize Data

Matrix Chart

15. EVALUATION

An evaluation form was completed by each team member. The Facilitator decided to use this information in planning for the next meeting.

Organize Data

Observation

Team Meeting Evaluation Form

Please complete and return to the Facilitator within one week of the meeting. Place a check mark (✔) next to each observation that applies to you, the Team, the Leader, the Facilitator, the Process and the Outcomes.

Participation	Myself	Team	Leader	Facilitator
Listened to others	❏	❏	❏	❏
Participated generously	❏	❏	❏	❏
Sought additional facts	❏	❏	❏	❏
Encouraged others	❏	❏	❏	❏
Came prepared	❏	❏	❏	❏
Explored alternatives	❏	❏	❏	❏
Problem solved effectively	❏	❏	❏	❏
Suggested solutions	❏	❏	❏	❏
Agreed to actions	❏	❏	❏	❏
Agreed to accountability	❏	❏	❏	❏

Process & Outcomes	Yes	No
Meeting notice helpful	❏	❏
Agenda followed	❏	❏
Tools used appropriately	❏	❏
Entire team participated	❏	❏
Actions clear and targeted	❏	❏
Outcomes useful and targeted	❏	❏

What were the most positive aspects of this meeting?_____

_____

_____

What needs improving?_____

_____

_____

Summary

The team felt that working together to identify and develop strategies for moving the organization forward over the coming 12 months was an invaluable experience. They learned from each other as well as developed a shared vision for the future.

Tool Selection

These process and tool selection worksheets were used during Steps 6 and 7. The team reviewed the *Agenda* items and completed the worksheets in order to focus the process and select tools.

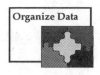

Worksheet

Process and Tool Selection Questions

Use this set of questions to identify appropriate processes and tools for meeting facilitation. (Designed to be used with the *15 Steps to Facilitating a Successful Meeting*.)

Gather Data

- ❑ Do you have data?
- ❑ Do you have enough data?
- ❑ Does it represent all areas of concern?
- ☑ Should the team be collecting more data?

What data should the team be collecting?

Expectations of team members around working together as a team.

What would this data collection tell you?

The data would reveal expectations of team members which would allow them to either meet expectations or to adjust expectations and make them more realistic.

What tools(s) should the team use to collect the data?

Questions/Survey

Organize Data

- ❑ Is the data organized?
- ❑ Is it organized in a manner that is usable for the team?
- ☑ Should the team better organize the data?

How could the team better organize the data?

The data could be better organized by listing the tactics associated with each strategy and asigning accountability.

What would this organized data tell you?

The tactics for accomplishing the strategies and the individual(s) responsible for completing each tactic.

What tools(s) should the team use to organize the data?

Matrix (L-Shaped)

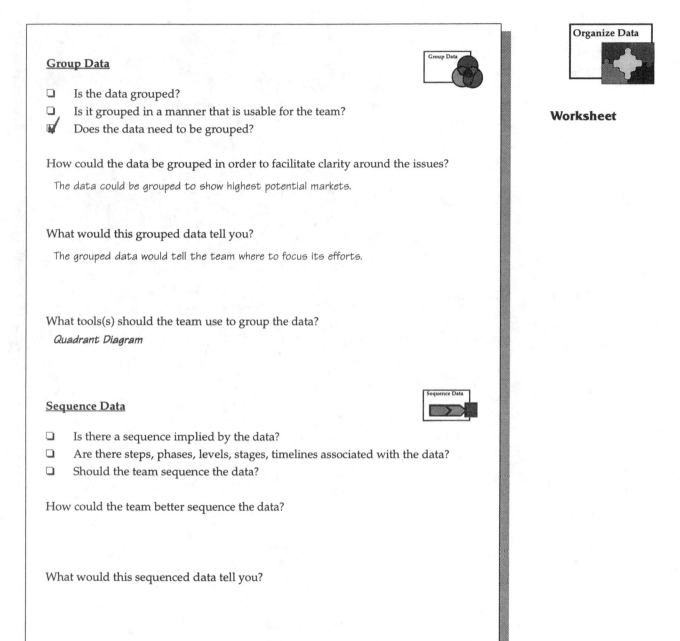

Group Data

❏   Is the data grouped?

❏   Is it grouped in a manner that is usable for the team?

☑   Does the data need to be grouped?

How could the data be grouped in order to facilitate clarity around the issues?

The data could be grouped to show highest potential markets.

What would this grouped data tell you?

The grouped data would tell the team where to focus its efforts.

What tools(s) should the team use to group the data?

Quadrant Diagram

Sequence Data

❏   Is there a sequence implied by the data?

❏   Are there steps, phases, levels, stages, timelines associated with the data?

❏   Should the team sequence the data?

How could the team better sequence the data?

What would this sequenced data tell you?

What tools(s) should the team use to sequence the data?

Worksheet

<u>**Breakdown Data**</u>

❑   Is the data in manageable chunks?

✓   Should it be broken down so that the various parts become evident?

❑   Are the components and relationships among the data in their simplest form?

❑   Is the data broken down in a manner that is usable?

How could the data be broken down in order to facilitate clarity around the issues?

The data could be broken down to visually show the relationships of the sales and marketing strategic priorities.

What would this broken down data tell you?

The data would show the relationships of the sales and marketing strategic initiatives.

What tools(s) should the team use to break down the data?

Circle Diagram (Relathonships)

<u>**Map Data**</u>

❑   Is it important to understand the flow of the data and/or process being addressed?

❑   Can the data and/or processes be mapped to visually show the flow?

❑   Should the team map the data?

How could the data be mapped in order to facilitate clarity around the issues?

What would this mapped data tell you?

What tools(s) should the team use to map the data?

Organize Data

Worksheet

Display Data

❑   Is the data easy to understand in its current form?
☑   Should it be displayed so that the various parts become evident?
❑   Are the components and relationships among the data evident?
❑   Is the data displayed in a manner that is usable?

How could the data be displayed in order to facilitate clarity around the issues?

The data could be displayed as comparative information.

What would this displayed data tell you?

The displayed data would visually show which markets to target.

What tools(s) should the team use to display the data?

Bar Graph

Case Study

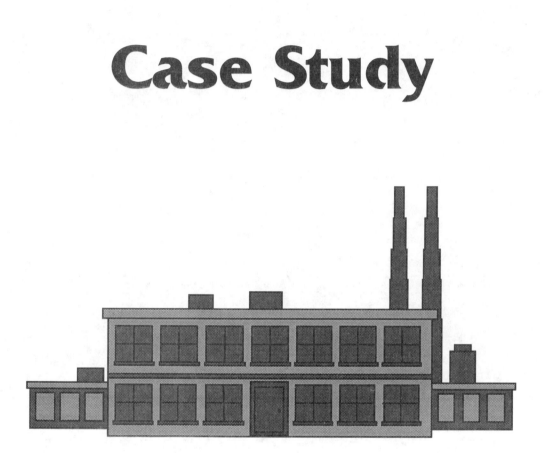

Manufacturing

Heavy Equipment
Valve Production Process Improvement

MANUFACTURING

HEAVY EQUIPMENT

VALVE PRODUCTION PROCESS IMPROVEMENT

Worksheet

Agenda

1. Meeting Purpose/Outcome(s):

The 10% error rate of the Valve Process Line does not meet the 0 error rate target.

2. Boundaries (Beginning and Ending):

The Boundaries **begin** with research and analysis of the problem and **end** when the process problems are defined and solutions targeted.

3. Meeting Objectives (These become the Agenda Item(s) below.):

Review the Current Situation   Develop Improvement Strategies

Research and Analyze the Current Situation   Establish Accountability and Controls

Identify Improvement Opportunities

4. Owner(s):

The Valve Department owns the problem.

5. Agenda Item(s)	6. Process	7. Tool(s)	8. Responsibility	9. Time
Review Current Situation	Display Data	Line Graph	Leader	1/2 hour
Research & Analyze the	Breakdown Data	Work Breakdown Structure	Team	2 hours
Current Process	Organize Data	Worksheet	Inspector/Leader	1 1/2 hours
		Check Sheet		
Identify Improvement	Organize Data	T-Chart	Team	1 1/2 hours
Opportunities				
Develop Improvement	Organize Data	Consensus Card	Team	1/2 hour
Strategies		Method		
Establish Accountability	Organize Data	Matrix (Plan)	Team	2 hours
& Controls				

9a. Total Time Needed: 2 half day work sessions

10. Roles:

      Leader: Valve Dept. 1st-Line Supv.   **Facilitator:** Trainer/Set-Up Assoc. **Recorder** Inspector

      Presenter(s): None

      Participants:

1. Machinist	**5.** _____	**9.** _____
2. Valve Machine Operator	**6.** _____	**10.** _____
3. Valve Machine Operator	**7.** _____	**11.** _____
4. Valve Machine Operator	**8.** _____	**12.** _____

11. Logistics:

      Date: 2 consecutive Fridays   **Time:** 7:00 a.m. - 11:30 a.m.. **Location:** Department meeting room

12. Materials Needed: Flip Charts (4), Felt-Tip Pens, Consensus Cards, Multi-Colored Dots, Sticky Notes, Pens, Pencils, Notepads, Masking Tape, Butcher Paper

Background

A new First Line Supervisor was recently appointed to provide leadership to the Valve Production Department. The Supervisor transferred from another supervisory assignment specifically to address the problems of scrap and rework in the Valve production line. The line had been running at a 10% error rate. The Supervisor's goal was to reduce the error rate to 0.

> This case study has been streamlined to model team process and tools and is not comprehensive. There were many more steps in the team's problem solving process. Several different solutions with varying degrees of success were tried before the desired goal of 0 valve defects was achieved. The team did obtain a couple of "quick wins" up front however, which resulted in reducing the production error rate by 50% within the first 2 weeks of effort. The entire process actually took about 6 months overall.

Pre-Meeting Preparation

Refer to the *Agenda,* and the *Process and Tool Selection Questions* at the end of this case study for clarification

1.   **MEETING PURPOSE/OUTCOME(S)**

    Prior to the meeting, the Supervisor (Leader) defined the problem as:

    The 10% error rate of the Valve Process Line does not meet the 0 error rate target.

2.   **BOUNDARIES (BEGINNINGS AND ENDINGS)**

    The Leader also predetermined the problem Boundaries. *The Boundaries **begin** with research and analysis of the problem and **end** when the process problems are defined and solutions targeted.*

3.   **MEETING OBJECTIVES (THESE BECOME THE AGENDA ITEM(S) LATER.)**

    The Leader met with the Valve Department Trainer/Set-Up associate. They defined the objectives of the work to be:

    Review the Current Situation

    Research and Analyze the Current Process

    Identify Improvement Opportunities

    Develop Improvement Strategies

    Establish Accountability and Controls

4. **OWNER(S)**

    The Valve Department First-Line Supervisor owns the problem. The Supervisor has the ultimate responsibility to ensure that the production line error rate is reduced from 10% to 0.

5. **AGENDA ITEM(S) (TAKEN FROM THE MEETING OBJECTIVES.)**

    Review the Current Situation

    Research and Analyze the Current Process

    Identify Improvement Opportunities

    Develop Improvement Strategies

    Establish Accountability and Controls

Based on the objectives and agenda, questions 6 - 9 were handled together.

6. PROCESS

7. TOOL(S) (SEE *PROCESS AND TOOL SELECTION QUESTIONS* **AT THE END OF THIS CASE STUDY.)**

8. RESPONSIBILITY

9. TIME

9A. TOTAL TIME NEEDED

The Leader determined that the team would need an initial 1/2-day meeting. A second 1/2-day follow-up meeting was also scheduled for the purpose of reviewing findings and setting actions for improvement. At the end of the second meeting, the need for further meetings and timing would be determined based upon team recommendations.

The graph in the Agenda was used to determine the Process, Tools, Responsibility and Time needed. This was done prior to the meeting by the Leader and the Trainer/Set-Up associate. The Process and Tool Selection Questions *were also used to complete the Process and Tools columns of the graph.*

5. Agenda Item(s)	6. Process	7. Tool(s)	8. Responsibility	9. Time
Review Current Situation	Display Data	Line Graph	Leader	1/2 hour
Research & Analyze the Current Process	Organize Data	Work Breakdown Structure	Team	2 hours
		Worksheet	Inspector/Leader	1 1/2 hours
		Check Sheet		
Identify Improvement Opportunities	Organize Data	T-Chart	Team	1 1/2 hours
Develop Improvement Strategies	Organize Data	Consensus Card Method	Team	1/2 hour
Establish Accountability & Controls	Organize Data	Matrix (Plan)	Team	2 hours

Organize Data

Matrix Chart

10. ROLES

Leader

The Valve Department First-Line Supervisor was the Leader. The meeting was initiated, planned and directed by the First-Line Supervisor.

Facilitator

The First-Line Supervisor asked the Trainer/Set-Up associate to facilitate the meetings. This associate had extensive experience in facilitating meetings and would later be instrumental in the successful completion of the team's recommendations.

Recorder

The Leader asked the production line Inspector to record and document the team's actions and decisions. The Inspector had experience with record keeping and documentation since much of the inspection job consisted of these activities. The Inspector was also felt to have a good grasp of the Valve Department line operation.

Participants

The team was comprised of the Valve Department First-Line Supervisor, the Trainer/Set-Up associate, the Inspector, a Machinist, and the three Value Machine Operators. There were 7 members on the team.

The Cut-Off Machine First-Line Supervisor was later brought into the process. This process preceded the Valve Department production line and some of the team's findings had to do with the parts that were received from the previous line.

11. LOGISTICS

Date

The first meeting was arranged for Friday of the current week. The second meeting was planned for the following Friday. Any additional meetings would be determined at the end of the second meeting.

Time

The meetings were scheduled to be held from 7:00 a.m. to 11:30 a.m. since that was part of the regular work day for the Operators. The team would take the normal morning break and quit just before lunch.

Location

The Department meeting room was reserved and the team members were notified.

12. MATERIALS NEEDED

The Trainer/Set-Up associate determined the need for a number of materials to be used throughout the meetings. The room was equipped with these materials: flip charts (4), felt-tip pens, Consensus Card tents, multi-colored sticky dots, sticky notes, pens, pencils, notepads, masking tape and butcher paper.

The room consisted of a conference table with 14 chairs, a coffee maker and a coffee warmer for tea. The walls were blank except for a white board located at the head of the conference table. It was felt that this room arrangement would accommodate any actions of the team.

During the Meeting Activities

13. GROUND RULES

The team contributed to, and agreed to, the following Meeting Ground Rules:

Ground Rules

✔ Be on time for each meeting

✔ Attend all meetings

✔ Come prepared to contribute

✔ Keep meeting discussions confidential

✔ Address issues or processes — do not blame people

✔ Take turns making coffee & tea

✔ Listen to each other

✔ Follow through on commitments

Organize Data

Brainstorming

14. ACTIONS

The team took these actions during the meeting.

Review Current Situation

The Leader shared the Production Reports with the team and pointed out the 10% scrap and rework problem. The problem and goal of this activity was also explained.

> **Problem:** The team was not familiar with the Production Reports and was not aware of the extent of the scrap and rework problem.

> **Goal:** Show the team the summarized Production Reports which visually show the extent of the scrap and rework problem.

The top report showed the total production for the month of July. The production went from 300 the first week, to 400 the next, to 700, and then to 900 parts produced overall for the month. The second Line Graph/Run Chart showed the scrap and rework numbers in the same way. The overall scrap and rework was 10% of the total production. In the final Line Graph/Run Chart a revised production report is shown. This chart suggests that if the scrap and rework could be eliminated, a 10% gain in production would result.

Once the team reviewed the information, they began to speculate on the reasons why the numbers were so bad. Some speculated that the errors were caused by faulty equipment, some suggested that human error was to blame. Lack of training and the recent flu epidemic were also mentioned. After a brief discussion, the team agreed that they really did not have enough information to properly diagnose the real problems and should obtain additional data to confirm or deny these charges.

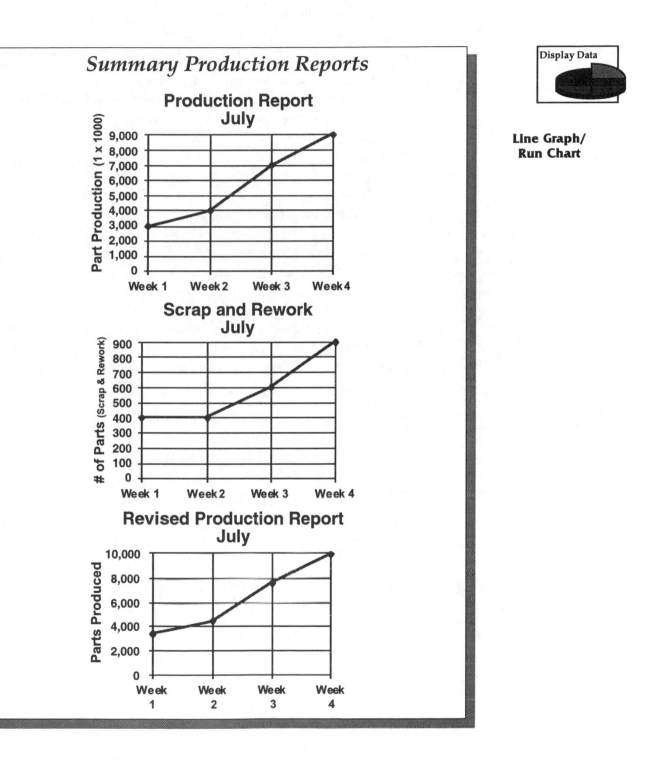

Summary Production Reports

Production Report July

Scrap and Rework July

Revised Production Report July

Display Data

Line Graph/ Run Chart

Research and Analyze the Current Process

The Trainer/Set-Up associate facilitated the team toward understanding the work activities involved in the Valve production process. The problem and goal for this activity was stated as follows:

>**Problem:** The team members lack understanding of the overall Valve production operations and would have difficulty identifying problems or offering solutions.

>**Goal:** Gain a detailed understanding of the overall Valve production operation.

The team developed a Work Breakdown Structure (WBS) showing all of the activities and tasks involved in each operation of the Valve production line.

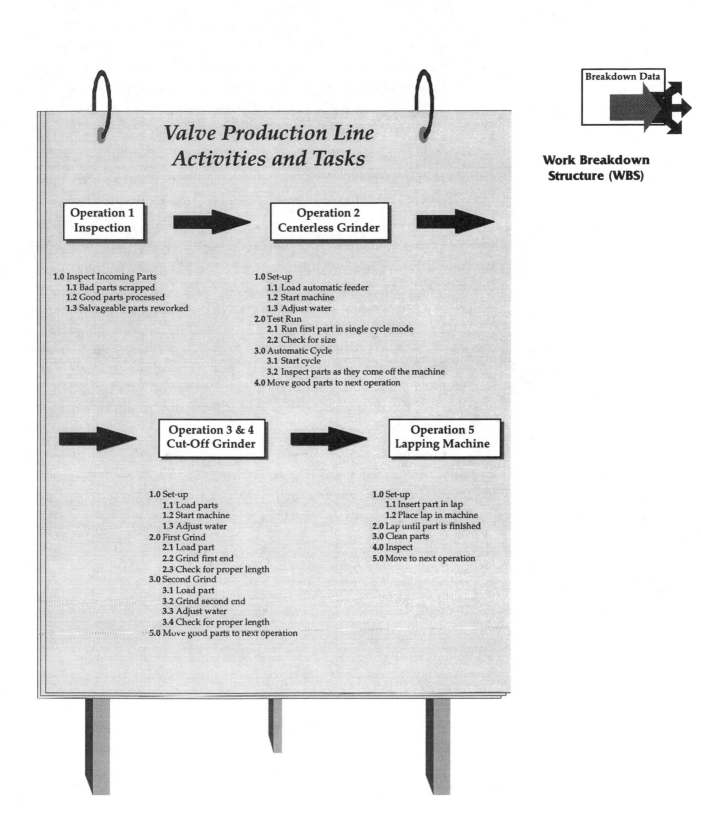

Breakdown Data

**Work Breakdown
Structure (WBS)**

Valve Production Line
Activities and Tasks

Operation 1
Inspection

1.0 Inspect Incoming Parts
   1.1 Bad parts scrapped
   1.2 Good parts processed
   1.3 Salvageable parts reworked

Operation 2
Centerless Grinder

1.0 Set-up
   1.1 Load automatic feeder
   1.2 Start machine
   1.3 Adjust water
2.0 Test Run
   2.1 Run first part in single cycle mode
   2.2 Check for size
3.0 Automatic Cycle
   3.1 Start cycle
   3.2 Inspect parts as they come off the machine
4.0 Move good parts to next operation

Operation 3 & 4
Cut-Off Grinder

1.0 Set-up
   1.1 Load parts
   1.2 Start machine
   1.3 Adjust water
2.0 First Grind
   2.1 Load part
   2.2 Grind first end
   2.3 Check for proper length
3.0 Second Grind
   3.1 Load part
   3.2 Grind second end
   3.3 Adjust water
   3.4 Check for proper length
5.0 Move good parts to next operation

Operation 5
Lapping Machine

1.0 Set-up
   1.1 Insert part in lap
   1.2 Place lap in machine
2.0 Lap until part is finished
3.0 Clean parts
4.0 Inspect
5.0 Move to next operation

The WBS gave the team a detailed snap shot of each step along the production line. The team also felt that they should develop a data collection plan to better understand where and how the scrap and rework problems were occurring. Decisions would then need to be made regarding priority and possible solutions for each problem. They stated the problem and goal of this activity to be:

Problem: The team did not know where the scrap and rework problems were occurring, nor what the problems were.

Goal: Determine where the scrap and rework problems were occurring and what the problems were.

To research and analyze this problem, the team decided that they would isolate 200 parts and track them through each operation in the Valve Production Line. Each of the 200 parts would be tracked using a peg board. Each peg in the board would provide a home for each part. The parts would be taken, one at a time, and processed through the line, one operation at a time. At the completion of each operation, each part would be inspected, recorded and placed back into its original peg. This would continue until each operation was completed, and each part inspected and recorded throughout the entire production process.

The team then spent the next hour designing a Worksheet that would track the necessary information. They used the Job Instruction Sheets (JIS) to build the questions since the JISs provided job instructions for each operation.

Worksheet

Part Processing Worksheet
(Questions taken from Job Instruction Sheet (JIS))

PART # ___36___   Inspector:_____

Cut-Off Department **Final Operation JIS**	The Cut-Off Department JIS required that these questions be answered before the part could be moved to the Valve Department. Operation 1 below re-checked these requirements.
Is the the Overall Length (O.A.L) accurate? Is the Outside Diameter (O.D.) accurate? Have the burrs been removed?	

Valve Department	Scrap	Rework
Operation 1 - Inspection		
Is the Overall Length (O.A.L) accurate?		
Is the Outside Diameter(O.D.) accurate?		
Have the burrs been removed?		
Operation 2 - Centerless Grinder		

Are the diameters within manufacturing tolerance?
    Diameter #1
    Diameter #2
    Diameter #3		

These were tracked together. If one diameter was off, *the part was considered to be scrap. The specific* *diameter was not important.*		
Operation 3 & 4 - Cut-Off Grinder		
Is the process dimension accurate? The tolerance is ± .002. Part 36 measured .006 - <u>UNDERSIZE.</u> Is the Overall Length (O.A.L.) dimension accurate?	✔	
Operation 5 - Lapping Machine		
Does the part pass function test (metal to metal seal)?		

Once all of the 200 parts had been processed through the Valve Production Line, the Inspector would take each individual part Worksheet and transfer the information onto a summary report. This report was to provide a summary as to where the problems were occurring and what the problems were. The team adapted the Part Processing Worksheet to also serve as a Check Sheet for summarizing where the problems originated and what they were.

The team spent 1-1/2 hours deciding on the direction that they wanted to take and designing the Worksheet and Check Sheet. This concluded the first 1/2-day session.

Check/Tally Sheets

Summary Part Processing Check Sheet
(Questions taken from Job Instruction Sheet (JIS)

ALL PARTS   Inspector:_____

Cut-Off Department **Final Operation JIS**	The Cut-Off Department JIS required that these questions be answered before the part could be moved to the Valve Department. Operation 1 below re-checked these requirements.
Is the the Overall Length (O.A.L) accurate? Is the Outside Diameter (O.D.) accurate? Have the burrs been removed?	

Valve Department	Scrap	Rework
Operation 1 - Inspection		
Is the Overall Length (O.A.L) accurate? Tolerance is ±.005. Parts were .005 out of tolerance.	II	
Is the Outside Diameter (O.D.) accurate?		
Have the burrs been removed? Print required burr-free parts. These had burrs.		III
Operation 2 - Centerless Grinder		
Are the diameters within manufacturing tolerance? Diameter #1 Parts were both UNDERSIZED and Diameter #2 OVERSIZED. Diameter #3	III	
These were tracked together. If one diameter was off the part was considered to be scrap. The specific diameter was not important.		
Operation 3 & 4 - Cut-Off Grinder		
Is the process dimension accurate? Too much material removed from part. UNDERSIZED	IIII	
Is the Overall Length (O.A.L.) dimension accurate? Too much material removed from part. UNDERSIZED	II	
Operation 5 - Lapping Machine		
Does the part pass function test (metal to metal seal)? 5 were scrap due to damage to tip and one rework due to failure of functional test.	NN	I

Identify Improvement Opportunities

At the beginning of the second 1/2-day session, the Inspector presented the results of the 200 test-group valves. The team reviewed the summary Check Sheet data and decided to further examine the problems and offer solution alternatives. The problem and goal for this activity are stated below:

Problem: The test group data had been collected and organized, but the problems had not been clarified to any extent and solution alternatives had not been generated.

Goal: Analyze the test data, create a complete list of problem opportunities, and identify solution alternatives.

The team listed the 5 line operations and the problems that had been identified in each of these operations. They also brainstormed and listed possible solutions.

T-Charts

Problem/Solution Identification

Problem	Solution
Operation 1 - Inspection	**Operation 1 - Inspection**
• Burrs were in some of the parts when received from the Cut-Off Department.	• Talk with First-Line Supervisor of the Cut-Off Department regarding the burrs received in the parts sent to the Valve Department.
Operation 2 - Centerless Grinder	**Operation 2 - Centerless Grinder**
• One of the grinding guides was worn and caused the part diameters to be inconsistent in size.	• New grinding guide should be installed.
Operation 3 & 4 - Cut-Off Grinder	**Operation 3 & 4 - Cut-Off Grinder**
• Part of the grinding fixture was scratching the large diameter. This diameter was a critical area on the part being processed.	• Contact the Tool Designer to adapt the tool fixture design drawing so that the tool can be modified.
• Undersized part diameters from the Centerless Grinder would slip in the fixture on the Cut-Off Grinder.	• Control diameters on Centerless Grinder.
Operation 5 - Lapping Machine	**Operation 5 - Lapping Machine**
• Use of the Lapping Machine required a sensitivity to the feel of the part in the process. Some people were able to lap effectively while others were not.	• Try the following steps. Stop when the problem is solved. *Step 1:* Train all lapping operators *Step 2:* Test for effectiveness *Step 3:* Re-train only those who need it *Step 4:* If they still cannot lap, move them to another department. *Step 5:* Replace with those who can lap or can be trained to lap.

Develop Improvement Strategies

The Consensus Card Method tents were then used to establish consensus among the members regarding the priorities of each of the problems and solutions. The activity problem and goal statement follows:

Problem: The team had not prioritized the problems and solutions to address.

Goal: Prioritize the process problems and target solution opportunities.

Consensus Card Method

A final T-Chart was completed summarizing the priority problem areas and the targeted solutions. The team now had a specific list of actionable items. The problem and goal of this activity is stated below:

Problem: The decisions of the team were not summarized into actionable items.

Goal: Prioritize and summarize the process problem areas and targeted solutions.

T-Charts

Priority Problem/Solution Areas

Problem	Solution
Operation 1 - Inspection	**Operation 1 - Inspection**
Burrs were in some of the parts when received from the Cut-Off Department.	Talk with First-Line Supervisor of the Cut-Off Department regarding the burrs received in the parts sent to the Valve Department.
Operation 2 - Centerless Grinder	**Operation 2 - Centerless Grinder**
One of the grinding guides was feeding the parts incorrectly. the guide was worn and out of alignment.	New grinding guide should be installed.
Operation 3 & 4 - Cut-Off Grinder	**Operation 3 & 4 - Cut-Off Grinder**
Part of the grinding fixture was scratching the large diameter. This diameter was a critical area on the part being processed.	Contact the Tool Designer to adapt the tool fixture design drawing so that the tool can be modified.
Operation 5 - Lapping Machine	**Operation 5 - Lapping Machine**
Use of the Lapping Machine required a sensitivity to the feel of the part in the process. Some people were able to lap effectively while others were not.	Try the following steps. Stop when the problem is solved. Step 1: Train all lapping operators Step 2: Test for effectiveness Step 3: Train only those who need it Step 4: If they cannot lap, move them to another department Step 5: Replace with those who can lap or can be trained to lap

Establish Accountability and Controls

The meeting concluded with the team developing an action plan from which the members could establish accountability and controls over the problem solving process. The problem and goal of this activity is stated below.

> **Problem:** There were no accountability and controls for the actions that were identified by the team.

> **Goal:** Establish accountability and controls for the targeted team actions.

Because the Valve Department Line process problems were just beginning to be addressed, a future meeting date was identified with suggested next steps included.

Matrix Chart

Valve Production Process Team
Action Plan

Tasks/Activities	Responsible	Resources	Outcome	Helper	Start	Finish
Work with Cut-Off Valve Supervisor to eliminate burrs received into the Valve Production Line.	Valve Superv.	Time	No Burrs	Team	Now	Next Week
Install new Centerless Grinding Guide.	Machine-Tool Repairer	New Guide	Good Parts	Operator	Now	3 days
Work with Tool Designer to modify tool fixture design. Have the tool modified to meet new specifications.	Valve Superv.	Modified Fixture	No Scratches	Operator	Now	1 month
Address Lapping Machine operator proficiency.	Trainer/Set-Up associate	Time	Ecquipped associates	Operators	Now	2 months

15. EVALUATION

A Team Meeting Evaluation Form was given to each member. The evaluation was done to allow team members to review their personal team behaviors as well as provide feedback for future meeting interactions.

Observation

Team Meeting Evaluation Form

Please complete and return to the Facilitator within one week of the meeting. Place a check mark (✔)next to each observation that applies to you, the Team, the Leader, the Facilitator, the Process and the Outcomes.

Participation	Myself	Team	Leader	Facilitator
Listened to others	❏	❏	❏	❏
Participated generously	❏	❏	❏	❏
Sought additional facts	❏	❏	❏	❏
Encouraged others	❏	❏	❏	❏
Came prepared	❏	❏	❏	❏
Explored alternatives	❏	❏	❏	❏
Problem solved effectively	❏	❏	❏	❏
Suggested solutions	❏	❏	❏	❏
Agreed to actions	❏	❏	❏	❏
Agreed to accountability	❏	❏	❏	❏

Process & Outcomes	Yes	No
Meeting notice helpful	❏	❏
Agenda followed	❏	❏
Tools used appropriately	❏	❏
Entire team participated	❏	❏
Actions clear and targeted	❏	❏
Outcomes useful and targeted	❏	❏

What were the most positive aspects of this meeting?_____

_____

What needs improving?_____

_____

Tool Selection

These process and tool selection worksheets were used during Steps 6 and 7. The team reviewed the *Agenda* items and completed the worksheets in order to focus the process and select tools.

Worksheet

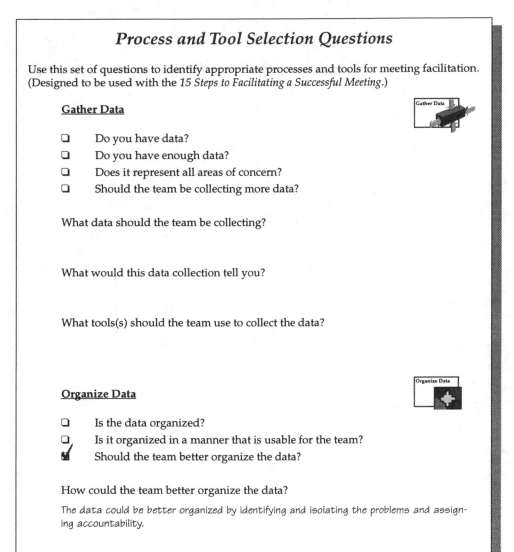

Process and Tool Selection Questions

Use this set of questions to identify appropriate processes and tools for meeting facilitation. (Designed to be used with the *15 Steps to Facilitating a Successful Meeting*.)

Gather Data

- ❑ Do you have data?
- ❑ Do you have enough data?
- ❑ Does it represent all areas of concern?
- ❑ Should the team be collecting more data?

What data should the team be collecting?

What would this data collection tell you?

What tools(s) should the team use to collect the data?

Organize Data

- ❑ Is the data organized?
- ❑ Is it organized in a manner that is usable for the team?
- ☑ Should the team better organize the data?

How could the team better organize the data?

The data could be better organized by identifying and isolating the problems and assigning accountability.

What would this organized data tell you?

The organized data would help the team identify and target priority actions for planning purposes.

What tools(s) should the team use to organize the data?

Worksheet	Consensus Card Method
Tally Sheet	Matrix (Plan)
T-Chart	

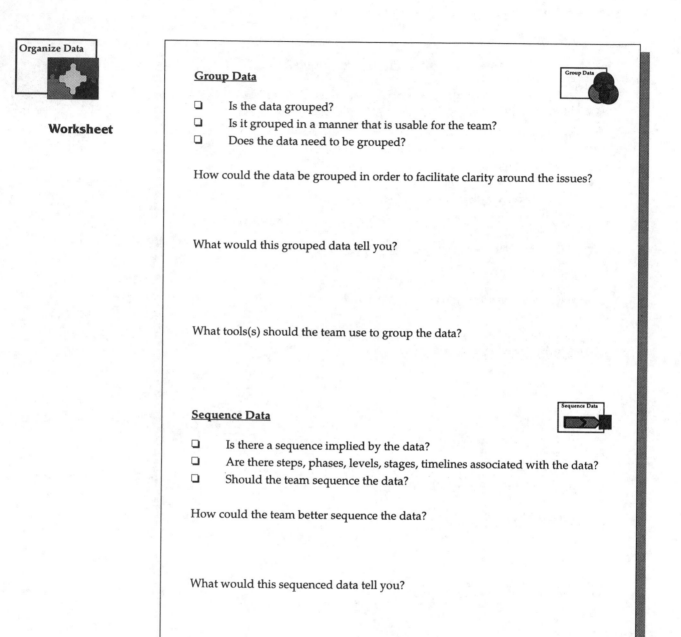

Organize Data

Worksheet

Group Data

❑   Is the data grouped?
❑   Is it grouped in a manner that is usable for the team?
❑   Does the data need to be grouped?

How could the data be grouped in order to facilitate clarity around the issues?

What would this grouped data tell you?

What tools(s) should the team use to group the data?

Sequence Data

❑   Is there a sequence implied by the data?
❑   Are there steps, phases, levels, stages, timelines associated with the data?
❑   Should the team sequence the data?

How could the team better sequence the data?

What would this sequenced data tell you?

What tools(s) should the team use to sequence the data?

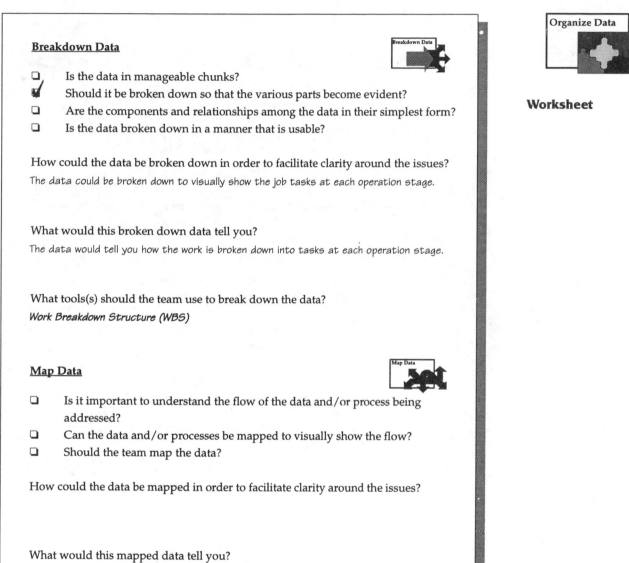

Breakdown Data

☐ Is the data in manageable chunks?
☑ Should it be broken down so that the various parts become evident?
☐ Are the components and relationships among the data in their simplest form?
☐ Is the data broken down in a manner that is usable?

How could the data be broken down in order to facilitate clarity around the issues?

The data could be broken down to visually show the job tasks at each operation stage.

What would this broken down data tell you?

The data would tell you how the work is broken down into tasks at each operation stage.

What tools(s) should the team use to break down the data?

Work Breakdown Structure (WBS)

Map Data

☐ Is it important to understand the flow of the data and/or process being addressed?
☐ Can the data and/or processes be mapped to visually show the flow?
☐ Should the team map the data?

How could the data be mapped in order to facilitate clarity around the issues?

What would this mapped data tell you?

What tools(s) should the team use to map the data?

Organize Data

Worksheet

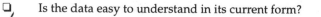

Display Data

- ☐   Is the data easy to understand in its current form?
- ☑   Should it be displayed so that the various parts become evident?
- ☐   Are the components and relationships among the data evident?
- ☐   Is the data displayed in a manner that is usable?

How could the data be displayed in order to facilitate clarity around the issues?

The data could be displayed as representation of the problem.

What would this displayed data tell you?

The displayed data would visually show the production report error percentages, which are the targets for improvement.

What tools(s) should the team use to display the data?

Line Graph

Appendix

How to Use

This book contains many tool examples that can be used in facilitating team meetings. The Appendix has been created so that the tools are in a format that can be copied for use in these meetings.

The book and forms have been copyrighted and permission to make copies of the Appendix tools is given only to the purchaser of the book. Please honor this requirement.

Organization

Each tool is shown on the right-hand page. Many are complete and can be used just as they are. Others are simply shells to be completed as appropriate to the business circumstance.

The left-hand page gives the group icon from which the tool is taken, the name of the tool, and the page(s) describing its use. These elements are provided as an easy reference for usage.

Not all of the tools described in this book are provided in this Appendix. Many of the tools are not included because usage necessitates other media requirements. Media requirements such as sticky notes, 3 X 5 cards, computer generated graphs, symbols and branching arrows can best be performed using a flip chart, white board or butcher paper.

Worksheet

Meeting Planning

Pages 1-18

Agenda

1. Meeting Purpose/Outcome(s):

2. Boundaries (Beginning and Ending):

3. Meeting Objectives (These become the Agenda Item(s) below.):

4. Owner(s):

5. Agenda Item(s)	6. Process	7. Tool(s)	8. Responsibility	9. Time

9a. Total Time Needed:

10. Roles:

Leader: _____   Facilitator: _____   Recorder: _____

Presenter(s): _____

Participants:

1. _____   5. _____   9. _____
2. _____   6. _____   10. _____
3. _____   7. _____   11. _____
4. _____   8. _____   12. _____

11. Logistics:

Date: Time: Location:

12. Materials Needed:

Worksheet

Meeting Planning

Pages 1-18

Process and Tool Selection Questions

Use this set of questions to identify appropriate processes and tools for meeting facilitation. (Designed to be used with the *15 Steps to Facilitating a Successful Meeting*.)

Gather Data

- ❑ Do you have data?
- ❑ Do you have enough data?
- ❑ Does it represent all areas of concern?
- ❑ Should the team be collecting more data?

What data should the team be collecting?

What would this data collection tell you?

What tool(s) should the team use to collect the data?

Organize Data

- ❑ Is the data organized?
- ❑ Is it organized in a manner that is usable for the team?
- ❑ Should the team better organize the data?

How could the team better organize the data?

What would this organized data tell you?

What tool(s) should the team use to organize the data?

Worksheet

Meeting Planning

Pages 1-18

Group Data

❑　　Is the data grouped?
❑　　Is it grouped in a manner that is usable for the team?
❑　　Does the data need to be grouped?

How could the data be grouped in order to facilitate clarity around the issues?

What would this grouped data tell you?

What tool(s) should the team use to group the data?

Sequence Data

❑　　Is there a sequence implied by the data?
❑　　Are there steps, phases, levels, stages, timelines associated with the data?
❑　　Should the team sequence the data?

How could the team better sequence the data?

What would this sequenced data tell you?

What tool(s) should the team use to sequence the data?

Worksheet

Meeting Planning

Pages 1-18

Breakdown Data

- ❑ Is the data in manageable chunks?
- ❑ Should it be broken down so that the various parts become evident?
- ❑ Are the components and relationships among the data in their simplest form?
- ❑ Is the data broken down in a manner that is usable?

How could the data be broken down in order to facilitate clarity around the issues?

What would this broken down data tell you?

What tool(s) should the team use to break down the data?

Map Data

- ❑ Is it important to understand the flow of the data and/or process being addressed?
- ❑ Can the data and/or processes be mapped to visually show the flow?
- ❑ Should the team map the data?

How could the data be mapped in order to facilitate clarity around the issues?

What would this mapped data tell you?

What tool(s) should the team use to map the data?

Worksheet

Meeting Planning

Pages 1-18

Display Data

❑   Is the data easy to understand in its current form?

❑   Should it be displayed so that the various parts become evident?

❑   Are the components and relationships among the data evident?

❑   Is the data displayed in a manner that is usable?

How could the data be displayed in order to facilitate clarity around the issues?

What would this displayed data tell you?

What tool(s) should the team use to display the data?

Observation

Meeting Planning

Pages 1-18

Team Meeting Evaluation Form

Please complete and return to the Facilitator within one week of the meeting. Place a check mark (✔) next to each observation that applies to you, the Team, the Leader, the Facilitator, the Process and the Outcomes.

Participation	Myself	Team	Leader	Facilitator
Listened to others	❑	❑	❑	❑
Participated generously	❑	❑	❑	❑
Sought additional facts	❑	❑	❑	❑
Encouraged others	❑	❑	❑	❑
Came prepared	❑	❑	❑	❑
Explored alternatives	❑	❑	❑	❑
Problem solved effectively	❑	❑	❑	❑
Suggested solutions	❑	❑	❑	❑
Agreed to actions	❑	❑	❑	❑
Agreed to accountability	❑	❑	❑	❑

Process & Outcomes	Yes	No
Meeting notice helpful	❑	❑
Agenda followed	❑	❑
Tools used appropriately	❑	❑
Entire team participated	❑	❑
Actions clear and targeted	❑	❑
Outcomes useful and targeted	❑	❑

What were the most positive aspects of this meeting?_____
_____
_____

What needs improving?_____
_____
_____
_____

Questions/Surveys

Meeting Planning

Pages 1-18

Meeting Planning Checklist

☐ **Determine if the meeting is necessary.**
Team process needed
Alternatives examined and eliminated

☐ **Establish Meeting Purpose/Outcomes.**
Problem/Issue/Process/Project identified
Problem/Issue/Process/Project Boundaries specified (Beginning & Ending)
Objectives stated
Problem/Issue/Process/Project Owner(s) established

☐ **Prepare Agenda.**
Sequenced topics/steps/information/activities listed
Process(es) to be used identified
Tools/Methods for accomplishing outcomes (e.g. debate, panel, presentation,
      open discussion, facilitation) selected
Responsible person for each item named
Time allocations specified

☐ **Identify Group Roles.**
Leader - Plan the meeting, set direction and establish accountability
Facilitator - Move the meeting along and keep it focused
Recorder - Document process, decisions, actions, and outcomes
Presenters - Prepare and present specific information
Participants - Participate through input, discussion, and feedback

☐ **Identify meeting participants.**
Those with pertinent information included
Those with authority to act considered
Those with a stake in the outcome included
Those needing development in this particular area considered
Those with pertinent expertise included
Those with functional responsibility for outcomes included
Number of people necessary to accomplish goals selected

☐ **Establish Meeting Schedule/Date/Time.**
Before, during, after work, or over weekends explored
Consecutive days considered
A few hours a week over a period of time examined
Conflicting company activities accounted for
Conflicting holidays or vacations accounted for
Conflicting schedules of critical members accommodated

Questions/Surveys

Meeting Planning

Pages 1-18

❑ **Select a Meeting Location.**
Away from the work environment considered
Near the work environment examined
In an office contemplated
In a conference room analyzed
Shop facilities investigated
Restaurant accommodations scrutinized
Hotel facilities explored
Conference center facilities researched

❑ **Prepare Pre-Meeting Materials.**
Participant pre-work assignments considered
Presentation data prepared
Individual assignments requested
Information and data documentation obtained and assimilated

❑ **Determine Room Set-up.**
Audio-visual equipment needs reviewed
Flip Charts, Chalk Board, White Board needs examined
Table and chair configuration(s) explored
Comfort accounted for
Lighting/Heating scrutinized
Break and lunch facilities investigated
Walls to display team's work inspected

❑ **Establish Ground Rules.** (Teams often sign to show their commitment.)
Expectations agreed to:
 Frequency of meetings
 Time of meetings
 Attendance at meetings
 Objectives for meetings
 Biggest hopes/worries
 Prioritization of work/activities
Behaviors agreed to:
 Resolution of problems/conflicts
 Decision making process
 Communication styles/methods
Team performance evaluated:
 Measurement of productivity/quality
 Improvement continuous and ongoing
Accountability established:
 Feedback individual performance
New team-member expectations set

Questions/Surveys

Meeting Planning

Pages 1-18

❑ **Conduct Meeting.**
Agenda followed
Ground Rules followed
Time managed
All team members heard from
Meeting facilitation tools used

❑ **Agree on Next Steps.**
Work completed - No next steps
Action Plans developed
Further meetings planned
Report written
The way business is done is changed

❑ **Evaluate the Meeting.**
Self evaluated
Team evaluated
Leader evaluated
Facilitator evaluated
Process evaluated
Outcomes evaluated

❑ **Feedback Meeting Data.**
Minutes furnished
Presentation materials supplied
Decisions made
Actions taken
Information shared
Contributions rewarded and/or recognized

❑ **Clean-up.**
Equipment returned
Room configuration reconstructed

Brainstorming

Pages 24-26

Integrity Publishing   © 1995   **Tools for Facilitating Team Meetings**

Brainstorming

Pages 24-26

Observation

Pages 27-30

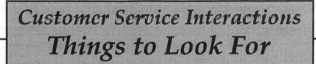

Customer Service Interactions
Things to Look For

1. **Greets Customer**

2. **Repeats Customer's Name**

3. **Asks If Customer Needs Help**

4. **Helps Customer**

5. **Invites Customer to Return**

Observation

Pages 27-30

1. **Greets Customer**

2. **Repeats Customer's Name**

3. **Asks If Customer Needs Help**

4. **Helps Customer**

5. **Invites Customer to Return**

Observation

Pages 27-30

Title: _____

Desired Attributes	Observed Attributes

Questions/Surveys

Pages 31-35

Instructions

1. Choose someone that you do not know to be your partner.
2. Take turns asking each other the questions listed below.
3. Record each others answers.
4. Introduce your partner and share her/his answers with the rest of the group.

   You have 15 minutes to ask the questions

   We will spend 15 minutes sharing the answers

Getting to Know You Icebreaker

1. **What is your name?**

2. **What department do you work in?**

3. **What do you do there?**

4. **What is your favorite movie?**

5. **What is your favorite pastime outside of work?**

6. **What is your favorite song?**

7. **If you were to describe your feelings about today's meeting using a color, which color would you choose?**

Questions/Surveys

Pages 31-35

Put Yourself in the Customer's Shoes

1. Who is your customer? What do they want from you?

2. The customer comes to your department. What happens?

3. Is this customer happy about the way your department handles things?

4. What would need to change in order for the customer to be delighted with your department's services?

5. Do you have the power to make these changes? If not, who does? How can you convince him/her to allow you to make the changes?

6. What will you do now to make things better for your customer? Name at least three things that you will do differently.

Mystery Shopper

Pages 36-37

Mystery Shopper Guidelines

1. How is the customer approached and greeted?
   By Your Organization   By Competitor's Organization

2. What is the sales experience the customer receives?
   By Your Organization   By Competitor's Organization

3. Does the customer receive accurate product knowledge?
   By Your Organization   By Competitor's Organization

4. Is the customer's experience friendly and helpful?
   By Your Organization   By Competitor's Organization

5. Does the customer experience initiative and enthusiasm when they visit?
   By Your Organization   By Competitor's Organization

6. Is the customer offered upselling opportunities?
   By Your Organization   By Competitor's Organization

7. Does the customer experience efficiency, speed and service?
   By Your Organization   By Competitor's Organization

8. Does the customer receive a quality product?
   By Your Organization   By Competitor's Organization

9. Does the customer experience a clean and organized facility?
   By Your Organization   By Competitor's Organization

10. Is the customer introduced to special promotions?
    By Your Organization   By Competitor's Organization

Interviews

Pages 38-41

Creativity Team Interview Questions

CANDIDATE _____ INTERVIEWER _____

1. Do you consider yourself to be creative? Why? How?

2. Tell me about a person that you believe to be creative. How are they creative?

3. Do you dream in color? Describe one.

4. If you had to give this room a name, what would it be? Why?

5. Describe as many ways as you can think of to get home from work.

6. If you could describe the perfect creativity team, what would it look like?

7. Name 5 methods for improving creativity thinking. Why did you choose these?

8. If you could draw your feelings on a piece of paper right now, what would you draw?

9. The employee cafeteria needs a new look. What ideas do you have that would improve the look and entice more employees?

<u>Comments</u>

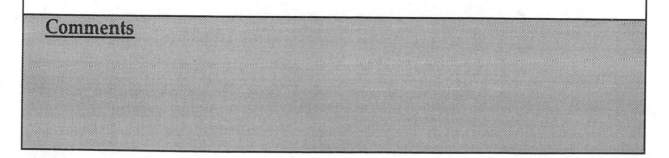

Interviews

Pages 38-41

Team Disclosure Interviews

Instructions

- Interview all team members and record their answers. (Sample questions are listed below.)
- Write a bibliography for each team member to share with the entire group.
- The team will share its findings about each other at the next meeting.
- One at a time, each team member will share a bio. Other members may add information about the member under discussion. Each member will continue to be discussed until no one has anything new to add.
- Then the next team member will read a bio and the process will continue until all team members have been discussed thoroughly.

1. Tell me about some things that you are doing well in your life. Can be work or home.

2. Tell me about a missed opportunity.

3. What are the most important values in your life?

4. Tell me about a change that you successfully made in the last year.

5. What would you like for your obituary to say about your life?

6. What do you like to do more than anything else in the world?

7. Whom do you admire the most?

8. Tell me about someone else's experience you observed that taught you an important lesson.

9. Describe something you would like to change and how you would change it.

10. If you were an animal, which one would you choose to be?

11. If you won the lottery tomorrow, what would you change about your life?

12. Describe the best boss you have ever had.

13. Describe your favorite co-worker.

14. Tell me something you are learning in your life right now.

15. What is the best team experience you ever had?

16. What do you think your life will be like 15 years from now?

17. What is the one thing people most misunderstand about you?

Matrix Chart

Pages 51-58

Title: _____

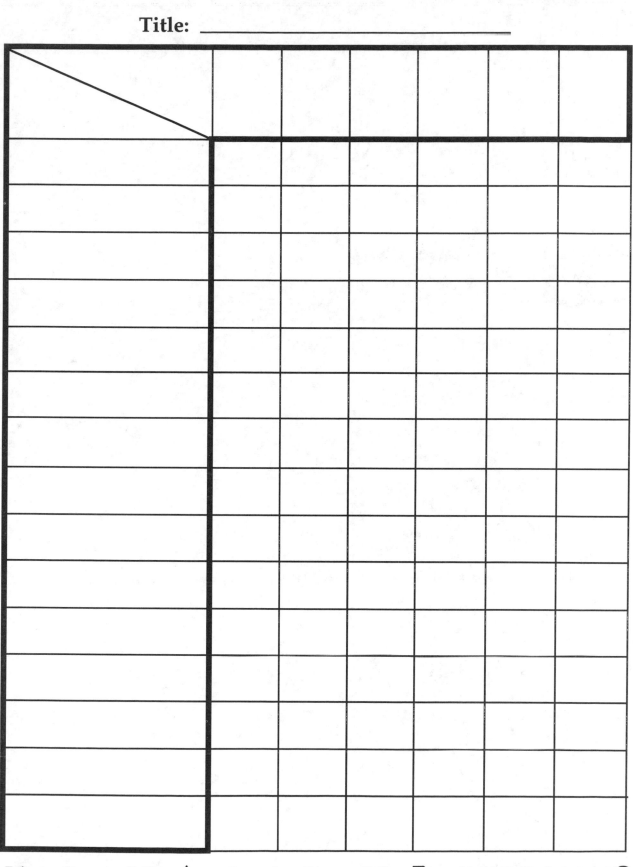

Primary Responsibility ▲   Secondary Responsibility ❑   Need To Be Informed ○

◆ Integrity Publishing   © 1995   **Tools for Facilitating Team Meetings**

Matrix Chart

Pages 51-58

Title: _____

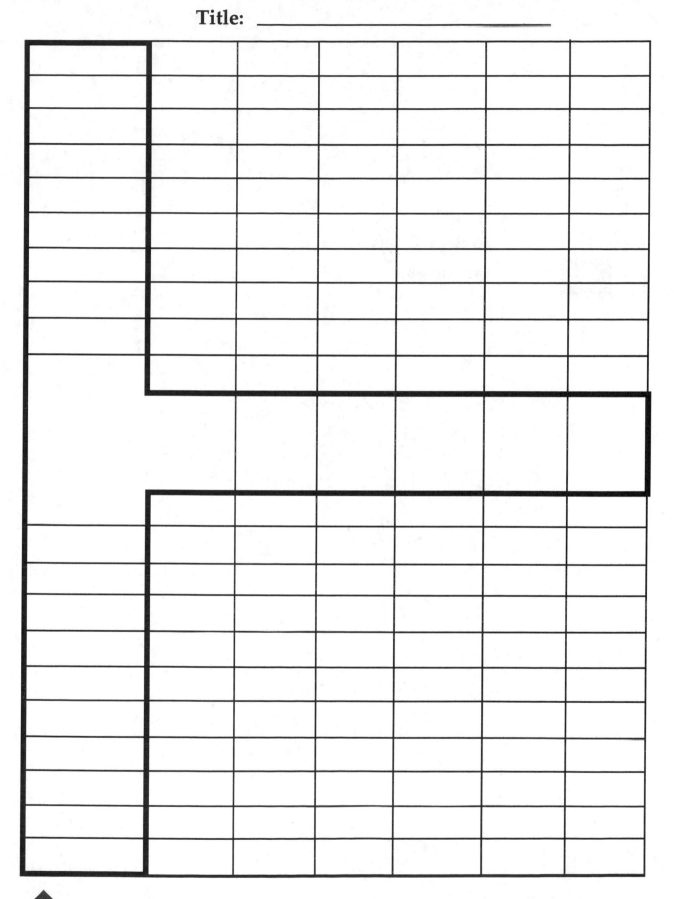

Integrity Publishing   © 1995   **Tools for Facilitating Team Meetings**

Matrix Chart

Pages 51-58

Is/Is Not Matrix

	IS When does this situation occur?	IS NOT When does this situation NOT occur?	THEREFORE What could explain this situation?
Stage 1			
Stage 2			
Stage 3			
Stage 4			

Matrix Chart

Pages 51-58

Decision Matrix

Name of Activity	Purpose of Activity	Type of Activity	Frequency of Activity	Assessment of Activity

Matrix Chart

Pages 51-58

Planning Matrix

Project: _____

Project Team: _____

Project Start Time: _____

Project Finish Time: _____

Tasks/Activities	Key Responsibility	Team Helpers	Resources	Outcome/ Deliverable	Who Needs to Know	Deadlines	
						Start	Finish

Organize Data

Matrix Chart

Pages 51-58

Planning Update Matrix

Project: _____

Responsible Team: _____

Report Date: _____

Tasks/Activities	Key Responsibility	Team Helpers	Deadlines		Project Status to Date
			Start	Finish	

Organize Data

Matrix Chart

Pages 51-58

Dimension Selection Grid

Selection Criteria

Dimensions

1.

2.

3.

4.

5.

6.

7.

8.

9.

10.

11.

12.

Paired-Choice Matrix

Pages 62-64

Title: _____

	■							
	X	■						
	X	X	■					
	X	X	X	■				
	X	X	X	X	■			
	X	X	X	X	X	■		
	X	X	X	X	X	X	■	
								■

Totals	
Topic	**Score**

Force Field Analysis

Pages 68-71

Title:_____

Driving Forces →	← Restraining Forces

Force Field Analysis

Pages 68-71

Force Field Analysis Worksheet

This worksheet is an aid for developing strategies for moving the Forces in one direction or the other once they have been identified. The goal is to develop solutions for weakening the Restraining Forces and strengthening the Driving Forces so that change can take place.

As a team:
1. Identify additional forces that might be used to help carry out the goals.

2. List the Driving Forces and Restraining Forces in rank order (per area, not in an integrated manner).

3. Take each one of these ranked Forces and brainstorm ideas for increasing the Driving Forces and decreasing the Restraining Forces.

4. Identify the forces that can be influenced by the group.

5. Identify the forces that the team has no ability to impact for change.

6. Together, develop action plan(s), assign duties and identify appropriate time frames.

Activities/Tasks	Responsibility	Deadline

Organize Data

Worksheet

Pages 72-75

Better Leader Worksheet

Name_____Title_____

Work Group_____Telephone Number_____

1. Identify the best leader that you have ever known. This should be someone that you have either worked with or for.

2. What are the leadership qualities or traits that you admire in this person?
   a.   f.
   b.   g.
   c.   h.
   d.   i.
   e.   j.

3. How do these qualities or traits compare with your own leadership style?

4. List the major steps you will take to align your leadership style more closely with that of your "best leader".

5. Share your action plan with others in the group so you can hold each other accountable for follow-up. Identify those with whom you are sharing your plan.

Worksheet

Pages 72-75

Requirements Worksheet

Describe your Product and Services	What do I need to change in order to meet the customer's requirements?	
Products	Products	Services
Services		
Identify the specific Customer Requirements		
Products		
Services		

Worksheet

Pages 72-75

Resource Identification

Resource	Resource Necessary? Yes/No	Resource Available? Yes/No	Resource Obtainable? How?
Money			
Time			
People			
Equipment			
Skill, Ability			
Facilities			
Knowledge			
Influence			
Energy			
Interest			

Integrity Publishing   © 1995   **Tools for Facilitating Team Meetings**

Check/Tally Sheets

Pages 76-79

Check/Tally Sheet

Data Collector Name _____**Time Frame**_____

Criteria	Un-satisfactory	Satisfactory	Above Average	World Class	Totals
Totals					

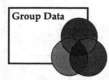

Venn Diagram

Pages 88-91

Title: _____

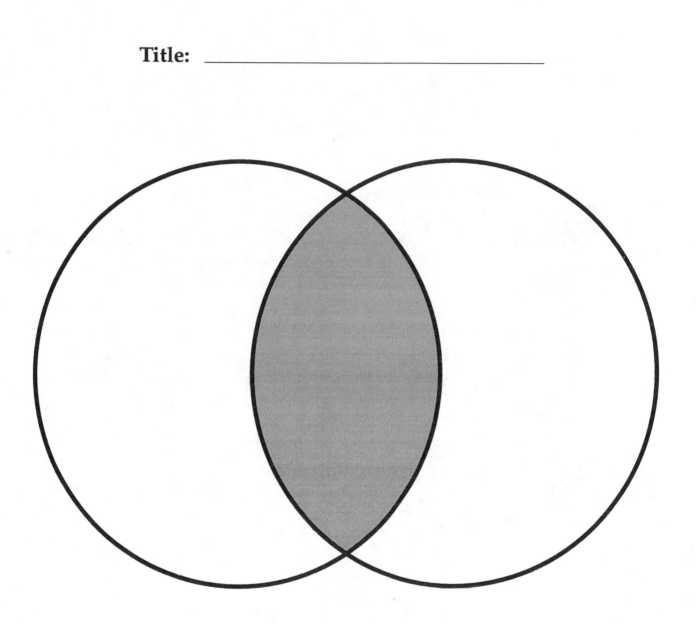

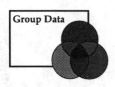

Quadrant Diagram

Pages 92-94

Cost/Benefit Analysis

	Low Cost	High Cost
Maximum Benefit		
Minimum Benefit		

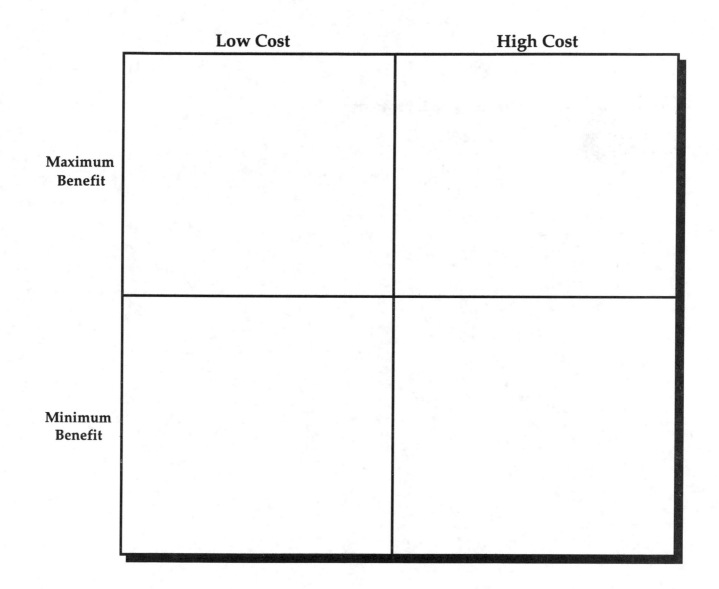

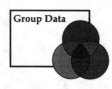

Quadrant Diagram

Pages 92-94

Cost/Benefit Analysis

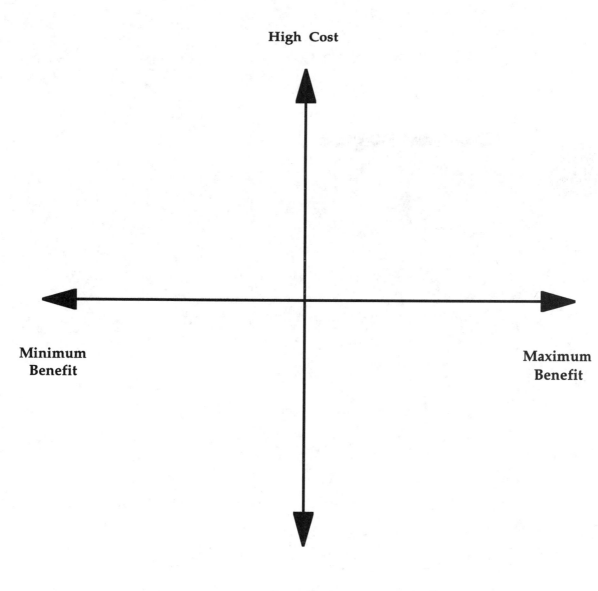

High Cost

Minimum Benefit

Maximum Benefit

Low Cost

 **Integrity Publishing**   © 1995   **Tools for Facilitating Team Meetings**

Group Data

Quadrant Diagram

Pages 92-94

Impact/Control Analysis

STEP 1: *Issue Analysis*

1. What is the organizational **impact** of this issue?
2. How much **control** do you have over addressing this issue?

	Issues	Impact	Control
A			
B			
C			
D			
E			
F			
G			
H			
I			
J			
K			
L			
M			
N			
O			
P			
Q			
R			

STEP 2: *Impact and Control Distribution*

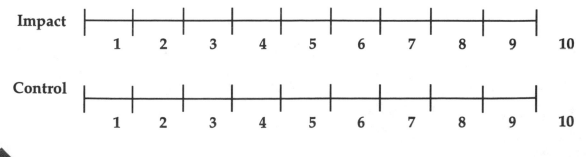

Impact   1   2   3   4   5   6   7   8   9   10

Control   1   2   3   4   5   6   7   8   9   10

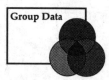 Group Data

Quadrant Diagram

Pages 92-94

STEP 3: *Impact to Control Relationship*

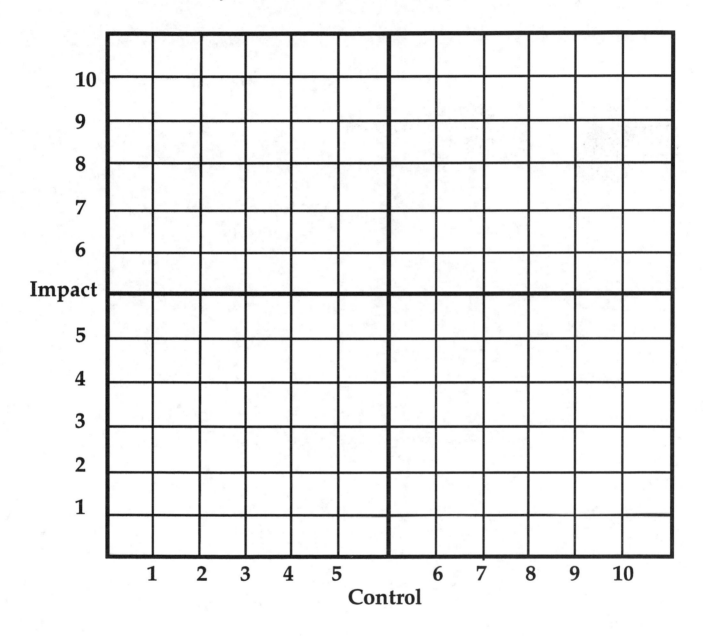

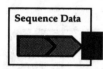 Sequence Data

Continuums

Pages 96-99

Time Line

 **Integrity Publishing**   © 1995   **Tools for Facilitating Team Meetings**

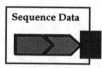
Sequence Data

Continuums

Pages 96-99

5-Step Process

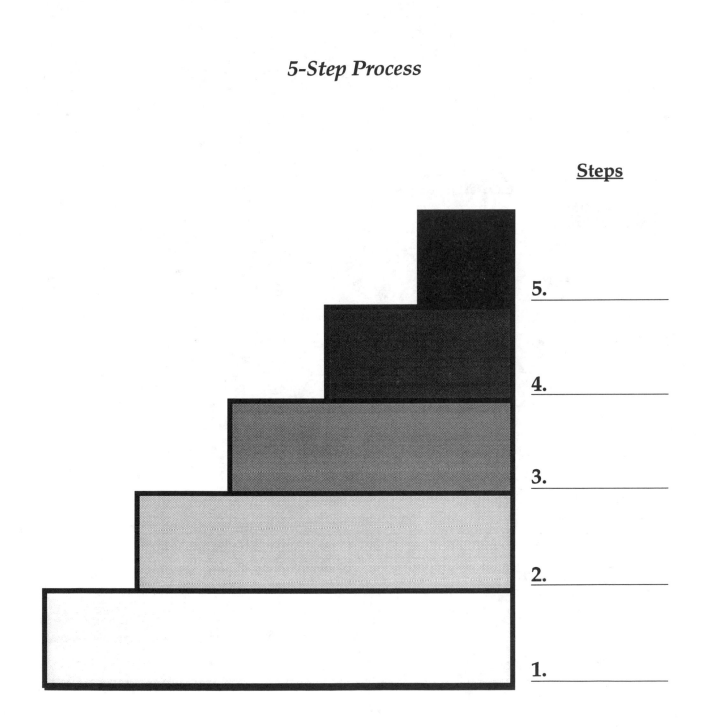

<u>Steps</u>

5. _____

4. _____

3. _____

2. _____

1. _____

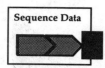

Continuums

Pages 96-99

Title: _____

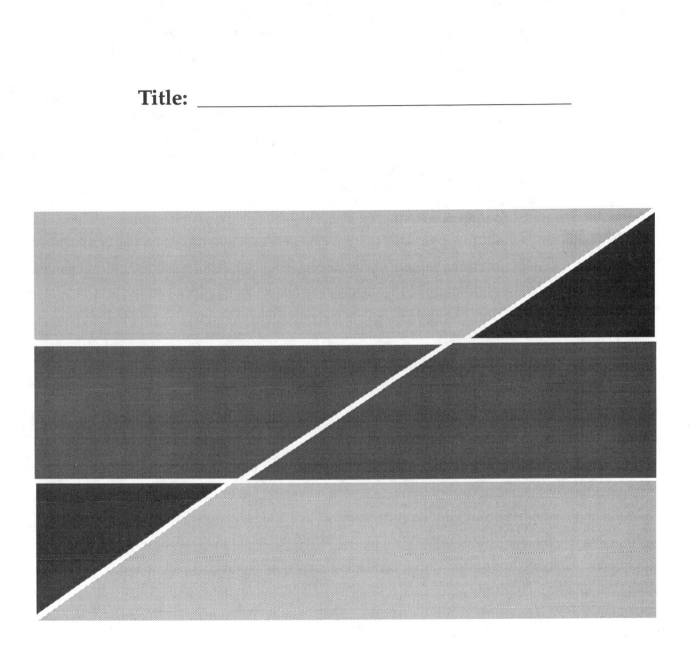

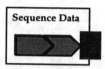

Stages

Pages 100-102

Title: _____

Stage	Activity

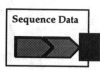

Stages

Pages 100-102

Career Stages

Novice ➤ Growth ➤ Competent ➤ Sponsor/Mentor

_____   _____   _____   _____

_____   _____   _____   _____

_____   _____   _____   _____

_____   _____   _____   _____

_____   _____   _____   _____

_____   _____   _____   _____

_____   _____   _____   _____

_____   _____   _____   _____

_____   _____   _____   _____

_____   _____   _____   _____

_____   _____   _____   _____

_____   _____   _____   _____

_____   _____   _____   _____

_____   _____   _____   _____

Levels

Pages 103-105

Behavior Anchor Rating Scale (BARS)

1.

2.

3.

4.

5.

6.

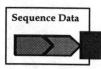

Levels

Pages 103-105

Candidate Evaluation

Level of Importance	Skills/Knowledge/Abilities
Primary Importance	
Secondary Importance	
Important	
Would be Nice	

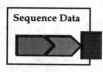

Gantt Chart

Pages 106-107

Title:_____

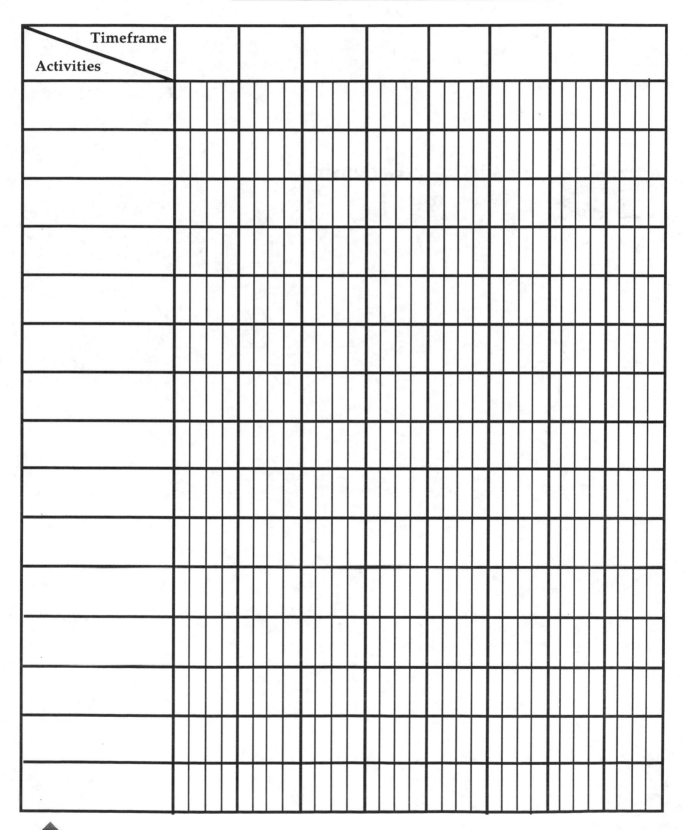

Timeframe / Activities								

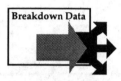

Circles (Relationships)

Pages 118-122

Title: _____

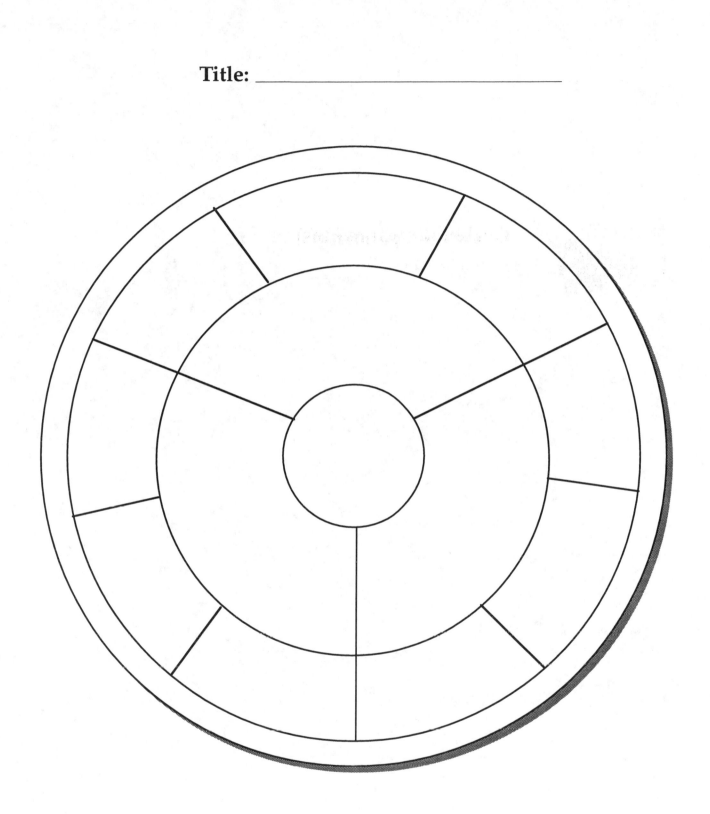

Circles (Relationships)

Pages 118-122

Title: _____

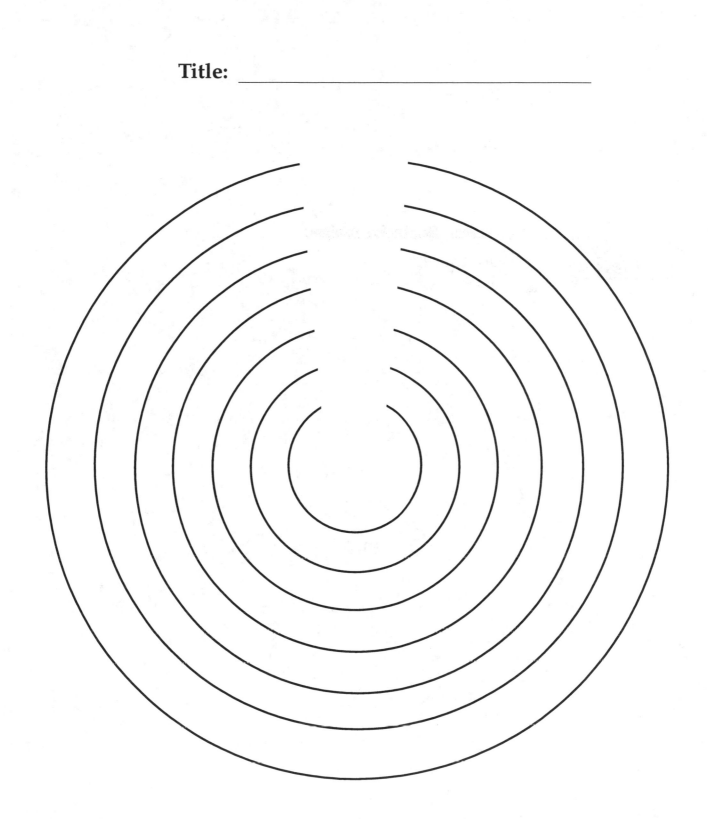

Circles (Relationships)

Pages 118-122

Title: _____

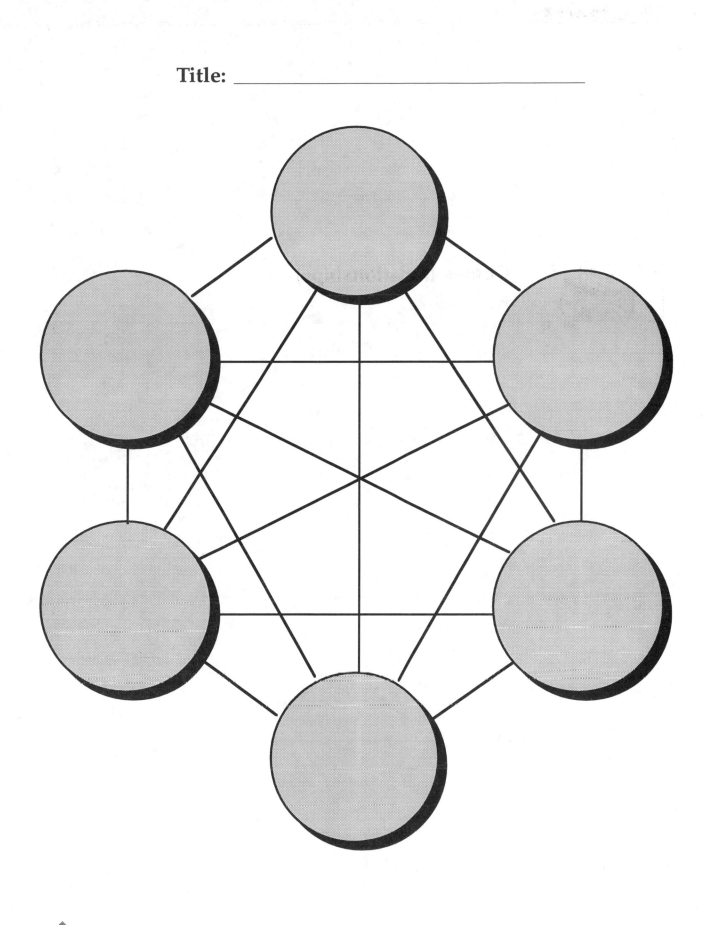

Circles (Relationships)

Pages 118-122

Title: _____

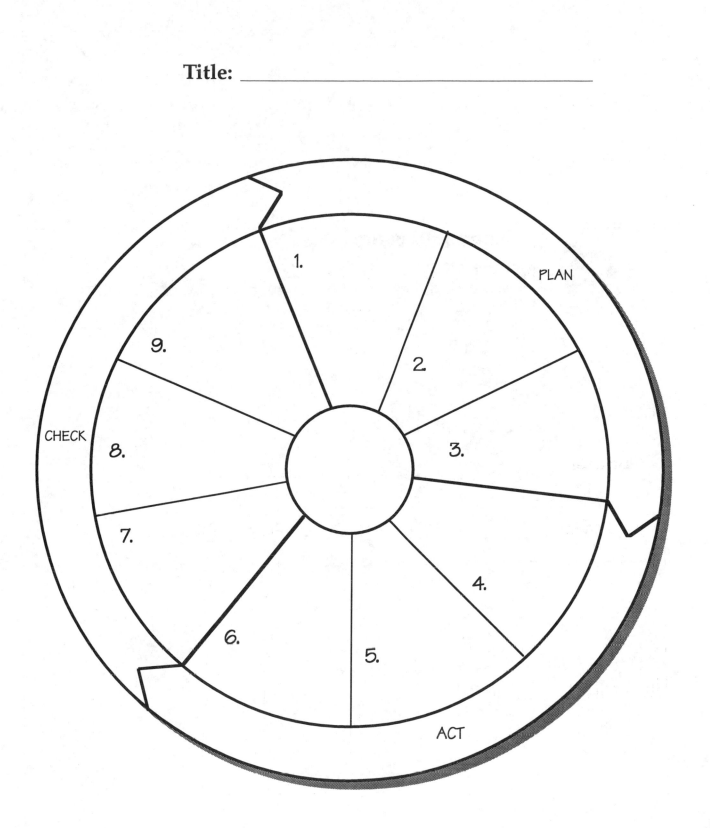

Iceberg Diagram

Pages 123-125

Title: _____

Visible

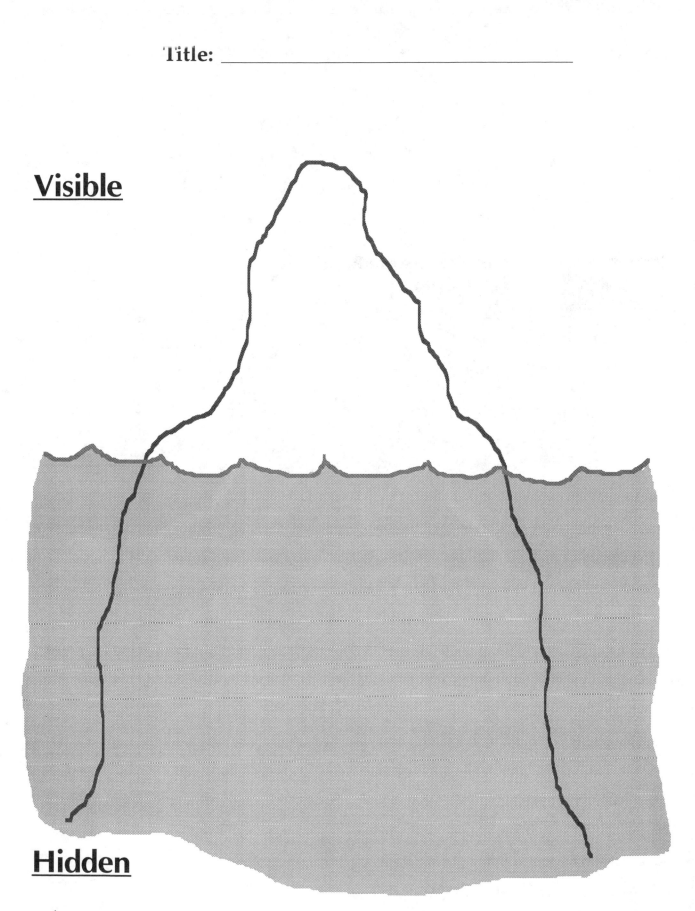

Hidden

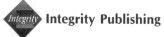 Integrity Publishing   © 1995   **Tools for Facilitating Team Meetings**

Deployment Process
Flow Chart

Pages 134-137

Title: _____

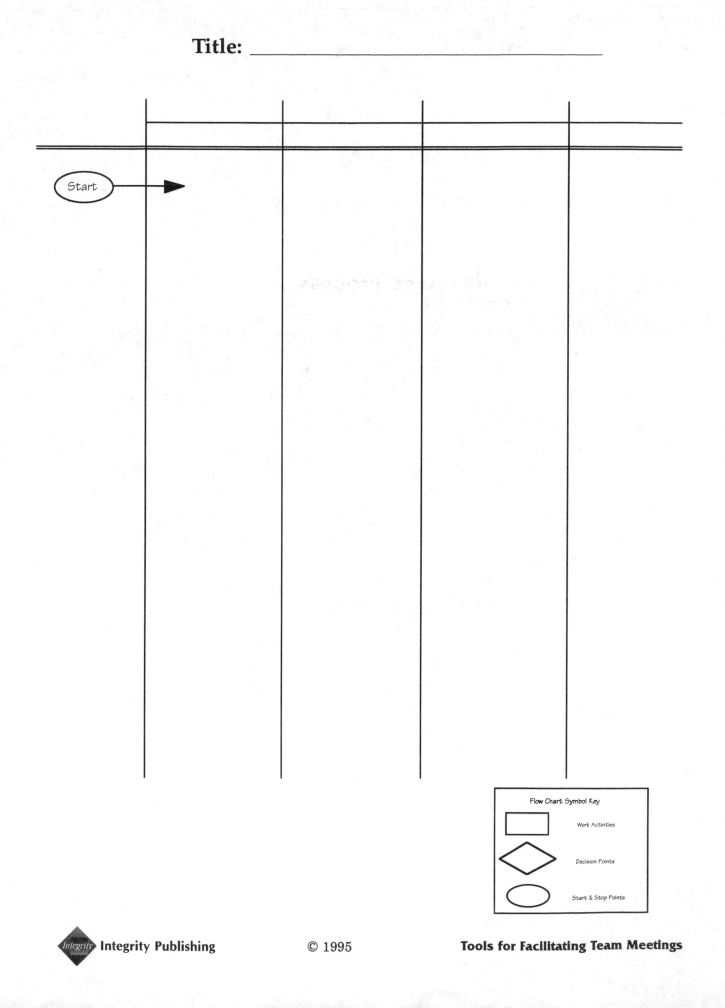

Flow Chart Symbol Key

Work Activities

Decision Points

Start & Stop Points

Start

Deployment Process
Flow Chart

Pages 134-137

Title: _____

Task / Who					Time

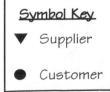

Symbol Key

▼ Supplier

● Customer

 **Integrity Publishing**   © 1995   **Tools for Facilitating Team Meetings**

Area Graph
Bar Graph
Line Graph/Run Chart

Pages 142-151

Title: _____

Area Graph
Bar Graph
Line Graph/Run Chart

Pages 142-151

Title: _____

Tool Index

A

Affinity Diagram
Case Studies
Guest Check-In Process Issues,
171
Description, 82-84
Types
Human Resources Activities
that Affect the Bottom Line, 84
Variations, 84

Area Graph
Appendix, 347, 349
Description, 142-143
Types
Quarterly Sales by Region. 143
Variations, 143

B

Bar Graph

Appendix, 347, 349
Case Studies
Local Market Data, 195
Description, 144-147
Types
Quarterly Sales by Region,
145-147
Variations, 146

Brainstorming
Appendix, 259, 261
Case Studies
Ground Rules, Finance, 191
Ground Rules, Manufacturing, 215
Ground Rules, Service, 163
Description, 24-26
Types
Management Development
Needs, 26
Things to Do Today, 25
Variations, 26

C

Check/Tally Sheets
Appendix, 305
Case Studies
Summary Part Processing
Check Sheet, 223
Description, 76-79
Types
Absenteeism, 79
Customer Satisfaction, 78
Variations, 79

Circles (Relationships)
Appendix, 333, 335, 337, 339
Case Studies
Local Market Strategic Initia-
tives, 199
Description, 118-122
Types
Business Requirements Rela-
tionships, 121
How to Use This Book, v
Human Resources Service
Strategy, 119

Individual as Core of Organization, 120
Machinists New Project Process,
122
Variations, 120

Consensus Card Method
Case Studies
Problem/Solution Decision
Making, 227
Description, 59-61
Types
Consensus Tent, 61
Thumbs Approach, 61
Variations, 61

Continuums
Appendix, 317, 319, 321
Description, 96-99
Types
15-Step Process, 5
5-Step Hiring Process, 99
Apprentice Learning Time
Frames, 98
Quality Meetings, 99
Steps for Planning a Successful
Meeting, 18
Subsidiary Visit Plans, 97
Variations, 98-99

D

Deployment Process Flow Chart
Appendix, 343, 345
Description, 134-137
Types
Career Transition Plan, 136
Mail Distribution Sequence
Flow Chart, 137
Variations, 137

Double T-Charts
Description, 47-50
Types
Meeting Leader Roles, 49
Organization Change Analysis, 48
Project Planning Steps, 49
Works - Does Not Work
Analysis, 48
Variations, 50

F

Force Field Analysis

Appendix, 295, 297
Description, 68-71
Types
Continuous Improvement
Analysis, 70-71
Variations, 71

G

Gantt Chart
Appendix, 331
Description, 106-107
Types
New Information System
Project Plan, 107
Variations, 107

I

Iceberg Diagram
Appendix, 341
Description, 123-125
Types
Company Survival Analysis, 125
How Things Get Done, 124
Variations, 125

Interrelationship Diagram
Description, 85-87
Types
Family Vacation, 87
Variations, 87

Interviews
Appendix, 275, 277
Descriptions, 38-41
Types
Creativity Team Interview
Questions, 40
Team Disclosure Interviews, 41
Variations, 41

L

Levels
Appendix, 327, 329
Description, 103-105
Types
Manager Behavior Anchor
Rating Scale (BARS), 104
Shop Manager Candidate
Evaluation, 105
Variations, 105

Line Graph/Run Chart
Appendix, 347, 349
Case Studies
Summary Production Reports,
217
Description, 148-151
Types
Quarterly Sales by Region, 149-
151
Variations, 150

Link Pin Diagram
Description, 116-117
Types
Corporate to Business Unit
Linkages, 117
Variations, 117

M

Matrix Chart
Appendix, 279, 281, 283, 285,
287, 289, 291
Case Studies
Agenda Items Matrix, Finance,
187
Agenda Items Matrix, Manu-
facturing, 213
Agenda Items Matrix, Service,
161
Guest Check-In Planning
Matrix, 175
Tactics and Accountabilities,
201
Valve Production Process Team
Action Plan, 231

Description, 51-58
Types
Dimension Selection Grid, 52
Is/Is Not Matrix, 56
L-Shaped Matrix, 53
Materials Selection Matrix, 22
Meeting Decision Matrix, 58
Project Planning, 55
Project Update, 55
Roles and Functions Matrix, 57
T-Shaped Matrix, 54
Variations, 53

Multi-Voting
Case Studies
Guest Check-In Process Bound-
aries, 159
Description, 65-67
Types
Reasons for Lack of Customer
Focus, 67
Variations, 67

Mystery Shopper
Appendix, 273
Description, 36-37
Types
Mystery Shopper Guidelines,
37
Variations, 37

O

Observation
Appendix, 251, 263, 265, 267
Case Studies
Team Meeting Evaluation Form,
176, 202, 232
Description, 27-30
Types
Customer Service Interactions
Things That Were Observed,
29
Things to Look For, 28
Desired and Observed Attri-
butes, 30
Team Meeting Evaluation Form,
14
Variations, 29

P

Paired-Choice Matrix
Appendix, 293
Case Studies
Guest Check-In Process Paired-
Choice Matrix, 173
Description, 62-64
Types
Team Member Replacement
Analysis, 64
Variations, 64

Process Flow Chart
Case Studies
Guest Check-In Process Map,
166-167
Description, 131-133
Types
Guest Check-In Process Map,
132-133
Variations, 133

Q

Quadrant Diagram
Appendix, 309, 311, 313, 315
Case Studies
Local Market Opportunities,
197
Description, 92-94
Types
E-Mail Cost/Benefit Analysis,
93
Impact - Control Priority Analy-
`sis, 94
Variations, 94

Questions/Surveys
Appendix, 253, 255, 257, 269,
271
Case Studies
Pre-Work Questionnaire,
Finance, 189, 193
Description, 31-35
Types
All Employee Cafeteria Survey,
34
Getting to Know You Ice-
breaker, 33
Meeting Planning Checklist,
15-17
Put Yourself in Your Customer's
Shoes, 35
Variations, 34

S

Stages
Appendix, 323, 325
Description, 100-102
Types
Career Stages of Engineers,
102
Manual Design Project, 101
Variations, 102

Storyboard
Description, 128-130
Types
From Medical School to
Physician, 129-130
Variations, 129-130

T

T-Charts
Case Studies
Problem/Solution Areas, 229
Problem/Solution Identification,
225
Description, 44-46
Types
Comparisons and Differences,
45
Opposite or Opposing, 45
Organize Relationships, 46
Shifts, 46
Variations, 45-46

Tree Diagram
Case Studies
Guest Check-In Process Break-
down, 169
Description, 110-113

Types
Guest Check-In Process, 112
Linkage of Organizational
Mission Statements, 113
Variations, 113

TT-Charts (see Double T-Charts)

V

Venn Diagram
Appendix, 307
Description, 88-91
Types
Attributes of Leaders and
Managers, 91
Filing Duties, 90
Product Design Relationships,
89
Variations, 90

W

Work Breakdown Structure (WBS)
Case Studies
Valve Production Line Activi-
ties and Tasks, 219
Description, 114-115
Types
Find a New Job, 115
Variations, 115

Work Flow Diagram
Description, 138-140
Types
Library as Open System, 140
Machinist Traffic Patterns, 139
Variations, 140

Worksheet
Appendix, 241, 243, 245, 247,
249, 299, 301, 303
Case Studies
Agenda, Finance, 184
Agenda, Manufacturing, 210
Agenda, Service, 158
Part Processing Worksheet,
221
Process and Tool Selection
Questions, Finance, 204-
207
Process and Tool Selection
Questions, Manufacturing,
233-236
Process and Tool Selection
Questions, Service, 178-181
Description, 72-75
Types
Agenda, 9
Process and Tool Selection
Questions, 10-13
Better Leader Worksheet, 73
Customer Requirements Work-
sheet, 74
Team Resource Identification,
75
Variations, 74

PRODUCTS AND SERVICES

Text   **$29.95**

Tools for Facilitating Team Meetings is today's most complete tool book on meeting facilitation. Whether you are an experienced facilitator or are new to facilitating — this is the book for YOU! Use these step-by-step planning tools to:

Plan. Learn to write detailed agendas which identify the meeting purpose or outcomes, boundaries (beginnings and endings), objectives and owner.

Organize. Use the 100+ facilitating tools from this book to establish the flow of your meeting by selecting the agenda items, process tools, responsible person(s), timing, roles, logistics and materials.

Conduct. Set meeting ground rules for operating and building action plans that encourage accountability and define time frames.

Evaluate. Measure the success of your meeting by examining participation effectiveness of the team, leader, facilitator and yourself as well as the process and outcomes.

Tool   **(Minimum 20 block orders only)**   **Call for Pricing**

Now you can optimize your team decision making through utilization of the *Consensus Tent* tool described in **Tools for Facilitating Team Meetings.** By displaying the Green (Agree), Red (Disagree) or Yellow (I Can Live With It) sides of the table tent, each team member provides real-time decision making input. The easy-to-store *Consensus Tents,* should be kept on hand in all meeting facilities and can be effortlessly transported to off-site locations by unfolding and stacking flat.

Workshops   **Call for Pricing Schedule**

Workshop 1:

Have fun while learning in these interactive 1-day **Tools for Facilitating Team Meetings** workshops. Following the 15-step meeting planning process, workshop participants will learn through forming teams to plan, organize, conduct and evaluate team meetings. Facilitation tool utilization will be demonstrated and teams will participate in choosing from the 100+ tools mentioned in the book as they plan their team meetings. Enhanced learning will occur as teams share their meeting planning decisions with other workshop participants.

Workshop 2:

Customized workshops focused on specific team or group outcomes provide "learn-while-doing" experiences. Teams can have fun, learn and solve problems.

Consulting   **Prices vary per Assignment - Call or Send Request for Proposal**

As an author, publisher and consultant, Johnna L. Howell has worked with numerous organizations internationally. She has facilitated organizational strategic planning, design and restructure efforts with senior corporate leaders, led and managed large professional staffs, conducted hundreds of team meetings and delivered many training sessions. Ms. Howell is a recognized leader in the human resources field as evidenced by her numerous publications and professional awards.

TEXT AND TOOL ORDER FORM

NAME: _____

TITLE: _____

ORGANIZATION: _____

ADDRESS: _____

CITY, STATE, ZIP _____

TELEPHONE: _____ FAX: _____

Shipping and Handling: Add $3.50 for the first book and $1.00 for each additional book. For international orders, add an additional $2.00 per item. For expedited orders contact the Customer Service Center, (206) 524-5348.

QTY	Item	Unit Price	Total

Volume Discounts available.

Subtotal	
Less Discount	
Total	
WA Residents add Sales Tax	
Shipping and Handling	
TOTAL	

Phone Order   Fax Order   Mail Order

(206) 524-5348   (206) 524-5527   *Integrity* **Integrity Publishing**
7456 E. Greenlake Drive N.
Seattle, WA 98115

FAX

Your Payment Information:

Check or purchase order enclosed. (Purchase Order must accompany form.)

Charge my   ❏ **VISA**   ❏ **MasterCard**

Card #: _____   **Expiration Date:** _____

Signature _____   **Today's Date:** _____